Tourism Alternatives

KT-148-381

WITHDRAWN

A Publication of the International Academy
for the Study of Tourism

Tourism Alternatives

Potentials and Problems in the Development of Tourism

Edited by Valene L. Smith and
William R. Eadington

JOHN WILEY & SONS

Chichester · New York · Brisbane · Toronto · Singapore

Published in 1994 by John Wiley & Sons Ltd,
Baffins Lane, Chichester,
West Sussex PO19 1UD, England
Telephone (+44) (243) 779777

First published in the United States of America in 1992
by The University of Pennsylvania Press

Other Wiley Editorial Offices

John Wiley & Sons, Inc., 605 Third Avenue,
New York, NY 10158-0012, USA

Jacaranda Wiley Ltd, 33 Park Road, Milton,
Queensland 4064, Australia

John Wiley & Sons (Canada) Ltd, 22 Worcester Road,
Rexdale, Ontario M9W 1L1, Canada

John Wiley & Sons (SEA) Pte Ltd, 37 Jalan Pemimpin #05-04,
Block B, Union Industrial Building, Singapore 2057

British Library Cataloguing in Publication Data

A CIP catalogue record for this book is available from the British Library

ISBN 0 471 94881 0

Printed and bound in Great Britain by SRP Ltd, Exeter.

To Jafar Jafari

Founder and President of the International Academy for the Study of Tourism

Contents

List of Tables and Figures   ix

List of Contributors   xi

Preface   xiii
VALENE L. SMITH and WILLIAM R. EADINGTON

Introduction: The Emergence of Alternative Forms of
Tourism   1
WILLIAM R. EADINGTON and VALENE L. SMITH

Part I - Theoretical Perspectives   13

1. Alternative Tourism: Concepts, Classifications, and
Questions   15
DOUGLAS G. PEARCE

2. Alternative Tourism: The Thin End of the Wedge   31
RICHARD BUTLER

3. Making the Alternative Sustainable: Lessons from
Development for Tourism   47
EMANUEL DE KADT

4. Alternative Tourism: Tourism and Sustainable
Resource Management   76
JOHN J. PIGRAM

5. International Tourism Reconsidered: The Principle of
the Alternative   88
MARIE-FRANÇOISE LANFANT and NELSON H. H. GRABURN

Part II - Case Studies   113

6. Tourism as an Element in Sustainable Development:
Hana, Maui   115
BRYAN FARRELL

7. Boracay, Philippines: A Case Study in "Alternative"   133
Tourism
VALENE L. SMITH

8. Predisposition Toward Alternative Forms of Tourism
Among Tourists Visiting Barbados: Some Preliminary
Observations   158
GRAHAM DANN

9. Tourism by Train: Its Role in Alternative Tourism   180
MARTINUS J. KOSTERS

10. Tourism Alternatives in an Era of Global Climatic
Change   194
GEOFFREY WALL

Epilogue: A Research Agenda on the Variability of   216
Tourism
DENNISON NASH

References   227

Author Index   247

Subject Index   251

Tables and Figures

TABLES

Introduction
Table 1. International travelers: volume and expenditure
    patterns   2

Chapter 1
Table 1. Variables used in classification of tourism   23

Chapter 2
Table 1. Problems of tourism   33
Table 2. Tourism development strategies   36
Table 3. Agents of change and types of tourism   38
Table 4. Possible implications of alternative tourism   41
Table 5. Viewpoints in tourism development   45

Chapter 7
Table 1. Arrivals at Boracay, 1983–1986   142
Table 2. Arrivals by month and nationality   145
Table 3. Locally perceived effects of tourism, Boracay   153

Chapter 8
Table 1. Responses to "Have you been inside a Barbadian
    home?"   165
Table 2. Cross-tabulation of variables with entry to local
    homes   173
Table 3. Profile of tourists disposed to entering homes   178

Chapter 10
Table 1. Global climate warming scenario   202
Table 2. Leading international destinations, 1985   203

Table 3. Regional distribution of international tourism   204
Table 4. International tourism arrivals and receipts   205

FIGURES

Chapter 4
Figure 1. Tourism development and environmental
  quality   77

Chapter 7
Figure 1. Location map, Philippines   137
Figure 2. Map of Boracay Island   138
Figure 3. Beach Road with coconut trees   141
Figure 4. Thatched "stands" along Beach Road   144
Figure 5. Advertisement for "world's best beaches"   147
Figure 6. Hand water pump   149
Figure 7. Bridge built by students over drainage ditch   150
Figure 8. Hillside cottages built for "ocean view"   151

Chapter 10
Figure 1. Possible climatic changes from greenhouse effect   201
Figure 2. Periods with snow cover under various scenarios   213

Contributors

Richard Butler is Professor of Geography, University of Western Ontario, London, Ontario, Canada. Long active in tourism research, he is particularly noted for studies in the history of tourism and for analysis of the resort cycle.

Graham Dann is Senior Lecturer in Sociology at the University of West Indies, Bridgetown, Barbados. A frequent contributor to leading journals, his interests lie in motivation and image in international tourism.

Emanuel de Kadt, an economist and sociologist, is Director of the Institute of Development Studies, University of Sussex, Brighton, England. His interests in tourism date to the 1976 joint UNESCO-World Bank symposium on the Social and Cultural Impacts of Tourism, the proceedings of which he edited as *Tourism: Passport to Development?*

William R. Eadington is Professor of Economics and Director of the Institute for the Study of Gambling and Commercial Gaming at the University of Nevada, Reno, Nevada, U.S.A. He is an authority on the legalization and regulation of commercial gaming throughout the world. He has edited a variety of books on social and economic aspects of gambling, including *Gambling and Public Policy: International Perspectives* and *Indian Gaming and the Law.*

Bryan Farrell is Professor of Geography, University of California, Santa Cruz, California, U.S.A. An environmental scientist by training, he has written extensively on the environmental impacts of tourism. His best-known work, *Hawaii: The Legend That Sells,* is based on extensive field work in Hawaii.

Nelson H. H. Graburn is Professor of Anthropology, University of California, Berkeley, California, U.S.A. He has strong interests in the theory of tourism. His extensive list of tourism-related publications includes the book, *Tourist and Ethnic Arts: Cultural Expressions from the Fourth World.*

Martinus J. Kosters is Director of the Commercial Research Centre, National Hogeschool voor Tourisme en Verkeer, Breda, the Netherlands. Trained as an economist, he has research interests in transportation, tourism management, and government policy toward tourism.

Marie-Françoise Lanfant is Director of Research, l'Utite de Recherche et Studie du Tourisme Internationale (URESTI) du Centre Nationale de la Recherche Scientifique (CNRS), Paris, France. She is a sociologist whose research interests center on tourism as a social phenomenon and the philosophical implications of tourism.

Dennison Nash is Professor of Anthropology, University of Connecticut, Storrs, Connecticut, U.S.A. He enjoys doing research in the history and theory of tourism, and has been a frequent contributor to leading tourism journals and symposia.

Douglas G. Pearce is Professor of Geography, University of Canterbury, Christchurch, New Zealand. He is the author of two recent and comprehensive books, *Tourism Today: A Geographical Analysis* and *Tourist Development.*

John J. Pigram is Associate Professor of Geography and Planning, and Executive Director, Center for Water Policy Research, University of New England, Armidale, New South Wales, Australia. He is a contributor to academic publications in tourism and resource issues, and is a frequent development consultant to tourism industries.

Valene L. Smith is Professor of Anthropology, California State University, Chico, California, U.S.A. She was editor of and a contributor to the pioneering book *Hosts and Guests: The Anthropology of Tourism,* and is a frequent contributor to leading tourism journals and symposia.

Geoffrey Wall is Professor of Geography, University of Waterloo, Ontario, Canada. He is co-author of *Tourism: Economic, Physical, and Social Impacts,* and is currently directing a major multi-disciplinary research project in Indonesia and Bali.

Preface

Valene L. Smith and William R. Eadington

The growth of tourism as a social phenomenon and the tourist industry as an economic enterprise has been dramatic during the last half of the twentieth century. Tourism has become a major economic force in many countries and regions throughout the world, altering work patterns, living standards, and income distributions. The expansion of tourist activities has coincided with the significant cultural, political, and environmental changes identified with post-industrial technology of the past few decades. The effects of tourism development have been particularly conspicuous both in the cities and countries from which large numbers of tourists emanate, where tour operators, governments, and other economic interests compete through advertising and image creation to attract tourism customers, and in the destinations to which the tourists travel, where they—and the facilities built to service them—make a visible impact.

Although the concept of leisure time and its use has been studied by theorists and recreation practitioners for many years, the study of tourism as a leisure activity is still comparatively new. In many circles, and for some time, tourism was regarded as a relatively frivolous topic; but as social scientific inquiry has focused ever more critically on the dynamics of tourism, it has become evident that tourism is in fact a significant social institution.

Tourism can be studied: it has a history and a literature; it has an internal structure with operating principles; it waxes and wanes and is highly sensitive to external influences including natural and cultural events; and it can be analyzed in terms of economic and social transactions. In short, tourism is a suitable topic for scholarly inquiry.

The International Academy for the Study of Tourism was chartered in Santander, Spain in June 1988 under the aegis of the World Tourism Organization for the purpose of creating a scholarly body to investi-

gate the theoretical nature of tourism and its global role. Interdisciplinary in scope and limited to a worldwide membership of seventy-five
scholars, the Academy scheduled its first meeting for August 1989.
The Polish Institute of Tourism offered to host this historic first conference at Zakopane. Meanwhile, Willibald Pahr, then Secretary-General
for the World Tourism Organization, suggested to Academy president
Jafar Jafari that the mounting worldwide interest in "Alternative Tourism" would merit scholarly inquiry and that such fruitful discussion
would benefit the several training programs operated under World
Tourism Organization sponsorship. Twenty-four Academy members
from diverse disciplines convened, and their papers and discussions
constitute the genesis of this book.

The Table of Contents reflects the pervasive spirit of eclecticism that
dominated the week-long symposium, and, as Nash and Butler reported in the Academy newsletter (1989:2:3),

the sessions revealed a great variety of viewpoints among members and served
to clearly illustrate the difficulty of using an ambiguous and confusing term
such as "alternative tourism", which has a variety of meanings to different
users. Discussions ranged from the highly abstract to attempts to produce
acceptable definitions of the term. Attention was focused on both the tourist
resource base or supply and the impacts resulting from tourism, and also the
demand or tourist side of the equation. The relationship between all forms of
tourism and developments were discussed, as was the association of the concept of alternative tourism with the principles of sustainable development.
There was some support for the view that *sustainable tourism* was a more
accurate and meaningful term than *alternative tourism*. The group came to the
conclusion that the concept of alternative tourism has little scientific value and
that a more acceptable substitute phrase would be *alternative forms of tourism*.

The significance and timeliness of the subject matter of the Zakopane Conference can best be measured in the short term by the occurrence of other activities that have since emerged. *Cultural Survival
Quarterly* (1990:14:1–2) published two issues entirely devoted to case
studies illustrating the effects of the various alternative forms of tourism. In November 1989, the World Tourism Organization and the
Government of Algeria hosted forty-eight tourism specialists (with a
similar number of Algerian counterparts) at a five-day seminar on
alternative tourism, where three theoretical lead papers were presented and other participants offered comments and examples from
their field work and experiences. At this conference, as in Zakopane,
the participants completely rejected the term "Alternative Tourism"; in
this case, they selected instead the term "Responsible Tourism."

The essays which form this book constitute the first major attempt to
capture the interdisciplinary and theoretical puzzles put forward by

alternative forms of tourism. Tourism, as defined at the United Nations Conference on International Travel and Tourism in Rome (1963), includes business travel, conventions, pilgrimages, family gatherings, and visits to health spas, as well as travel by sightseers and vacationers. Thus, as a trillion dollar worldwide leisure time activity, tourism has become a major social institution with content and form, and participants in its activities include individuals of differing age, sex, sect, race, socioeconomic class, and culture, and reflect the full spectrum of educational and occupational backgrounds. Their motivations, expectations, and levels of visitor satisfaction are almost endless. As Crick (1989) has suggested, no single discipline can hope to address all facets of such a complex and dynamic entity, nor to draft a single theory of tourism. In the long term, the Zakopane Conference may well be viewed as a watershed event in the development of a social science of tourism, and this set of contributions may well become a benchmark for future endeavors.

This volume is organized into two major sections. The first section is essentially theoretical; the second includes case studies. The final chapter proposes an agenda for future research. Because the Academy is interdisciplinary in nature, the contributors bring a wide diversity of expertise and experience to their analysis. The list of contributors that follows points out the variety in training, interests, and affiliations of the contributing authors.

The editors would like to express their gratitude to Diana Elizabeth Eadington and Judy A. Cornelius for their assistance in completing this book, and to Patricia Smith of the University of Pennsylvania Press for her ongoing assistance on editorial matters. We would also like to thank our respective spouses, Stan McIntire and Margaret Eadington, for their ongoing support on this and related projects.

Introduction: The Emergence of Alternative Forms of Tourism

William R. Eadington and Valene L. Smith

I. Introduction

The latter half of the twentieth century has been marked with amazing changes in technology, transportation, and communication and, in varying degrees, a spread of geo-political stability that has accompanied economic affluence for many citizens in industrialized and developing countries throughout the world. These changes have triggered the development of a number of new industries and the substantial evolution of existing industries to address the needs of increasingly prosperous, educated, and sophisticated post-industrial societies. One of these industries, tourism, has quietly emerged to become an important force in many societies and economies in various parts of the world.

Though not usually thought of as a single cohesive industry, the growth of tourism since World War II has nonetheless been dramatic. Higher discretionary incomes, smaller family size, changing demographics, lower transportation costs, improved public health standards, infrastructure development, and hospitable environments for tourists in many destinations have made tourism, especially long-distance tourism, an activity within the reach and desires of many members of many nations. Furthermore, developments in marketing, management, vertical and horizontal integration, pricing, and tour packaging, as well as capital investments in physical facilities—"bricks and mortar"—and public infrastructure, have provided tourism with the necessary framework to allow the tremendous growth it has experienced over the past half century. Thus, tourism has indeed emerged as an "industry" which, according to the World Tourism Organization, in 1989 gener-

Table 1 International Travelers: Volume and Expenditure Patterns,
1950–1990

Year	Arrivals (millions)	Percent Increase	Expenditures (U.S. $ billions)	Percent Increase
1950	25.3		2.1	
1960	69.3	173.9	6.9	229
1970	158.7	145.0	17.9	159
1980	204.8	29.0	102.4	472
1990	425.0	107.5	230.0	125

Source: World Tourism Organization Secretariat 1991

ated approximately 74 million jobs in its direct and service-related industries, such as airlines, hotels, travel services, and publications.

At least at the international level, the growth and extent of tourism activity can be appreciated by examining the volume and expenditures of international travelers; data from the period 1950 to 1990 are presented in Table 1. Though these data include many who are traveling for other reasons, a good portion of the growth is attributable to tourism.

Many countries and regions which have possessed the necessary resources for tourism development have chosen, either consciously or otherwise, the path of developing large scale tourism as a major national or regional activity. Tourism has become a major employer, taxpayer, and physical and political presence in many jurisdictions. As a result, tourism has often altered the very nature of social, political, and economic interaction that occurs in these places. Frequently, the transformation has been no less dramatic than the shifts that took place generations before, as agrarian ways were pushed out by industrialization. Now, in industrialized countries, tourism is frequently pushing out (or more correctly, replacing) manufacturing, distribution, or extractive industry as the economic mainstay. In developing countries, the shift typically has been from an agrarian economic base to a touristic economic base, bypassing an industrial phase altogether.

The reasons for this explosion of growth in tourism are many and interrelated. At one level, transportation systems, especially with respect to the automobile and commercial air travel, have opened new opportunities for potential tourists by making transport from home to destination less expensive (in real terms), more convenient, quicker, and safer. Increases in real incomes since 1950, especially in the industrialized countries of Europe, North America, and Australasia, have expanded the numbers of potential long distance tourists from solely the upper classes to virtually all social strata. Shortened work weeks, increased leisure time, earlier retirement age, and extended life expectancies have provided many more people with the discretionary time and opportunities to undertake frequent holidays, or "get-aways," or to pursue lengthy exploratory excursions. Improved communications and information dissemination, ranging from travelogues on television, to movies filmed in exotic locations, to extensive word-of-mouth networking, have familiarized potential tourists with the far corners of the globe long before they consider visiting them. The desire to see famous natural or man-made sites, to experience new or familiar adventures, different cultures, or one's own historic or ethnic roots, or just to change one's environment from the cold chill of winter to the warmth of sun-drenched beaches has been enhanced and stimulated by the marketing efforts of such various components of the tourism industry as airlines, destination resorts, and tourism authorities in their efforts to increase volumes of business or visitorship to specific locations.

On the supply side, various improvements have been made which have catered to the tastes and preferences of potential tourists. No longer is long distance air travel considered a major ordeal. With the combination of increasingly experienced travelers and customer-sensitive airlines, trips that would have been considered extremely demanding only one or two generations ago are now taken in stride by all but the most fickle of travelers. The uncertainty of the availability or quality of accommodations that may have prevailed in the past has been replaced by worldwide reservation services, hotel franchises that guarantee quality standards and potable water, and the familiarity and assurances generated by prior visits, visits by friends, or observations by travel writers.

However, tourist development has not progressed without controversy. Disillusionment with "mass" tourism and the many problems it has triggered has led many observers and researchers to criticize vociferously the past methods and directions of tourism development and to offer instead the hope of "alternative tourism," broadly defined as forms of tourism that are consistent with natural, social, and community values and which allow both hosts and guests to enjoy positive and worthwhile interaction and shared experiences. To date, however, such reactions have been more notable for their harsh judgments against mass tourism than their positive contributions as to what "alternative tourism" means. As many of the articles in this volume point out, it is easier to grasp and speak against the negative results of mass tourism than it is to formulate a realistic and cohesive view of what "alternative tourism," however defined, can reasonably offer.

II. The History of Alternative Tourism

The flurry of research and publication concerning mainstream and alternative tourism in the past two decades can be placed in historical perspective. Most analysts recognize that tourism takes on forms appropriate to an era, and therefore historic styles develop consistent with population size, economic status, available modes of transport, and geographical habitats of home in comparison with destinations abroad. Public participation creates mainstream tourism, usually in several variations at any given time; and the needed infrastructure develops accordingly. In addition, the existence of "alternatives" to mainstream tourism is not new.

Sigaux (1966) documents the history of tourism from the time of the early Greeks to the period after World War II, and this chronology clearly shows both mainstream and "alternative" tourism for more than two millennia. According to Casson (1974), for example, during the Empire the seven hills of metropolitan Rome supported an estimated 1.5 million people, many of whom must have shared modern motivations for travel including the need for fresh air and a change of scene. Wealthy Romans traveled to Naples, where their vacation homes were constructed on piers built over the water, providing a fine view of Mt. Vesuvius reflected in the Bay. A fragment of etched glass depicting this salubrious scene may well be the first known tourist souvenir. Around this cluster of superior accommodations, lesser folk rented lodging in small rooms on side streets. The rich traveled by chariot from Rome to Naples and built private villas (*diversoria*) for their overnight stops along the highway. Even though used only three or four nights per year, these en route accommodations were elegantly furnished and maintained by a permanent staff of servants. Their gardens were filled with fruit and flowers, but water was so scarce in the hill country that it was necessary to "water" the plants with wine! To house the commoners who also toured, farmers whose land fortuitously fronted the Roman highway built *tavernas* to provide lodging, meals, and stables and soon were in business as innkeepers.

Not all Romans could travel so far. Early in the Imperial era Tivoli (originally *Tibur*), only a few miles outside Rome, became a popular holiday center noted for its gardens and waterfalls. "Second home" tourism also dates at least to Roman times in the many villas and spas constructed outside every major city of the Empire. Near Rome, Hadrian's Villa, built between 125 and 135 AD, is still a much-visited attraction.

Tourism became a major industry in the nineteenth century. The *Dictionnaire universale du XIXe siècle* of 1876 (quoted by Sigaux 1966:7) defines tourists as "people who travel for the pleasure of traveling, out of curiosity and because they have nothing better to do" and "even for the joy of boasting about it afterwards." Construction of railroads and the innovations of Thomas Cook and George Pullman created new forms of "mainstream" tourism such as group tours. In his first nine years in business (1857–1866), Thomas Cook alone handled more than a million customers, building an economic empire in mainstream tourism with his hotel vouchers, rail tickets, traveler's cheques, and a global travel agency network.

As Dennison Nash (1979b) details, European aristocracy (together with the gamblers, ne'er-do-wells, and voyeurs who followed them) created at Nice the first European winter resort where a cluster of palatial hotels with ballrooms and adjoining concert halls provided annual recreation for some 60,000 *hivernants* (winter visitors) amidst opulence, indoor toilets, and a discriminating hotel staff. And tiny adjacent Monaco attained its fame with the establishment of a resplendent casino to serve the so-called "international set."

But "alternative" forms of tourism also developed in Europe during this same period, as reported in the 1985 Special Issue: The Evolution of Tourism, of the *Annals of Tourism Research*. Noteworthy is the article on "tramping" by members of the British working classes for whom these "tramp trips appear to have become rites of passage to full male adulthood" (Adler 1985:339). The similar French *Tour de France* and the German *Wanderpflicht* provided European journeymen with an opportunity to gain work experience away from home, and thereby served to "regulate competition by geographically dispersing workers and delaying entrance to master craftsman status" for as long as four to five years. *Compagnonnage* as a rite of passage into manhood is said to have been one of the most powerful working class institutions ever developed in France (Adler 1985:340). For domestic tourism, Fichtner and Michna (1987) trace the rise of Europe's famous amusement parks, the forerunners of today's theme parks.

In the twentieth century, the first passenger jet service in 1958 is credited with inaugurating modern mass and charter tourism, with all its attendant problems of overcrowding and pollution. Thus mainstream tourism in subsequent decades has used airplanes for long-haul travel and autos on the local scene. The railroad which reigned supreme during the nineteenth century fell quickly into decline, as Martinus Kosters documents in this volume (Chapter 9). Mainstream tourism in this century has been primarily north-south (English 1986) because of climate and, as Hall observes (1984:540), "destination countries represent a much wider spread than originating countries, reflecting a spatial diffusion of tourists from the developed world across the globe, with fastest growth in the more remote regions of the Third World."

Rapid development of resort infrastructure to receive and accommodate airborne guests in favored spots was responsible for the Miami Beach/Waikiki atmosphere, advertising sun, sea, sand, and sex on beaches from Antigua to Zihuatanejo. Alternately sun, ski, snow, and sex have become winter sports attractions in resorts from the Arlberg to Zermatt, with the attendant gridlock on mountain access roads. By the 1990s, there is a sense that the public has become "tired" of the crowds, weary of jet lag, awakened to the evidences of pollution, and in search of something "new." Innovative but rapidly gaining in popularity as "alternative" vacations for this decade are walking tours (some of which are very costly because of the level of accommodations and cuisine provided), barge and canal tours (many of which are also deluxe and expensive), bicycle tours, home and farm stays (as discussed by Pearce in this volume), and, at least within the United States, an increase in domestic tourism.

Youth tourism has also taken many forms over time, most of which seem to have been a simple expression of youthful energy and curiosity about the world beyond their bounded society. Their travels were usually a form of "alternatives" to prevailing tourism. Historically, these have involved travels to medieval universities and such institutions as the "Grand Tour," with its year abroad for young scholars and their tutors. In recent years, the youth hostel movement encouraged "hitchhikers" (Mukerji 1978) and the 1960s generated the "hippies," followed by what Riley (1988) now terms the "long term budget traveler," as discussed by Valene Smith in Chapter 7 of this volume. This last group is to be distinguished from the "drifters" first described by Cohen (1973) whose deviant, drug-related behavior and counterculture still persist in some locales such as Thailand and Sri Lanka.

Thus, to seek "alternatives" to the tourist mainstream is a contemporary but by no means a novel theme. The history of tourism is replete with centuries of parallel examples.

III. Economic Trends and Byproducts in Mainstream Tourism

Because of the growing awareness of tourism as an activity, an industry, and a catalyst for economic growth and development, competition for the tourist and for tourism expenditures has been significant in recent decades. One result has been market segmentation and a considerable broadening of the perceived and actual opportunities available for potential tourists. Thus tourists can choose from "sun and sand" holidays, "adventure travel," "theater tours," "shopping sprees," summer or winter sports vacations, cultural immersion, historic re-enactments, and various other tourism experiences.

An interesting illustration of product identification and market segmentation is offered by two of the fastest growing tourism destinations in the United States: Orlando, Florida and Las Vegas, Nevada. Both of these tourist-dominated cities offer predominantly artificially created tourism experiences: Orlando with the presence of Disney World, Epcot Center, and MGM and Universal Studio "Hollywood"-themed parks; and Las Vegas with its variety of themed "must see" casino-hotel resorts such as The Mirage, Caesars Palace, and Excalibur, along with high-technology showroom extravaganzas and unparalleled convention facilities, all framing a wide variety of gambling opportunities. Both Orlando and Las Vegas offer escapism and fantasy in highly artificial environments and have been tremendously successful in doing so. It is no accident that Las Vegas is often referred to as providing an "adult Disneyland" for its visitors, whereas Orlando provides the "real" Disney experience. With the exception of the slot machines and gambling tables, there are strong similarities between these two rapidly growing tourism destination cities. Indeed, it may not be so farfetched to call Orlando, with all of its thrilling but nonetheless artificial attractions, an "adolescent's Las Vegas." It is worth noting that the economic success of both Las Vegas and Orlando has led to many recent attempts to emulate them; legalization or attempted legalization of casino-style gambling has been widespread in the United States, Canada, and Australia over the past fifteen years (Dombrink and Thompson 1990; Eadington 1990), and Mickey Mouse has gone abroad to France and Tokyo to found new Disney Worlds to conquer.

However, in spite of the many forms it has taken, not all tourism industries in the developed or the developing world have been beneficial. Success in attracting tourists and tourism-related investments has sometimes led to over-exploitation of tourism resources, which has deteriorated the tourism experience for visitors and hosts alike. Conflicts have arisen between natural and constructed tourism resources as governments and entrepreneurs have cooperated in competition with those of other locations to attract the economic benefits and prestige that popular destination resorts could bring. Sheer numbers of tourists have altered the "pristine" or "natural" experience that some regions initially offered. The development of high volume tourism facilities, such as high-rise hotels and tourist-oriented strip retail centers, with inadequate attention paid to traffic patterns, urban planning, infrastructure needs, or aesthetic considerations, has created more than a few "tourism disasters." It is clear in retrospect that, in many cases, the benefits linked to tourism development were quickly dissipated, either due to inadequate or inept planning or because of short-term, short-sighted exploitation.

Disillusionment with mainstream or mass tourism is reflected in the retrospective disappointment of many locals and tourists alike with the ultimate results of tourism developments. An interesting illustration is provided by the case study of Maui, Hawaii, written by Farrell in this volume. For the locals—the hosts—the concerns may be of promises unfulfilled, destruction of an older and simpler way of life, inadequacy of employment opportunities, or dissatisfaction with other economic changes which came with tourism development. For tourists the view is often summarized with statements such as "This used to be a nice place, but now it is ruined" because of overcrowding, overcommercialization, or overdevelopment. The "mass tourism," the tackiness, and the variety of problems experienced in such places as Niagara Falls, Waikiki, Spain's Costa Brava, and Australia's Gold Coast have too often created eyesores alongside beautiful natural settings; herded large numbers of tourists as if they were so many cattle; disrupted traditional cultures and occupational patterns by creating a pervasive tourism industry characterized by low-paying service jobs and manipulative values; and ignored the needs of local citizens and the community values that were inconsistent with pragmatic economic requirements of the tourism industry.

The decade of the 1990s has been predicted to become the "Decade of Eco-Tourism," and the travel industry is becoming sensitized to mounting global concern about the social costs and environmental damage created by too much tourism. In the past, planners in the private and public sectors have relied heavily on short and intermediate term economic and investment criteria for decision making and for resource allocation considerations regarding tourism projects. This has often led to problems of overdevelopment accompanied by rapid decline in a destination's general appeal to more upscale tourists. Select coastlines in Florida, Spain, and Mexico provide a variety of examples of this pattern of development.

One reason for this short-sightedness is that the market pricing mechanism and other economic processes do not always provide a full and complete accounting of all costs and benefits associated with tourist developments. In instances where important resources are held as the property of "all the people," or where individual property rights are poorly defined, externalities—defined as costs (or benefits) resulting from transactions undertaken between buyers and sellers but falling on otherwise uninvolved third parties—can and frequently do arise. Pristine beaches and alpine settings, for example, are usually

perceived as complementary resources for tourism development projects. Yet the attempt of too many projects to capture the common
benefits from such shared resources can lead to congestion, pollution,
and a general degradation of the value of such resources for tourism
purposes (Eadington and Redman 1991).

Thus local residents at tourist destinations, as well as the general public, often bear the costs of overdevelopment through diminished aesthetic or use value of the resources; by paying for mitigation, abate-
ment, or clean-up efforts through private endeavors or increased taxes;
or with lower wealth through foregone opportunities, diminished incomes, or depressed property values. There is also the socially de-
stabilizing issue of redistribution of income and wealth that invariably
follows rapid economic change. Tourism development creates "winners" and "losers" among the local residents, often without a common
acceptance as to the equity of such redistribution. Alternatively, many
of the "winners" might be outsiders who are then viewed as exploiters
of the native population and rapists of the land. Furthermore, the
changes in income and wealth are often viewed in light of the long term
depletion of an area's resource base; the ability of such destinations to
capitalize fully on their tourist resources in the future may become
permanently impaired because of rapid tourism development.

Good decision making procedures should take all such externalities
and their costs fully into account in planning for tourism development
and in directing the evolution of existing tourist industries. Private
market forces by themselves cannot rectify such external costs and
often ignore altogether—or treat amorally—the income and wealth
redistribution issues. When such situations occur, policy makers should
structure government intervention to stimulate more desirable outcomes. Regrettably, such enlightened planning is often not realized in
practice.

Awareness of such resource and social conflicts, however, and their
relationship to the health of a tourism industry is growing. Antonio
Savignac, Secretary-General of the World Tourism Organization, was
the keynote speaker at the International Travel Industry Expo 1990,
held in Chicago. Among his comments delivered to some 3,000 travel
agents and 400 industry suppliers were: "if the destination deterio-
rates, so do the profits." This conference dealt with "green tourism," or
tourism in the context of man's stewardship with nature, with the
development of rural tourism, and with the need to develop responsible tourism policies. It was emphasized that industry and tourism planners need to establish criteria which would determine carrying capacities, both physical and social, for many tourist destinations. Those
criteria then require implementation to insure a more enjoyable and

lasting experience for the guest and an economically and psychologically more rewarding environment for the hosts. This volume's article by Bryan Farrell provides discussion and a case study of the aspects and pitfalls of this process. In short, the direction of tourism planning in the 1990s should be toward enlightened self-interest and the value of preserving the quality and stability of both natural and human resources in tourism destinations.

IV. Conceptual Basis for Mainstream and Alternative Tourism

The concept of mainstream and alternative tourism needs to be reviewed in theoretical perspective. Although European guidebooks date to the fourteenth century and European scholars began to write about the phenomenon of tourism as early as 1899 (Cohen 1984), serious interest in tourism as an institution spans only two decades. Analyzing the literature to date, Jafar Jafari (1989a:20) has aggregated the individual opinions and writings about tourism into four groups, each with "a distinctive position or consolidated platform on tourism." The four platforms appeared in chronological order but are not mutually exclusive. One has not replaced the other, and all four platforms are still being individually used:

- *The Advocacy Platform* includes both private and public interests that "focus on tourism's importance to the economy" as a labor-intensive industry that generates foreign exchange, preserves environment, revives traditions of the past, and actively promotes cultural performances (Jafari 1989a:20). This viewpoint became a strong voice in the 1960s as nationalism swept many countries into independence, heightening their need for funds, and is still prevalent. It was recently expressed as the route to success "with mass tourism as a ticket to development" *Economist* (1989).
- *The Cautionary Platform* grew out of research and case studies largely undertaken in the 1970s by social scientists who questioned the validity of the benefit claims as contrasted to the realities of commoditization of culture and other negative impacts on a host society. An extensive literature supports the voiced concerns and challenges the Advocates.
- *The Adaptancy Platform,* benefiting from the arguments raised by its predecessors, seeks new strategies for tourism such as indigenous tourism, soft tourism, green tourism, sensitized tourism, responsible tourism, appropriate tourism, alternative tourism, cottage tourism, local level tourism. However, as Jafari has noted,

"the Adaptancy Platform has emerged as a partial remedy, but strategies have not been fully developed to accommodate the mass tourism generated globally. Tourism's forms and practices can be influenced but its volume cannot be curtailed" (Jafari 1977, 1989b).

- *The Knowledge-Based Platform* is the most recent development and "aims at positioning itself on a scientific foundation which simultaneously maintains bridges with other platforms . . . the many studies are intended to contribute to a holistic study or treatment of tourism; not just its forms or consequences. The main goal is the formulation of a scientific body of knowledge on tourism (Jafari 1989a:25)."

This Knowledge-Based Platform is therefore the *raison d'être* for the International Academy for the Study of Tourism and is the organizing principle for this volume.

V. Conclusions

As with many other aspects of modern life, tourism has brought with it benefits and costs, blessings and curses. Reflecting people's inherent curiosity, hedonism, desire for adventure and excitement, or just a need to change the pace and setting of everyday experiences, tourism has opened the door to many to seek out and fulfill their vacation needs. Furthermore, tourist industries have been the willing suppliers of the demanded services.

But all of this has not come without dissatisfaction. Perceived difficulties with mainstream tourism have encouraged planners, researchers, and social critics to rethink the logic of traditional tourist development, to examine the alternatives to mainstream or mass tourism, and to begin formulating better ways to integrate tourism into a broader range of values and social concerns that traditional tourism development has somehow put at risk. Fully understanding the benefits and costs of tourist development in terms of their sources, possibilities for mitigation, and implications of "alternatives" will we hope play a major role in correcting the mistakes of the past.

Every body of scholars, working in a particular time span, develop an explanatory mode appropriate to their frame of reference. Just as Jafari has developed a typology of tourism literature (as discussed above), most of the members of the International Academy for the Study of Tourism have been involved in tourism research and/or as consultants to various facets of the travel or transportation industry. As noted earlier, in the early 1960s the new self-rule of former colonies mandated an immediate search for new sources of foreign exchange and domestic employment. The World Bank and the United Nations recognized the potentials of tourism to meet those needs and negotiated loans and support for new resort developments, for modern airplanes, and for tax benefits for investors. The pace of this type of development has not yet slowed, both because of the development of new overseas destinations such as Boracay in the Philippines (see Smith, Chapter 7 in this volume) and because of the mounting interest in increased domestic tourism in virtually every country on the globe, including many Third World nations.

Of necessity, government planners and policy makers throughout the world are seeking direction for the management of their tourism industries. In many ways this book provides such direction. The contributors to this volume and the members of the Academy are mindful, however, of the intellectual and ideological alternatives to a tourism management perspective: the emerging interest in eco-tourism, in local level and privatized development, and the concerns and implications suggested in dependency theory and in ecumenical edicts. To a degree these issues are addressed here, but the body of data to test and verify theory in many of these areas is not yet at hand or is in need of refinement. Meanwhile, development goes forward, sometimes scarcely keeping pace with demand, and the need for direction and greater understanding by and for policy makers remains a most significant challenge. The pragmatic issue that can be useful to policy makers—understanding the broad implications of the various choices confronting them—constitutes the philosophical organizing core for many of the articles in this volume. It is hoped that this will serve as a major building block in the accumulation of knowledge of tourism and its various effects on societies.

Part I
Theoretical Perspectives

Tourism is a highly competitive industry which is often manipulated by forces in the marketplace to bring visitors to a destination by offering group travel discounts, incentive off-season rates, and volume commission overrides. Governments have the ability to limit visitor numbers or even exclude them entirely, as in Bhutan and Saudi Arabia respectively. Government policy makers and development agency planners can also at least partially regulate the social level of the inbound tourist by their control of aircraft landing rights. A charter aircraft with a passenger load of sunbathers destined for a foreign-owned beach hotel affects a community in ways entirely different from the individual tourist who opts to travel domestically by local bus and use bed-and-breakfast lodging in private homes. Thus the many forms of tourism available to an individual may appear to be his or her alternatives, but underneath is a complex matrix of operatives which are often difficult to discern. The essays which comprise Part I address the important theoretical issues which are fundamental to understanding the many variants inherent in the study of tourism.

Douglas Pearce, in "Alternative Tourism: Concepts, Classifications, and Questions," provides a useful review of the appropriate literature. From these sources he identifies the variables used in the classification of tourism and provides examples of the impacts associated with the differing alternative forms.

Richard Butler, writing about "Alternative Tourism: The Thin Edge of the Wedge," identifies six problems common to all forms of tourism and evaluates their short and long term impacts. As he observes, if the goal is to limit or reduce the numbers of tourists and thereby create alternatives to mass tourism, the economic, social, and political consequences must be carefully weighed.

"Making the Alternative Sustainable: Lessons from Development for Tourism" by Emanuel de Kadt identifies the key factors widely recognized and used in development policy, such as resource use and renewability, scale, the role of the state, economic power, and interest groups. He examines each with reference to tourism planning, especially to protect a destination from the misuse of nature and loss of culture.

John Pigram addresses the issues of policy planning and implementation in his essay "Alternative Tourism: Tourism and Sustainable Resource Management." With a background in geographic planning, he stresses the irreversibility of change and the consequent importance of mitigating conflicts between the various economic, social, political, and environmental entities involved in creating "safe minimum standards" for tourism at any level.

"International Tourism Reconsidered: The Principle of the Alternative" applies the French structuralist approach of Marie-Françoise Lanfant (with a translation and editorial interpretation by Nelson Graburn) to the definitions of alternative and tourism. They examine the challenge of international tourism, itself a multidimensional element, and the disjunction between the operative economic and cultural forces.

Taken together, the five chapters provide a wide spectrum of interpretation and many guidelines useful to the process of policy planning and implementation.

Chapter 1
Alternative Tourism: Concepts, Classifications, and Questions

Douglas G. Pearce

I. Introduction

Over the past decade the concept of "alternative tourism" has emerged in various guises in different parts of the world. In some cases, projects fostering new forms of tourism have been promoted, especially in developing countries (e.g., Britton 1977; Saglio 1979). Drawing in part on some of these examples and as part of a broader interest in the problem, attempts have been made to define "alternative tourism" and to clarify associated issues, both by individuals (e.g., Dernoi 1981, 1988; Cazes 1987; Cohen 1987) and at earlier conferences and workshops (e.g., Pearce 1980; Holden 1984; Broggi 1985; Britton and Clarke 1987). A number of alternative tourism networks and support groups have also been established in both developing and developed countries (Tüting and Krippendorf 1989).

Given the different backgrounds and concerns of these individuals and organizations, it is not surprising that no universally agreed or widely adopted definition of alternative tourism is to be found, nor that few explicit links between its different forms have been made. It is not the purpose of this essay to pursue the quest for an all-embracing single definition of alternative tourism, for such a goal will be elusive and ultimately fruitless. Many different forms of tourism exist (Pearce 1989); there is no dominant form with but a single alternative to it. What is required is a more systematic basis for distinguishing between and classifying different forms of tourism.

This essay attempts to provide such a basis and to identify relevant variables and dimensions by drawing on and reviewing systematically the literature on alternative tourism and on tourism typologies. Questions arising out of this review are then raised. For example, are different forms of tourism necessarily alternatives to each other, or are they complementary?

II. Origins and Concepts of Alternative Tourism

A number of projects and policies promoting "new" forms of tourism appeared in developing countries during the 1970s and early 1980s. Such projects were usually small scale and low key in nature and involved a high degree of participation by the local population. In the Caribbean, St. Vincent embarked on a policy of "indigenous and integrated" tourism in 1972 based on gradual, small scale, locally controlled development. However, the government lost power before the policy could be fully implemented (Britton 1977). Alternative accommodation on the island away from San Juan, notably villas and small *paradores* (country style inns), has been encouraged in Puerto Rico, while in Guadeloupe recent policy has stressed diversification in terms of both plant and location (Pearce 1987). Hotel development near Pointe-Pitre has been followed by official encouragement for small units, both private and communal, initially on the Île des Saintes and later on Marie-Galante and La Désirade. Similarly in French Polynesia, official emphasis has gone from luxury hotels *d'impact* on Tahiti, to bungalow type accommodation on Moorea and Bora Bora, to support for small family units in the more distant islands, particularly in the Tuamoto archipelago (Blanchet 1981). Ranck (1980) has examined different attempts to foster alternative tourism in some of the more isolated parts of Papua New Guinea, particularly in the form of clan-run guest houses.

The most widely cited of the officially sponsored alternative tourism programs is that of the Lower Casamance region of Senegal which is variously described as a "tourism for discovery project" or "integrated rural tourism" (Saglio 1979, 1985; Bilsen 1987). By 1983, nine small villages of traditional Diola dwellings had been built there.

The outward manifestations of these various projects are similar, with an emphasis on locally owned and operated, small scale traditional accommodation units. However, significant differences exist in their underlying policies and philosophies as well as between these and the policies of other alternative tourism groups. In the cases of French Polynesia and Guadeloupe, for instance, official encouragement of small family-run units appears to have been designed to maintain the population on the outer islands where this form of tourism was seen to offer some development opportunities. Such encouragement was a later stage in a policy which had initially attempted to launch tourism by concentrating large hotels on the main islands of the two groups so as to achieve economies of scale in infrastructural investments and to create sufficiently strong images to develop a tourist traffic from distant markets (Baptistide 1979). In the cases of St. Vincent and the Lower Casamance, on the other hand, the goal of development through local participation appears to have been reinforced or even initially stimulated by some reaction to mass tourism and by the strong and explicit goal of improving contacts between the hosts and their guests. Indigenous accommodation was seen not only as a way by which the local population could become involved in tourism, but also as a means of offering a more authentic, meaningful, and satisfying experience for both the visitor and the visited. Here the alternative is not only a different form of tourism but one which is perceived to be preferable.

Differences in the degree of emphasis given to form or underlying philosophy also occur in the various recommendations and definitions of alternative tourism which have been put forward by diverse individuals and groups in the past decade. A UNESCO-sponsored workshop involving South Pacific researchers and National Tourist Office (NTO) managers drew attention to the nature and extent of development which might result from different forms of tourism distinguished by accommodation type when it recommended in 1980

that studies be carried out in at least four Pacific Island countries to evaluate experience with alternative forms of tourism, for example, international hotels, locally owned hotels, smaller motels or guest houses, village accommodation. (Pearce 1980:viii)

Two years later, a Commonwealth Geographic Bureau workshop on tourism on small islands held in Fiji put forward "six Third World alternatives to large scale, capitalistic, foreign owned tourism" (Britton 1987:181). Here the existing mainstream form of tourism is spelled out and, instead of one, six alternatives are presented, essentially in terms of scale and ownership.

Dernoi (1981:253) initially defined alternative tourism by accommodation type:

In alternative tourism (AT) the "client" receives accommodation directly in or at the home of the host with, eventually, other services and facilities offered there.

However, he then went on to list a number of other features by which alternative tourism might be distinguished from "conventional/commercial tourism." These features essentially describe the nature of the enterprises, but he also recognized differences in possibilities for creating tension or improving understanding between tourists and locals. This latter aim is strengthened in his more recent definition:

Simply stated, AT/CBT [Community Based Tourism] is a privately offered set of hospitality services (and features), extended to visitors, by individuals, families, or a local community. A prime aim of AT/CBT is to establish direct personal/cultural intercommunication and understanding between host and guest. (Dernoi 1988:89)

The promotion of a better form of tourism is an explicit goal of the Ecumenical Coalition of Third World Tourism (ECTWT), a church-based network whose interests in and views on tourism have evolved during the 1970s and 1980s (Gonsalves 1987). For the ECTWT,

Alternative tourism is a process which promotes a just form of travel between members of different communities. It seeks to achieve mutual understanding, solidarity and equality amongst participants. (Holden 1984:15)

The stress here has been on facilitating and improving contacts between hosts and guests, especially through the organization of well prepared special interest tours, rather than on actual development of facilities. The social contact emphasis appears to have been in reaction to some of the excesses of mass tourism and, especially in Asia where most of the related conferences were held, to sex tours in particular.

Although some support groups exist in Europe (e.g., Tüting and Krippendorf 1989 and Dernoi 1981 cited examples of European rural tourism projects), the policies described so far have essentially concerned alternative tourism in developing countries. The European counterpart of this phenomenon is perhaps found in the concept of "sanfter Tourismus" or "soft tourism" which gained some popularity in the early 1980s, especially in the German speaking Alpine areas of Bavaria, Austria, and Switzerland. Many and varied definitions have been proposed and a number of related terms used, although "alternative tourism" is not one of them (Hasslacher 1984; Broggi 1985). While social and economic criteria are important, the distinguishing feature of "soft tourism" is the weight given to environmental matters and the promotion of ecologically sensitive development policies. A general definition of soft tourism is found in the 1984 Chur Declaration of the Commission Internationale pour la Protection des Régions Alpines (CIPRA):

By soft tourism, CIPRA denotes a form of tourism which leads to mutual understanding between the local population and their guests, which does not endanger the cultural identity of the host region and which endeavors to take care of the environment as best as possible. "Soft tourists" give priority to using infrastructures destined for the local population and do not accept substantial tourist facilities harmful to the environment. (Broggi 1985:286)

As noted earlier, some of these definitions are elaborated on by way of a systematic contrasting of the features of alternative tourism with those of what is perceived to be the dominant, mainstream variety: commercial/conventional (Dernoi 1981); "large-scale, capitalistic, foreign-owned" (Britton 1987); "hard tourism" (Hasslacher 1984). In other cases, the new form of tourism is an alternative to some general and ill-defined mass tourism. The distinction is usually between polar opposites, and there is scarcely any recognition of variations in the mainstream nor any evidence of the existence of intermediate cases. Another body of literature, dealing with tourism typologies, gives greater attention to these variations; classifications with three or more categories are not uncommon. Moreover, "alternative tourism," as variously defined above, rarely occurs as one of the classes in the typology literature.

III. Classifications

As the literature on the classification of tourist development has recently been reviewed elsewhere (Pearce 1989), only the salient features will be examined here. First, it should be noted that this literature is not extensive; relatively few writers have tried to identify and clarify different types or processes of tourist development. Much of the literature on tourism is ideographic in nature with few attempts being made to compare case studies, let alone generalize from them. Even where an effort has been made to model a process, this has sometimes suggested that only a single development path exists, as in some cases from the Caribbean (e.g., Lundberg 1974:197–98; Hills and Lundgren 1977). The typologies that have been proposed serve the useful purpose of highlighting the fact that different processes of development can and do occur. More importantly, the criteria used in deriving these typologies can provide a means of analyzing tourism in other situations for, as Preau (1968:139) points out: "A rigorous classification is less important than an analytical method of examining reality." This would especially appear to be the case when addressing the question "an alternative to what?"

Most typologies have been confined to local and regional developments in particular environments, notably in coastal and alpine areas, with some research also being carried out in Third World destinations. Comparatively little attention has been directed to classifying urban and rural tourism. With the exception of the Third World classifications and some of the work on tourists themselves, most of the typologies have been derived in Europe. North Americans in particular have neglected this problem in the same way that they have largely ignored alternative tourism.

The seminal typology on tourist development along the coast was Barbaza's (1970) regional study of the Mediterranean/Black Sea coastline, where three types of development were distinguished. Other recent writers (Priestley 1986; Morris and Dickinson 1987), while not proposing typologies as such, have underlined factors resulting in differences in the degrees and types of tourist development that have occurred along the Costa Brava and brought about significant local variations on the broad regional theme introduced by Barbaza. These later studies suggest that the depiction of the Costa Brava as a single region given over to mass charter tourism is an oversimplification. The only American attempt at classifying tourist development appears to be that by Peck and Lepie (1977) who developed a threefold typology which they applied to small coastal communities in North Carolina.

Ski-field development in the French Alps has been examined and classified by, among others, Preau (1968, 1970), Pearce (1978), and Raynouard (1986), while in the larger Alpine arc Barker (1982) identified differences in the scale, intensity, and form of tourist development between the western Alps (France, western Switzerland) and the eastern Alps (eastern Switzerland, northern Italy, Austria, Bavaria).

Similar typologies of rural tourism are difficult to find, although two three-stage models of second home expansion in rural or peri-urban areas have been proposed by Lundgren (1974) drawing on the Canadian experience and by Boyer (1980) examining the Paris basin. Other studies from France have highlighted local variations in second home development in the Marais de Monts region (Lefevre and Renard 1980) and in Provence-Côte d'Azur (Bromberger and Ravis-Giordani 1977). Again, the message is one of local if not regional variation.

Despite the large amount of effort given over to research on tourism in the Third World, comparatively little attention has been directed to examining systematically the way in which tourism has developed there. All too often, tourism in developing countries is portrayed as being the exclusive realm of large multinational hotel chains or tour operators. Closer analysis in particular countries has shown that different forms of tourism do indeed exist. Large, intermediate, and small accommodation types, for instance, have been identified by Haider (1989) on Tobago and Rodenburg (1980) on Bali. Wong (1986) has produced a more complex classification on the east coast of Peninsular Malaysia while Young (1977) showed diversity within the Caribbean, where she derived categories of comprehensive luxury and plantation tourism.

Other writers have been less concerned with typologies of tourism than with classifying tourists themselves. Gray (1970), for example, distinguishes between wanderlust and sun lust tourists, Plog (1973) between psychocentrics and allocentrics, and Pearce (1978) between circuit and destination tourists. Smith (1977) has derived a sevenfold typology based on tourist numbers and their adaptation to local norms. Market researchers have presented innumerable different segmentations based on socioeconomic, psychographic, and other factors. As an example of the great diversity of tourist demand which may exist, Oppedijk van Veen and Verhallen (1986) cite a Dutch survey of over 2,000 holiday makers of whom forty percent had unique vacations. The largest group having similar vacations (a two-person summer vacation, abroad, in the mountains, with hotel or apartment accommodation, transport by private car, and no advance reservations) consisted of no more than two percent of the sample.

Many variables and techniques for distinguishing among different groups of tourists and forms of tourism have also been used for the purposes of analyzing the spatial structures of tourism (Pearce 1987). Included here are measures of accommodation (type, capacity, occupancy, ratio of beds to host population, . . .), attractions (type, number of visitors, . . .), economic impact (expenditure, employment, revenue, . . .), and tourists (number, origin, seasonality, length of stay, . . .). Often, selected single measures are used to map spatial variations but occasionally more complex, composite classifications are attempted, as with typologies of tourism in Romania (Molnar, Milhail, and Maier 1976; Swizewski and Oancea 1978). The use of these variables and techniques shows that considerable geographical variations in tourism occur although certain regularities in its spatial structure are also to be found. These diverse studies clearly show that many different forms of tourism and types of tourist can be identified. Many differences also occur in the criteria used and the types of classification devised.

These differences reflect actual variations in the situations studied, the purposes for which the typologies were derived, and the backgrounds and interests of the researchers. In general, there is little justification of the variables used; and only rarely is a new classification related to earlier typologies. As in other fields of tourism, the typology literature is fragmented, lacks cohesion, and is without much sense of common purpose and central direction. A major reason for this is the multifaceted nature of tourism which makes any comprehensive analysis or classification very difficult, and consequently has led researchers to concentrate on certain aspects (e.g., demand, development, or impact), to focus on particular types of tourism (e.g., coastal or alpine), or to limit themselves to selected areas (e.g., the Mediterranean, the Black Sea coast, or the North Carolina coast).

This is not to suggest that a detailed, comprehensive, and global classification scheme is essential for addressing all or even most tourism problems, even if its preparation were immediately feasible. However, a better, systematic basis for discriminating between different forms of tourism would not only provide a firmer foundation for exploring further aspects of alternative tourism but would also go a long way toward establishing some common ground on which a more theoretical and unified approach to the study of tourism might be developed. Attempts at assessing the impacts of tourist development, a major preoccupation with tourism researchers, would clearly benefit from a more systematic appraisal of the different processes which have given rise to those impacts in the same way that market researchers have increasingly emphasized the need for better segmentation in marketing tourism and understanding demand (Pearce 1989). It may be, for example, that the deleterious effects of tourism, such as water pollution through the discharge of inadequately treated sewage, are much less in a large, planned resort than with smaller scale spontaneous developments lacking appropriate infrastructure.

Development of a more comprehensive classification of tourism is clearly a daunting task, but one which needs to be addressed. Drawing on the literature reviewed above, the remainder of this analysis limits itself to a discussion of the basic questions which might be asked and variables that might be used. No attempt will be made to apply these to a given situation, but a number of points will be raised relating back to the earlier review of alternative tourism.

IV. Classifying Tourism—A Synthesis

Table 1 attempts to summarize the major variables which different writers have employed to derive their classifications or to distinguish alternative tourism from conventional or mass tourism. Further details are to be found in the references cited; in some cases, Table 1 represents a synthesis of more specific variables as with Hasslacher's (1984) distinction between "hard" and "soft" tourism.

Table 1 indicates a wide range of variables have been used to classify different types of tourism. Some, such as those relating to scale and ownership, have been used more frequently than others (e.g., context or markets), but none occurs consistently from one classification to the next. This may suggest either a marked disagreement among the authors as to what is relevant or, as is perhaps more likely, it may reflect the complex multifaceted nature of tourism.

The diversity of criteria used may also result from the availability of relevant material. Assembling the data or information on each of these

TABLE 1 A Synthesis of Variables Used in the Classification of Tourism[a]

Context	Barbaza, Préau (68), Young.
Facilities	
Type	Britton (87), Haider, Pearce (80). Young,
Scale	Barker, Britton (87); Dernoi (81); Young, Jenkins, Haider, Rodenburg, Wong
Quality, service, prices	Dernoi (81), Haider, Pearce (78)
Location	
Localized/extensive	Barbaza, Barker, Dernoi (81), Young
Isolated/incorporated	Barker, Jenkins, Pearce (78), Préau (70)
Developers/ownership	
Origin and type	Britton (87), Dernoi (81), Haider, Hasslacher, Pearce (78), Peck & Lepie, Préau (70), Raynouard, Rodenburg
Attitudes and motives	Dernoi (81), Hasslacher, Préau (70)
Development process	
Requirements	Britton (87), Dernoi (81), Préau (68, 70)
Time	Hasslacher, Pearce (78), Peck and Lepie, Préau (68, 70)
Planning	Barbaza, Hasslacher, Pearce (78)
Process	Hasslacher, Raynouard, Wong
Form	Barker, Pearce (78).
Markets and Marketing	
Origin of tourists	Haider, Jenkins
Other tourist characteristics	Gray, Pearce (87), Plog, Smith (77)
Promotion and packaging	Boerma, Saglio
Impacts	Britton (87), Dernoi (81), Hasslacher, Peck and Lepie

[a]Bibliographic citations for each author appear in the References to this volume.

variables so as to incorporate them in the classification of tourism for any particular area or study is obviously a challenging task. A useful approach in addressing this array of potential variables (and the list in Table 1 is by no means exhaustive) is to go through a series of basic questions as follows:

1) What are the contexts in which tourism has developed?

Consideration of contextual characteristics, such as the physical, social, cultural, and economic environments, is important because the context will influence the way in which tourism evolves and will condition the impact which tourism will have.

2) What is being developed?

Surprisingly little attention has been given to important aspects of this question. The type of facility considered is usually limited to different means of accommodation, but significant variations also occur in the attractions sector (natural/constructed, public/private, purpose built/converted/shared, . . .), modes and types of transport (road/rail/air/etc., public/private, scheduled/chartered, . . .), supporting services, and infrastructure. As has been recognized in Table 1, the scale of development of these facilities is a crucial factor.

3) Where is tourism being developed?

This question can be addressed at several spatial scales. First, a distinction can be made between different physical regions such as coastal, alpine, rural and urban areas. Second, the localized or extensive nature of the development is related to this to the extent to which the tourism projects are isolated or incorporated into the existing settlement network.

4) Who are the developers?

There has been increasing recognition over the past decade that the nature of the developers and the form of ownership and control are critical factors which influence the nature and extent of tourism's contribution to development. Questions to be asked here relate to the origin and type of developer (public/private, foreign/local, individual/corporate, . . .) and developers' attitudes to tourism and the host society (profit or people oriented, aggressive/defensive, . . .).

5) How has tourism developed?

The way in which tourism develops can be described in terms of the inter-relationship of a number of factors, such as the economic and physical inputs required, the rate of development, the nature and extent of planning, the processes involved, and the form of the resulting resorts.

6) Who are the tourists?

As well as estimating the numbers and spending patterns of tourists, information is also needed on their characteristics and motives. Attention should also be directed at how these tourists travel and how their trips and vacations are promoted and packaged. While an extensive tourism marketing literature exists, this has often not been incorporated into broader classifications of tourism.

7) What impacts are generated?

Tourism impacts have been widely studied, but comparatively few attempts have been made to incorporate these impacts into tourism typologies. If this were more commonly done, it would facilitate bringing together cause and effect in the manner outlined by the authors cited.

Of course, derivation of a classification of tourism types involves more than just asking these questions. In each case, specific measures of each variable used must be established, either in quantitative or qualitative terms. For instance, how big must development be to be classified as large or small scale? As Britton (1987:182) notes:

There are alternative definitions of scale (physical size, retail turnover, minimum capital requirements and tariff of product sold) and ownership (varying degrees and forms of control, shareholding, management contracts, joint-stock holding, and family, individual, cooperative, or public proprietorship).

Moreover, different units of measurement might be used. The average second home as an individual unit is small compared with most commercial accommodation forms but, in the aggregate, second homes may constitute a very sizeable proportion of total capacity in particular resorts. Likewise, should a chain hotel be considered separately or part of a larger organization? Are 500 beds in a single hotel the same as 500 beds in one hundred second homes? Such questions need to be asked with regard to each of the variables to be used.

Having established the different criteria to be taken into account, how are the different variables to be combined? While there may be a general tendency for certain classes to come together—large hotels may be owned by external developers and oriented largely to foreign markets, while small guest houses are locally owned and serve predominantly domestic tourists—it would be a mistake to assume that this pattern is universal and that all forms of tourism can slot neatly into a series of logically defined categories. Bromberger and Ravis-Giordani (1977), for example, cite the case of Savines (Provence) where the Socialist mayor encouraged the development of a social tourism center, bringing into the development process a major developer but one who was not profit oriented, rather than permitting the proliferation of second homes, as this may more readily have resulted in the loss of local control (second-home owners have local voting rights and may "take over" a council if they become numerous). In other examples, Bromberger and Ravis-Giordani also show that local control is not per se the "good thing" that many writers imply, particularly where that control is in the hands of development-driven local politicians. A similar point is made by Morris and Dickinson (1987) regarding the Costa Brava.

The challenge here with classification is to be as comprehensive as possible without succumbing to unwieldy complexity. One response to this problem has been to reduce the range of variables used and to limit the number of examples included, as when threefold typologies are illustrated by three examples.

Consideration must also be given to the appropriate scale of analysis. While Barbaza's classification of the Costa Brava holds up at the level of the Mediterranean-Black Sea, closer inspection shows significant local variations (Priestley 1986; Morris and Dickinson 1987). Likewise, Barker's (1982) division of the western and eastern Alps is useful at one scale, but the more detailed analysis within the French Alps also highlights the existence of different forms of tourism there. As the scale of analysis becomes smaller, it may be appropriate to include more variables in the classification.

Attention to the stage of development is equally important. Tourism evolves, and criteria which indicate classification in one category may suggest inclusion of the same area in a different class at a later period. Most of the 150 hotels in Belize, for instance, are small, locally owned, family-run establishments, often built by enlargement of existing dwellings and offering modest standards of service and comfort (Pearce 1984). It is debatable, however, whether this situation represents a form of alternative tourism or the initial pre-take-off stage in a more traditional form of development (van Doorn 1979). If change does occur, at which point is the transition from one category to another made?

V. Questions, Applications, and Conclusions

Having devised some classification, or at least a set of variables by which tourism can be systematically analyzed, a number of problems can be more effectively addressed while other points may be raised. For example, tourism in developed and developing countries has traditionally been seen as two separate phenomena, with few links being made between the two and of which there exist two fairly distinct bodies of literature. A more systematic appraisal reveals that, while differences are indeed to be found, many close parallels also exist in some cases (Pearce 1989).

One of the key features identified with tourism in the Third World is enclavic development, the development of isolated, usually large scale projects undertaken often with a considerable degree of external participation, whether by means of investment assistance from international aid agencies or active involvement by multinational corporations, primarily for foreign visitors (e.g., Hills and Lundgren 1977; Jenkins 1982). In physical and financial terms, however, such enclaves have their parallels in developed countries such as France. The integrated ski resorts of the French Alps and the development of the new beach resorts of Languedoc-Roussillon have much in common with the sun-sand-sea enclaves of Bali, Mexico, the Caribbean, or the South Pacific. The main reason for this is that the advantages of economies of scale and the freedom to develop an isolated site apply as much to resorts created ex nihilo in developed countries as to those built in the Third World.

Nevertheless, differences do occur. The "external" developments in the French case are essentially external to the community or region rather than to the country. International aid agencies scarcely play a role in enclavic development in developed countries. The clientele in the French case remains overwhelmingly domestic, and for this reason the social considerations of enclaves are much less significant there than in developing countries where contrasts between local residents and the predominantly foreign visitors can be marked. Moreover, in France there is a large proportion of independent holiday makers not channelled through tour operators or travel agencies. That these differences are perhaps not that great, particularly in parts of the French Alps, is testified by assessments of tourism's contribution to development in which recent French writers (Dorfmann 1983; Gurin 1984) present arguments similar to those advanced by Hills and Lundgren (1977), Britton (1982), and others for the Caribbean and South Pacific.

Similarities and differences are also to be found in more modest types of tourism in developed and developing countries. In many respects the "alternative tourism" of developing countries discussed earlier has its counterpart in the rural tourism of Europe, particularly in farm tourism. Both involve small scale developments closely linked to the existing community and way of life. These usually feature traditional dwellings or modifications to them. On the basis of accommodation type and ownership, European farm tourism clearly fits several of the earlier definitions of "alternative tourism" and was recognized as such by Dernoi (1981). It has generally not been promoted explicitly to improve host/guest contact, however, or to foster a "more just form of travel." Getting to know farmers and rural life certainly features in some of the advertising, but farm tourism in Europe has generally developed spontaneously by farmers seeking to increase or diversify their income, or has been officially encouraged as a means of rural or regional development. Farmstays in Ireland have been particularly successful, but officially approved Irish Farmhouses must have a minimum of three guest bedrooms and separate dining and living rooms for guests. It is recognized that while guests like contact, they also appreciate comfort and privacy. How "alternative" is this form of tourism?

For a variety of reasons, "alternative tourism" in developing countries has been much more limited and less successful (Ranck 1980; Blanchet 1981) than the farm tourism of Europe (FAO/ECE 1982). Farm tourism in Europe is accessible to a large domestic and international market which can drive to individual farms or *gites ruraux*, whereas the alternative projects in the Third World are frequently handicapped by the costs of international travel in the first place and poor local connections within destinations in the second. Differences in culture and standards of living between hosts and guests are less pronounced in Europe than in the Third World. A shared language greatly facilitates communication between host and guest and eases overall organization. Farm tourism in Europe has also been developed with the help of a variety of advisory and support services. Finally, and perhaps most significantly, European farmstays have been marketed much more effectively. The activities of the Irish Farm Holiday Association provide a good example of what can be done in this field with strong leadership, enthusiasm, and limited resources.

What is apparently the most successful of the alternative tourism projects, that in the Lower Casamance, also shares some of these latter characteristics. The Senegalese project was initiated under the guidance of a French ethnologist (Saglio); some financial assistance with construction costs was provided, for example, by the Agence de Cooperation Culturelle et Technique and by the Canadian Government; and the Department of Tourism has played a role in coordinating and marketing this new form of tourism. Contacts were also developed with travel agencies specializing in youth travel. More recently, attention has turned to non-profit-making travel associations (Saglio 1979, 1985).

However, the Casamance example and several of the others cited earlier (e.g., French Polynesia and Guadeloupe) raise questions about whether such alternative projects could have been established and survived without the prior growth in mass tourism and the accompanying markets and infrastructural support such as, for example, international air connections. Some initial demand for the Casamance projects was generated by way of short overnight excursions from the Club Méditerranée. In other words, can such low-key alternative developments survive in developing countries, or elsewhere, without having some other form of tourism to be an "alternative" to?

The non-promotion of farm tourism in Europe as "alternative tourism" might be seen as instructive in this regard. In many cases, as in Ireland, the farmstay is presented as part of the overall tourist product, and it complements other forms of accommodation rather than replacing them.

In certain areas, there may be only limited possibilities for developing tourism. Farm tourism or some other low-key variety may be the only viable form that can be promoted. In the sense that there is really little choice, such tourism, despite its outward manifestations, scarcely constitutes an alternative, unless it is so to some other form of economic development. In Germany, for example, the Grüne Band has been successful in initiating short stay, cycle tourism in parts of the Münsterland, attracting a small but growing number of visitors from the nearby Ruhr area through collective efforts. Such development fulfills the conditions of "sanfter Tourismus," but the area was scarcely in danger of "hard" tourism developing and the future likelihood of this occurring also seems remote. Soft tourism was not an alternative; given the resources and markets, it was the only real possibility.

Having established with the earlier typologies that different forms of tourism do occur, more consideration now needs to be given to identifying the conditions that permit or restrict choices being made in any given situation. With regard to developing countries, Britton notes:

It is necessary to recognize that the technological prerequisites of some tourism functions preclude certain enterprise types. The technical, management, and marketing needs of international transport, tour wholesaling, advertising, ticketing and reservations are beyond the capacity of some of the alternative types of tourism enterprises. One implication of this is that criteria used to evaluate costs and benefits of any tourism type must be related to the facilities needed to (1) establish a viable tourist industry and (2) ensure that tourism complements development goals. (1987:183)

In his study of the Cook Islands, Milne (1987) highlights the tension that may exist between different development goals and the role of different strategies in attaining them. The two major objectives of the Cook Islands government with regard to tourism are shown to be maximizing gross tourist revenue generation on the one hand and maximizing local participation on the other. Intensification of the present pattern of development characterized by large foreign or European-owned establishments with minimal local linkages might enable the first objective to be met but local control would be sacrificed. Conversely, encouragement of alternative tourist development would enhance local participation and reduce leakages, but at the expense of lower tourist expenditure per day. Milne's study is a further example of the value of systematically analyzing different forms of tourism, in this case with regard to the specific impacts of each and the implications this might have for future development. He suggests that an optimal solution continues to lie along a path between the two poles.

More account must also be taken of demand. The propensity for travel has long reached a level in developed Western economies that provision for this demand is such that "alternative tourism," as narrowly defined in the introduction to this analysis, could never be expected to cope. If the rights to holidays are accepted as a legitimate need for all, then mass tourism—defined simply in terms of sheer numbers—will continue to expand, not only in developed countries, but increasingly in the Third World.

This is not to imply that because demand exists, it should be catered to unthinkingly at the expense of the environment, society, or economy of tourist destinations. Rather, it should be recognized that a variety of different forms of tourism will be needed. By considering a broader spectrum of possible development paths, by relating more closely demand to supply, impact to process, then it may be possible to avoid some of the excesses which have provoked the explicit "alternative tourism" policies in the past, to cope with tourist pressures, and, indeed, even derive some benefits from tourism.

What is required now is a better understanding of the many possible forms of tourism. It is hoped that this review has provided some firmer base to address this problem and that the questions and issues raised will provide some challenges for those involved in the study of tourism.

Chapter 2
Alternative Tourism: The Thin Edge of the Wedge

Richard Butler

I. Introduction

Alternative tourism has emerged as one of the most widely used and abused phrases of the last decade. Like sustainable development it sounds attractive, it suggests concern and thought, a new approach and philosophy toward an old problem, and it is hard to disagree with. Even the most ardent proponent of tourism or the ugliest of "ugly tourists" will probably acknowledge that tourism creates a wide range of problems, even though it may have tremendous economic and social benefits. Thus the idea of a different approach is something most people will accept instinctively, at least in principle, and may perhaps actively promote even if they do not completely understand it, at least if it does not apply to them directly. As with sustainable development, the phrase can mean almost anything to anyone. It is necessary, however, to evaluate carefully just what is meant by the term and, more to the point, what the implications of this alternative form are to existing and potential destination areas.

What is alternative tourism? Alternative to what? It is obviously not alternative to all other forms of tourism, but rather to the least desired or most undesired type of tourism, essentially what is known as mass tourism, the "Golden Hordes" of Turner and Ashe (1975) or the mass institutionalized tourist of Cohen (1972). It is an alternative to the Costa Bravas, the Daytona Strips, Atlantic Citys, and Blackpools of the world, and an alternative also to large numbers of people, tasteless and ubiquitous development, environmental and social alienation, and homogenization. So far, to many academics, jaded travel writers, and intellectuals, alternative tourism sounds good. Like many appealing alternatives, however, there are both problems and costs associated with the alternative. This analysis argues that the problems, the implications, and potential costs have generally been ignored by many proponents of alternative tourism, and that in some situations the "cure" may be worse than the symptoms.

The rejection of mass tourism is not new. Thomas Cook's tourists aroused great opposition from the elite individual tourists they encountered on their travels in the nineteenth century. Christaller (1963) wrote of the transformation of peripheral tourist places because of large numbers of mass tourists and associated developments, concluding that "all who seek real tourism move on." Social scientists have long expressed concern over the effects of tourist related development and visitation on human values, traditions, and behavior in host destinations (Smith 1977).

These concerns have met two fairly significant problems: first, the economic value of mass tourism, at least at national and perhaps regional levels, and second, the fact that many people seem to enjoy being mass tourists. They actually like not having to make their own travel arrangements, not having to find accommodations when they arrive at a destination, being able to obtain goods and services without learning a foreign language, being able to stay in reasonable and sometimes considerable comfort, being able to eat relatively familiar food, and not having to spend vast amounts of money or time to achieve these goals. Mass tourists are prepared to give up genuine one-on-one authentic local cultural contact and the harsh realities of a Third World or Old World existence in return for these conveniences, seen by them as benefits.

It is necessary to ask therefore, why anyone should want to promote alternative forms of tourism, given the "success" and appeal of mass tourism. The answer would appear to lie in an assumption that the alternative forms of tourism (and tourist) will have fewer and less severe negative effects on destination areas and their populations without diminishing the positive economic effects, that is, achieving the best of all worlds. Obviously this is a laudable and eminently desirable goal to many host communities and decision makers.

It is equally reasonable to ask why one would be critical of such alternatives. There are several reasons: the nature of tourism; the nature of the development process; the dismal record of dealing with tourism by most communities and agencies; naive assumptions about all of the above; and, most seriously, human nature.

An attempt is made in Table 1 to identify some of the fundamental problems of tourism. They have been discussed by this writer elsewhere (Butler 1989) but a brief comment is appropriate. In general, there is remarkable ignorance and inaccurate perception of the dimen-

TABLE 1 Problems of Tourism

Ignorance
Of dimensions, nature, power of tourism

Lack of ability
To determine level of sustainable development, i.e., capacity

Lack of ability
To manage tourism and control the development

Lack of appreciation
That tourism does cause impacts, is an industry, and cannot easily be reversed

Lack of appreciation
That tourism is dynamic, and causes change as well as responding to change

Lack of agreement
Over levels of development, over control, over direction of tourism

---

Source: Butler 1990:80

sions of tourism. Few people, even decision makers, are aware of its true magnitude, economic and social linkages, and political significance. At present there is little evidence of any real ability to manage and control tourism at the international level, and even less ability to identify, accept, and maintain appropriate levels of tourism. Thus even if it were possible to determine the "optimal" visitation, there are few examples of how to achieve but not exceed this amount of tourism. Related to the first point noted above is a lack of recognition that tourism is, and behaves, like most other industries: it causes impacts and its development can be self-sustaining and not easily reversible. Tourism is also extremely dynamic, constantly changing and causing change. All these elements combine to produce, in many areas, virtual anarchy in coordination and planning of tourism.

II. The Problems of Tourism

A brief examination of what appear to be major effects resulting from tourism development is in order. They include price rises (labor, goods, taxes, land); change in local attitudes and behavior; pressure on people (crowding, disturbance, alienation); loss of resources, access, rights, privacy; denigration or prostitution of local culture; reduction of aesthetics; pollution in various forms; lack of control over the destination's future; and specific problems such as vandalism, litter, traffic, and low-paid seasonal employment. These problems are common to many forms of development and in many cases represent dissatisfaction with one or both of change from the status quo and overreaching of acceptable levels of impact.

It is necessary, therefore, to consider whether the real problems with status quo or non-alternative tourism are endemic and unavoidable or a function of dimensions and numbers. It is argued here that they are essentially a function of both factors. The nature of tourism to some degree determines the nature and pattern of growth and, unless checked and controlled, will inevitably create a set of problems.

In many areas for many years, tourism was promoted as a panacea, a soft option, with few negative effects. "Tourists take nothing but photographs and leave nothing but footprints" was until recently an advertising slogan of one Canadian provincial government trying to encourage its citizens to welcome visitors. Why anyone would want to welcome people leaving film wrappers and footprints was not clear, but a little note in the advertisement to the effect that tourists spent several billion dollars in Canada may be part of the explanation. In reality, it has become increasingly apparent that tourism creates impacts of various types and levels of seriousness (Mathieson and Wall 1982).

Some of these impacts are almost unavoidable, while attempts at mitigation for others can cause other problems. It is possible almost completely to prevent contact between tourists and locals, for example, if contact is viewed as a problem or cause of social change (Brougham and Butler 1981). Tourist enclaves can be staffed by imported labor and tourists can be encouraged not to venture out of the enclave, as, for example, in many Third World casinos or Club Med-type resorts. However, some authorities would bemoan the lack of contact between tourists and locals and complain of tourist ghettoes, while others would see such developments as a missed opportunity for much needed employment and further alienation of resources for use as imperialistic playthings.

Tourism is an industry, but it is also a form and agent of development and change and must be recognized as such. Controlled and managed properly, it can be a non- or low-consumptive utilizer of resources and can operate on a sustainable basis. However, if developed beyond the capacity of the environment, the resource base, and the local population to sustain it (as discussed by Bryan Farrell in this volume), it ceases to be a renewable resource industry and it instead becomes, as Murphy (1985) has noted, a "boom-bust enterprise."

Such comments, it is suggested here, apply equally to mass tourism and to alternative tourism. The process of development of mass-tourism resorts and destination areas has been discussed widely, including the life-cycle concept proposed by this author (Butler 1980).

What needs to be stressed, however, is that without control and responsibility there is almost inevitably the overreaching of some or all capacity limits and degradation, decline, and change in the tourism product, which includes both environmental and human elements. There is a strong and clear analogy to the "tragedy of the commons " identified by Garrett Hardin.

In Hardin's (1969) essay, the real tragedy of the commons was the inevitability of destruction because of a lack of assigned responsibility and the fact that each individual stood to benefit in the short term by deliberately exceeding the capacity of the resource. Hardin's example was the grazing of too many cattle on the common, while in the case of tourism it could be the presence of too many tourists for the destination to withstand (although with tourism there are many variations on this scenario). While not all the problems of tourism result simply from exceeding capacity limits, many do. Brugger et al. (1984:615) note, "The market for tourism is not in a position to guarantee a path of development which in the long run is in its own best interest." Nor, one might add, is it in a position to guarantee a level or magnitude of development in anyone's best interest. The highly fragmented and extremely competitive nature of the tourism industry, in both the public and private sectors, mitigates against self or internal control. Thus in Cyprus, for example, the Cyprus Tourist Board sees the need for selective marketing and limited specific development, but hoteliers and would-be hoteliers push for rapid growth of all segments of the market (Androniku 1988).

To promote another form of tourism as a solution to the multiple problems which can be caused by extensive and long term tourism development is somewhat akin to selling nineteenth-century wonder medicines, and such promotion needs to be evaluated carefully and objectively. Making simplistic and idealized comparisons of hard and soft, or mass and green tourism, such that one is obviously undesirable and the other close to perfection, is not only inadequate, it is grossly misleading (Table 2). The examples listed in Table 2 are illustrative of such simple and possibly purposefully naive comparisons and do not make for realistic recommendations or intellectually sound debate. Mass tourism need not be uncontrolled, unplanned, short term, or unstable; and green tourism is not always and inevitably considerate, optimizing, controlled, planned, and under local control. To hope that it will be may be the ideal scenario, but it is not always a realistic one. Even if it begins that way, if the tourism industry grows there is little if any evidence that it could always remain so. Some of the worst examples of mass tourism in the world involve concentrated development, such as the wall-to-wall hotels on Queensland's Gold Coast, while build-

TABLE 2 Tourism Development Strategies

Mass tourism	Green tourism
Development without planning	First plan, then develop
Project-led schemes	Concept-led schemes
District level planning only	Regional co-ordination of district plans
Scattered development	Concentrated development
Building outside existing settlements	Development within existing settlements
Intensive development in areas of finest landscapes	Fine landscape conserved
New building and new bed capacity	Re-use existing buildings—better utilisation of bed capacity
Building for speculative unknown future demand	Fixed limited to development
Tourism development everywhere	Development only in suitable places, and where local services already exist
Development by outside developers	"Native" developers only
Employment primarily for non-natives	Employment according to local potential
Development only on economic grounds	Discussion of all economic, ecological and social issues
Farming declines, labour force into tourism	Farm economy retained and strengthened
Community bears social costs	Developer bears social costs
Traffic "plan" favours cars	Traffic "plan" favours public transport
Capacity for high season demand	Capacity for average demand
"Natural" and historical obstacles removed	"Natural" and historical obstacles retained
Urban architecture	Vernacular architecture
High technology and mechanised tourist installations	Selective mechanised development—"low-tech" development favoured

Source: Lane 1988, quoting Krippendorf.

ing outside existing settlements may in some situations be much more socially and environmentally sound than development within existing settlements.

When the approaches of mass tourism and its alternatives are compared in this way, there is little wonder that the concept of soft, green, alternative tourism seems particularly attractive, certainly compared to the much maligned Costa Brava, "El Cid," or "Ugly American" images ascribed to mass tourism. It is in many ways dangerous and problematical to represent something in the manner that alternative tourism is often presented. To promote the acceptance and development of alternative forms of tourism without being confident of the end result can potentially be more harmful for a destination and its population than no development at all, or even limited mass tourism.

III. Evaluating the Alternatives

In properly and appropriately evaluating the relative merits of mass and alternative forms of tourism it is necessary to consider not only the dimensions, behavior, and traits of visitors and the requirements of these forms of tourism, but also their inherent characteristics and their relationships with the agents of change associated with tourism. While the state of research in tourism is such that we cannot yet produce the definitive list of all agents of change associated with tourism, we can identify at least some which are generally acknowledged as significant. They are illustrated in Table 3 and have been subdivided into four broad areas: factors relating to the tourists, factors relating to the resource base, factors relating to the economic structure, and factors relating to the political structure of the destination area. This is certainly not claimed as a total list of all factors, and in some cases a wide range or a large number of elements are subsumed under one category; for example, contact is treated as a single category but actually varies in amount, nature, location, duration, and other factors.

The purpose of Table 3 is to illustrate that a simplistic (big/small, rapid/slow development) type of comparison is not acceptable. Rather, if we examine, even simplistically, the characteristics of mass and alternative forms of tourism with respect to the related agents of change, we see a potentially very different picture. In the short term there is little doubt that alternative tourism appears, and almost certainly is, much less conducive to causing change in destination areas than mass tourism, in part because of its dimensions and in part because of the need for fewer and smaller facilities. However, as time goes by, some factors can assume greater significance under alternative tourism and result in greater and more serious long-term change. Contact is one such example. While total contact (measured in visitor/host interaction occasions, for example) may occur less under alternative tourism, duration may be greater per occasion, the nature may be more intensive involving considerable discussion, and the location may be more sensitive and personal as, for example, with a home in comparison to a hotel lobby.

In Table 3 the tourist characteristics noted refer to total numbers of visitors, the behavior of the majority, their location in the destination, the time spent at the destination (length of stay), the amount and nature of host/guest contact or interaction, and the degree of similarity

TABLE 3 Principal Agents of Change Relating to Types of Tourism

	Conventional tourism		Alternative tourism	
	Short term	Long term	Short term	Long term
Tourists				
Numbers	Small, rapid growth	Large, perhaps decline	Small, slow growth	Small, consistent
Behaviour	Sedentary	Sedentary	Explorer	Explorer
Location	Limited/ resorts	Resorts	Communities, households	Widespread, households
Time	Short	Short, definite	Long, indefinite	Medium, definite
Contact	Some, economic	Great, shallow	Some, intensive	Intensive
Similarity	Little	Little	Very little	Very little
Resource				
Fragility	Possible pressure	Possible ruination	Little pressure	Pressure
Uniqueness	Possible pressure	Possible ruination	Little pressure	Pressure
Capacity	Problem	Probably exceeded	Minor problem	Problem
Economy				
Sophistication	Some	Developed	None	Very little
Leakage	Some	Some	Maybe lots	Maybe lots
Political				
Local control	Some	Little	Most	Some vulnerable
Planning extent	Some	Little/ reactive	Little	Little

between the two groups. Thus in the short term or early stages of mass tourism, numbers are small but grow rapidly, and visitors are sedentary and primarily in resorts, staying for brief periods, with little interaction with locals except of an economic nature, and are generally quite different from them.

The resource characteristics most related to tourism-induced change are the degree of fragility in the area, the area's uniqueness, and the general capacity or limits to development. Thus in the early stages of conventional tourism there is likely to be pressure on both the fragile and unique characteristics of the resource, and capacity limits may be ignored. In the long term scenario for alternative tourism, one could see equally heavy pressure on the unique and perhaps most fragile resources because of their specific appeal to alternative tourists, with their very limited capacity a major problem to be faced. It is not impossible or unrealistic to see in the long term a conventional tourism scenario in which the unique and most fragile resources are under little pressure because they do not appeal to the mass tourist.

Two characteristics of destination area economies are felt to be significant in terms of potential changes caused by tourism: the sophistication of the host economy, and the degree of leakage of tourist expenditures from the destination area. In the context of conventional tourism, local economies tend to become more sophisticated and more developed as tourism grows, but there is always some leakage. In alternative tourism areas, the economies are normally very simple with high levels of leakage, thus retaining only a smaller amount of tourist expenditures in the area. This greater leakage may reduce or contain the rate of change or it may mean a great deal of work for relatively little financial gain.

Finally, with respect to the political arrangements of destination areas, the degree of local control and the extent of planning practices are two key factors. In most mass tourism areas local control exists initially to varying degrees but tends to be less effective as development becomes international. Similarly, the planning process often becomes more conceptual and less realistic, and finally completely reactive. In the alternative tourism scenario, local control over areas is quite common, in many cases because of the remoteness of such areas, but over time becomes equally vulnerable to external pressures. Planning is often totally absent and, if introduced, may be too late and reactive.

One conclusion which can be drawn is that, at least potentially, alternative forms of tourism penetrate further into the personal space of residents, involve them to a much greater degree, expose often fragile resources to greater visitation, expose the genuine article to tourism to a greater degree, proportionally may result in greater leakage of expenditure, and may cause greater political change in terms of control over development than traditional or mass tourism.

Alternative tourism is often used as a synonym for appropriate tourism. In this context, however, it is necessary to ask the question: appropriate for whom? Furthermore, one should also ask for how long, under what conditions, and by whose decision is it deemed appropriate? Tourism has rightly often been regarded as yet another form of imperialism, furthering the domination by and subservience to Developed Countries of Third World or Lesser Developed Countries (Roekaerts and Savat 1989). Surely academics from developed countries pontificating on what is appropriate tourism is hardly much better, particularly when such authorities cannot guarantee the long term results of their recommendations.

In fact, one might argue that at the root of much of what is being proposed as alternative tourism is really disguised class prejudice. Large numbers of middle and lower class tourists are not welcome, nor are "hippies" in any number, but small numbers of affluent, well educated and well behaved tourists are welcome. While this may seem a harsh criticism, descriptions such as "the hippie, preaching his counterculture with drugs, loose sexual mores and poor hygienic standards," and "the average tourist—a consuming raping individual, who destroys or violates what he or she has come to look for" (Roekaerts and Savat 1989) do little to dispel such criticism. Even experienced researchers make similar comments. Holder (1988:10) writes: "The country resorts to mass tourism, attracting persons of lower standards of social behavior and economic power. This leads to the socio-environmental degradation of the tourist destination." This dislike of "low class" tourists and tourism manifests itself in a wide variety of areas. In Ontario, in one infamous episode, a coach load of tourists (day visitors) had stones thrown at their coach by residents of Niagara-on-the-Lake, and yet this small town is proud of, and enthusiastically promotes, a Shaw Theatre Festival which attracts large numbers of the "right kind of tourist" who will stay in rather expensive restored properties and spend a considerable amount of money in the process. In the book *Bermuda's Delicate Balance,* Hayward, Gomez, and Sterner (1981:57–59) are clear that the type of visitors they would prefer are "the very tourists that would be our ideal: the long-staying, high spending, committed, quality visitor." While all proponents of alternative tourism may not be guilty of class prejudice, in the majority of cases the type of tourist who would realistically be attracted to most forms of alternative tourism is highly educated, affluent, mature, and probably white. If this description fits many researchers (except the affluent label), it may explain why many academics are at least basically sympathetic to alternative tourism!

IV. The Implications of Alternative Tourism

The implications of alternative tourism need to be examined more closely. These include the reduction in numbers of tourists, the change in type of tourist, the education of all parties involved, and the impacts resulting from a new set of activities. Reducing numbers of tourists has two aspects: reducing numbers in areas where numbers are currently too great, and limiting potential visitors to levels compatible with ca-

TABLE 4 Possible Implications of Alternative Tourism

	Impacts		
	Social	Environmental	Economic
Tourists			
Numbers	Positive	Positive	Negative
Behaviour	Questionable	Slightly positive	Negative
Location	Negative	Negative	Negative
Time	Positive/Negative	Negative	Positive
Contact	Negative	Neutral	Neutral
Similarity	Negative	Slightly negative	Positive
Resource			
Fragility	Neutral	Negative	Neutral
Uniqueness	Neutral	Negative	Neutral
Capacity	Neutral	Slightly positive	Neutral
Economy			
Sophistication	Positive	Neutral	Negative
Leakage	Slightly positive	Neutral	Negative
Political			
Local control	Positive	Unknown	Neutral
Planning extent	Slightly negative	Unknown	Neutral

pacity parameters. It is extremely difficult to reduce numbers in a free market situation without prejudicing the viability of the industry. Revenues can be expected to decline (unless massive market replacement occurs at the same time), which can result in loss of employment and reduction in local standard of living. Local support is relatively unlikely, certainly not likely to be unanimous. A few places have seen this change, normally where relatively small numbers were involved, and even then not without opposition (Jayal 1986; Singh 1986). Limiting numbers before they become a problem is more attractive but assumes that capacity levels can be identified and agreed upon. Even if local preferences were accepted, there is no guarantee these would match the goals of alternative tourism proponents. In many cases, local entrepreneurs and politicians have been enthusiastic proponents of mass tourism development. Rural and indigenous peoples' environmental ethics often differ from those of their urban counterparts, and they see the imposition of environmental controls and protection as contradictory, limiting their development in order to satisfy the desires of the urban sophisticates.

Table 4 illustrates some possible implications of alternative tourism with respect to the elements listed in Table 3 in the context of the social, environmental, and economic systems of destination areas. It suggests that fewer tourists may have positive social and environmental effects but probably negative economic ones, while the longer length of stay of alternative tourists may have both positive and negative social effects, negative environmental ones, and positive economic effects. Resource implications are primarily environmental and are more likely to be negative than positive over the long term for reasons noted earlier. In economic terms, the impacts of alternative tourism are negative with respect to total amounts of tourist expenditure, the amount remaining in the local area, and the number of jobs created.

Politically, the implications of alternative tourism are even less clear but fascinating to speculate upon. Local control and initiative may be stimulated at first but lost to external institutions creating dissatisfaction. Preservation of resources and culture for alternative tourism may run counter to individual desires, and planning may be resented at the local level. More research is needed in this topic.

Changing the type of tourist is as difficult as limiting or reducing numbers. Plog (1977) and others have shown that different tourists have different preferences. Once an area is developed and markets established, it is next to impossible to change the type of visitor back to that which had come earlier in search of "real tourism" (Christaller 1963). Furthermore, if a destination aims itself at a specific (and hence limited) market, for example, ornithologists, photographers, amateur archaeologists, culture lovers, it faces the real risk that not only may there not be a large enough market but it may not be a repeat market. Visitors may decide that after seeing the Galapagos they will go to the Canadian Arctic, then to the Himalayas, then to Antarctica, and so on. In addition, while mass tourists are for the most part sedentary and spend their money in a limited number of locations, much of the expenditure of the alternative tourist may be pre-spent on packages or spent in small amounts in a wide variety of locations. Wall (1989) has shown that the true wilderness tourist spends little or nothing in the wilderness, because in the real wilderness there is nothing on which to spend money.

Educating people is an alternative that is hard for this author to reject, but it is a mammoth and long term project. Most people would probably accept the wisdom of the concept of sustainable development and developing "suitable" and low impact forms of tourism, but short term reality dictates that the window of opportunity is often limited and the time scales of most entrepreneurs are short. Time scales of a tourist spending a week on a beach are even shorter. It is not realistic, perhaps not even naively optimistic, to expect a tourist wishing to lie on a beach in the Caribbean to be too interested in the impact he or she may have on the social fabric of the island visited, especially when they may not wish to associate with local residents or move out of the hotel complex. The response is, with some justification, more likely to be that tourism is supplying jobs and investment and, because the government of that location obviously wants tourists, there is no problem.

The bottom line perhaps is that one cannot expect one's cake to remain after eating it. The much needed jobs and income will not necessarily come from alternative tourism. To have some tourism but not too much is similar to parenthood; the child grows and changes almost independent of the parent's influence. However environmentally sympathetic, every tourist can be damaging to the environment (Grosjean 1984), and few forms of alternative tourism are really amenable to a no-change scenario over time. In the social environment, a similar situation exists:

It is generally accepted that social change and impacts from tourism occur because of contact between tourists and the hosts and residents. One can therefore argue that tourism which places tourists in local homes, even when they are culturally sympathetic, and not desiring a change in local behavior, is much more likely to result in changes in local behavior in the long run than is a larger number of tourists in more conventional tourist ghettoes, where contact with locals is limited, if intensive, and in, what is to locals, and tourists, clearly artificial settings. The true local environment can still be found in areas into which tourists do not penetrate. To disperse tourists in space and time, i.e., to extend the season to avoid peaking, could and in some cases has, resulted in far more profound and permanent changes over a wider area, than when tourists are confined to small areas in large numbers for clearly defined seasons. (Butler 1990)

V. Conclusions

This analysis has been critical of alternative tourism, a position felt necessary because so much has been assumed to be positive about alternative tourism without critical evaluation. These criticisms should not be taken as a rejection of the concept per se, but rather as an expression of concern and doubt that enough is known about the topic to warrant wholesale support for it. In some areas, for some people, in some situations, it is certainly better than mass tourism. In many cases, however, such areas would most likely *not* experience mass tourism anyway. The question then should be: is alternative tourism an appropriate form of development, not *instead* of mass tourism, but in its own right? Can it be controlled and directed so that benefits go where they are intended, negative aspects are mitigated or avoided, and the developments remain sustainable and within capacity limitations, both human and physical? That would represent a truly alternative approach rather than the snake-oil panacea too often proposed at present.

This is not an attempt to dismiss alternative tourism as being impractical or undesirable, but even in the case of alternative tourism, perhaps even *more* so in that case, there needs to be more selective and deliberate planning, management, and control over development. An active rather than reactive approach (Edwards 1988:13) with an emphasis upon balance, as Holder (1988:19) notes, "between ecosystems, balancing economic and social goals, balancing the responsibility of the state with the rights of individuals and groups." This is not easy to do in any circumstances. As Cazes (1989b: 125) has pointed out, there is really no example of significant size which clearly and completely meets the alternative tourism model, including local priorities and control. Perhaps, in line with Cohen's (1989) excellent conclusions to his brief critique of alternative tourism, the real value of alternative tourism lies in aiding more realistic attempts to ameliorate the problems of conventional tourism rather than trying to do away with mass tourism and replace it with something else. Where would the millions of tourists who currently visit the Costa Brava go and what would they do? Perhaps just as important, what would the inhabitants of Lloret de Mar and neighboring communities do?

In realistic terms, we cannot and should not want to obliterate mass tourism. Alternative tourism could not replace it in economic terms, in personal preference terms, and certainly not in logistical terms. At best, perhaps, it can fulfill a number of roles. One is to complement mass tourism by increasing attractions and authenticity, as for example Meganck and Ramdial note (1984:4), allowing tourists "the chance to enjoy the natural areas and rich cultural history of the region." Another role is to serve the needs and desires of specific groups or categories of tourists including, for example, those interested in natural history, in language, or in photography. Another role, already well established in Europe, is to supplement incomes of primarily rural dwellers in marginal areas through, for example, farm tourism, guiding, crafts, and bed-and-breakfast enterprises. A fourth role may be to allow some tourism development in areas which cannot sustain major change because of environmental and/or social capacity limitations. As Norbu (1984) shows however, even as few as five thousand annual visitors can have an unacceptably high level of impact, depending upon their activities and needs.

Thus, the development of alternative tourism should be supported where it is clearly the most appropriate form of tourism, but reaching this decision requires consideration of much more than counting the negative effects of mass or conventional tourism. It means determining

TABLE 5 Viewpoints in Tourism Development

Viewpoints	Parties involved
Economic	Entrepreneurs (local and non-local), government, residents
Annoyance	Residents, tourists (if disappointed)
Environmental	Government(?), residents(?), external groups
Pleasure	Tourist
Political	Politicians, local residents, entrepreneurs
Mental/spiritual	Ecclesiastical, academic

the priorities and needs of an area and its residents (in conjunction with those residents), determining the capacity limitations of the destination environment (human and physical), and the reaction of the potential market. It is essential to incorporate a wide variety of perspectives in any assessment of an area for tourism development. One can expect to find a number of different and often contradictory viewpoints relating to tourism, as shown in Table 5. Traditionally, the economic viewpoint has had the most importance and tends to be supportive of tourism development. Furthermore, that viewpoint is common to all levels, from the individual to international corporations. Often in opposition to this perspective is one of annoyance, primarily limited to local residents suffering the negative effects of tourism and perhaps also tourists if their expectations are not met. The environmental viewpoint is often broad, including local residents, non-governmental organizations ranging from local groups to international bodies such as Greenpeace, and elements of various levels of government. The pleasure viewpoint is primarily that of the tourist, and the elements giving pleasure to the tourist may cause concern or annoyance to others. A political viewpoint is also appearing in some areas, where tourism and other forms of development and change may reflect or conflict with local or nationalistic aspirations, which in turn may differ from the preferences of the government of the day. Finally, there is a more abstract viewpoint (noted in Table 5 as "mental/spiritual") expressing a concern with morals, social mores, and aesthetics, most commonly but not uniquely held by ecclesiastics and academics, which may or may not become significant in decision making.

Alternative tourism is not effective if there are no tourists. There must be sufficient attractions to draw tourists, and at present most alternative tourists, like mass tourists, have many options open to them. Despite the desire not to attract the mass market, it is necessary for even alternative tourism destinations to attract a market. The main problems include identifying the market, reaching only it, and maintaining it at an acceptable size for a long time. Unless the type of tourism development proposed for an area is acceptable to all or most of the viewpoints shown in Table 5, the long term future for tourism in that area is unlikely to be very satisfactory. Opposing viewpoints will be exerting pressure constantly to alter the industry to fit their vision of development.

A major concern is that the process of tourism development would appear to be unidirectional; that is, alternative small scale tourism can change to mass conventional tourism, and perhaps will inevitably do so without strict management and control, but mass conventional tourism is highly unlikely to be able to change to alternative small scale tourism. Even if this latter change were possible, the consequences in economic, social, and political terms might be too severe ever to allow it to take place.

This analysis has tried not to take sides for or against either of these types of tourism but rather to argue for rational, objective evaluation of the merits and problems of all types of tourism in the context of the destination area. Development has the capacity to enhance enjoyment, economic return, and the environment if the type, scale, and timing are correct. It also has the power to degrade, corrupt, or bankrupt and despoil if any or all the elements are wrong. Claiming that one form of tourism is all things for all areas is not only pious and naive, it is unfair, unrealistic, and unwise.

Chapter 3
Making the Alternative Sustainable: Lessons from Development for Tourism

Emanuel de Kadt

I. Introduction

> We don't want tourism. We don't want you. We don't want to be degraded as servants and dancers. That is cultural prostitution. I don't want to see a single one of you in Hawaii. There are no innocent tourists.

A few years ago, in a short note published in *Annals of Tourism Research*, Georg Pfafflin approvingly quoted these sentiments of a native Hawaiian, expressed at a church-sponsored conference on tourism and the Third World. In that note, Pfafflin not only repeated the view that the chances for genuine encounters between tourists and host populations are extremely poor, but also wrote that "the public" in Europe "now realizes that tourism to the Third World is always connected with such North-South problems as hunger, the debt crisis and its poverty-producing effects, and the destruction of the ecological system" (Pfafflin 1987:577).

It is not obvious that Pfafflin is right about "the" public, nor is it easy to understand what mechanisms are involved in these very different connections. Yet however sweeping his view of the ill-effects of tourism and however much it ignores many years of patient work to distinguish different tourism situations from each other (Cohen 1988a), this view nevertheless needs to be taken into account. It is relevant to much that has been written about Alternative Tourism.

The concept of Alternative Tourism has been used in so many ways as to make it meaningless. Even so, many of the approaches share an undertone of moral indignation, of rejection of normal, mass or "mainstream" tourism in which political hostility to transnational capitalism mingles with cultural and ecological unease over modern mass-consumption society.

This undertone has also been present in the concept of "Alternative," or "Another," Development. However, it is not used in so bewildering a variety of ways as is Alternative Tourism. Alternative Development is a broader concept, which in some senses encompasses that of Alternative Tourism. The parallels and contrasts between these two "alternative" concepts and the evolution in both cases from a predominantly "moralistic" or normative approach to one which is more concerned with analysis and understanding are the focus of the present analysis.

II. Alternative Development

There have always been a variety of approaches to development, and no one paradigm or theory has ever attained absolute dominance. Most discussions would recognize at least three contenders in the field: the neo-classical, the Marxist, and the structuralist "schools" (Toye 1987). During the 1980s, the recognition has spread that all three theories have failed to give satisfactory overall explanations of the process of development, or of its "absence"; and practitioners—decision makers, planners, advisers—in both market and state run economies have been clamoring for new guidelines. Many have blamed the problems of development on the negative effects of a large scale direct role for the state in the economy, and a more or less hefty dose of neo-liberal ("Thatcherite") policies has been injected almost everywhere, even in many "socialist" economies. This has resulted in a broad and widely shared development "mainstream," but we are, it seems, not far from yet another turning point, one likely to reincorporate the view that the untrammeled operation of the market does not provide the ultimate answer and itself creates new problems. We can expect to see a measure of rehabilitation of the state's role in forcefully regulating the market, though not perhaps in the direct production of goods and services (IDS 1987, 1988).

The emergence into prominence, at least in Europe, of Green political parties (the political expression of one of the hitherto more remote "counterpoints" to that mainstream) is likely to push the issue of curbing the market higher up on the political agenda. A few years ago, those with a "green" approach to our planet and development were seen as cranks, their organizations as marginal. Since then, partly as a result of the success of their efforts in putting their views across and partly because of the remarkable impact of the Brundtland Commission (Brundtland 1987), itself a sign of the times, we have all been "greened" to a greater or lesser extent. In recent years environment, ecology and even "sustainable development" have moved progressively closer to the center of the stage of public concern and politics. It is no longer considered outlandish to speak of Alternative Development, or Sustainable Development.

There are many explicit and implicit definitions of Alternative Development. Their constituent elements have become rather more distinct over time, and some of the "evangelical" fervor has been lost. Concern with the environment has been there from the start. Among the Greens there are still some extreme antagonists to mainstream development in "a vocal ecocentric wing (which) continues its rather shrill opposition to the destruction of almost anything" (Brookfield 1988:127), but the more moderate demand for "ecologically sound" development is now heard in wide circles of public and government opinion. While environmental sensationalism and scientific amateurism still abound, there are also indications that among critics of mainstream development a more sober assessment of global ecological problems is emerging, in which less reliance is placed on discredited doom-laden predictions from the 1970s and more allowance is made for technical change and the probability that it will modify the problems as well as their solutions (Brookfield 1988; Pepper 1987).

In addition, the proponents of Alternative Development agree that scaling down the operations of production and government is both necessary and desirable. It is necessary if development is to become sustainable—defined by Brundtland as development that "meets the goals of the present without compromising the ability of future generations to meet their own needs" (Brundtland 1987:43). It is desirable in order to achieve a development which is more "people-oriented," in contrast to the present style. Such development revolves around maintaining economic growth without concern for the effects of such growth in ecological and social ("who benefits?") terms, especially with regard to the "essential needs of the world's poor" (Brundtland 1987:43).

Such scaling down involves encouraging smaller enterprises at the local level—paying attention to what has been called the "informal economy"—as well as promoting devolution of power from central political systems to local, self-reliant communities (Hettne 1985; Ekins 1986). The resemblance of the political prescriptions to those of the nineteenth-century anarchists is striking, and they can be criticized on similar grounds (Pepper 1987:335); some of the purer ideas on community production also smack of nineteenth-century utopianism. It is no wonder that these now dominant Alternative Development views are attacked from a more radical "red" perspective for disregarding the structural causes of ecological and other problems and for being naive about the political action required to change these structures (Pepper 1987:336ff). Yet the basic traits of Alternative Development are clear: ecological soundness, small-scale production, recognition of needs other than those of material consumption, equal consideration of the needs of all (including future generations), and political involvement from below. These are also, broadly, seen as the traits of development that is sustainable.

III. Alternative Tourism

As a concept, Alternative Tourism lacks even the tentative Gestalt which can be recognized in Alternative Development. While Alternative Development always refers to the developing economy or society, Alternative Tourism can have as its prime reference the host economy or society, the tourist, or the national or transnational tourism industry. In fact, Alternative Tourism means all things to all people: "nowadays all travellers who do not undertake a normal type of vacation are lumped together under the general heading of 'alternative tourism'" (Tüting n.d.:280). Some writers appear to suggest that anything other than mass tourism should be graced with the "alternative" label: the collection put together by the Ecumenical Coalition on Third World Tourism leaves such an impression (Holden 1984). Various recent studies, such as the article by Pearce in this volume, have attempted to put some order into this confusion, mainly by distinguishing the different people or situations to which the concept refers (Cazes 1987; Cohen 1987).

Nevertheless, there are a number of themes that recur in many discussions on Alternative Tourism which echo the central issues of Alternative Development. First, Alternative Tourism is applied to tourism which does not damage the environment, is ecologically sound, and avoids the negative impacts of many large-scale tourism developments undertaken in areas which have not previously been developed (Kozlowski 1985; Travis 1985). Second, Alternative Tourism is thought to consist of smaller developments, or attractions for tourists which are set in and organized by villages or communities. These are seen as having fewer negative effects, social or cultural, and a better chance of being acceptable to the local people than mass tourism (Saglio 1979; Bilsen 1987; Gonsalves 1984). Third, and following from this, there is the question of "who benefits." Certain kinds of tourism are called alternative because they are not "exploitative" of local people, because the benefits flow to local residents or in general to poorer communities (Yum 1984; Nielsen 1984). Conventional tourism demands large-scale organization and resources not usually available locally or even in the country; as a result its rewards flow away to distant townsfolk or abroad. Finally, a shared perspective with Alternative Development is an emphasis on cultural sustainability. Tourism which does not damage the culture of the host community is often called alternative; more than that, Alternative Tourism may actively try to encourage a respect for the cultural realities experienced by the tourists through education and organized "encounters." (Various examples can be found in Holden 1984.)

These last two characteristics dominate in the approach of church-oriented groups active in the promotion of Alternative Tourism. Holden's definition fairly captures this:

Alternative Tourism is a process which promotes a just form of travel between members of different communities. It seeks to achieve mutual understanding, solidarity and equality amongst participants. (Holden 1984:15)

While the symmetry of this approach may seem attractive, it is not the line followed in this analysis. Here we shall focus predominantly on tourism as seen from the perspective of the host country and its inhabitants, rather than concern with the motivations, attitudes, or behavior patterns of the tourists, let alone their ethos.

IV. Authenticity in Tourism and Meaning in Development

The idea of Alternative Tourism as centering on the search for authenticity would appear not to have an equivalent in Alternative Development. Authenticity as a characteristic of Alternative Tourism is wholly focused on the tourist; it concerns his or her perceptions of the reality encountered in the tourist experience (Riley 1988). Cohen's recent paper deals with this issue brilliantly and in detail, his main point being that authenticity does not have an "objective quality," but is attributed by moderns to the world "out there" and thus is a socially constructed concept with a connotation that is not given but "negotiable" (Cohen 1988a). In spite of all the nuances brought to the discussion, authenticity remains an issue of importance only to the tourists, or to the hosts insofar as they want to please the tourists; the questions it raises lie outside the realm where Alternative Development provides the pointers for comparison.

Nevertheless, there is an area of overlap, because authenticity deals with meaning, and meaning—for the subjects of development—is an important issue in Alternative Development also. As Dudley Seers noted more than twenty years ago, the question of meaning in development addresses the issue of values often disregarded in the development discourse. "The starting-point is that we cannot avoid what the positivists disparagingly refer to as 'value judgements.' . . . Development is inevitably a normative concept, almost a synonym for improvement" (Seers 1969). And however crucial it remains to the poor to have greater access to material goods, this does not define exhaustively what people regard as "improvement" nor what meaning they can discover in development.

Mainstream development is a child of Western civilization. With the growth of science and technology over the past four centuries, the manipulation and mastering of nature has become the driving force of material "progress." "Development," as it is now understood in mainstream Western thinking, translates this instrumental rationalism into action, constantly "transforming" and "improving" the world (Rist 1987). Beyond science and technology, economics dominates the social and human sciences. The mainstream theories of development focus mostly on the economic processes in that material transformation (economics as the science of the management of scarce resources) and devote less attention to the ecological, cultural, and sociopolitical context within which the economy operates. This has contributed to the dominance of economic policies in the political arena, with governments often paying scant attention to the impact of such policies on culture or nature (Theuns 1989) or to issues arising in these spheres in the first place. Innovation in production and the stimulation of an everchanging demand for the latest in consumption became the final hallmarks of Western "consumer society"; these have provided the meaning of development for "Westerners" and those influenced by them. Nature, culture, and community have been at the forefront of people's concerns in many non-Western societies. It is clear that in modern society these have moved backstage; they no longer provide the prime motivations for people's actions.

Proponents of Alternative Development want to change that and thereby give a new meaning to development. For even when their language is that of analysis and interpretation, the underlying thrust is political, ideological, and moral. "People-centredness" or "human-centredness" implies small scale institutions, a relocation of decision making, and a rearrangement of the locus of power. Yet Alternative Development enjoins people to relinquish the meaning they have given to everyday life through the products of the consumer society. They are called to reorient their *Weltanschauung* to the fulfillment of basic human needs, not only for themselves—the simplest life—but for all their fellow human beings (distributive justice) and their posterity (intergenerational justice). Included therein is a concern to achieve harmony with nature and its creatures (Hettne 1985; Friberg 1988; Ekins 1986). This ideological or moral streak in Alternative Development—and Alternative Tourism—has been prominent.

V. The Sense of Outrage

There are three areas in which this ideological concern has focused in regard to both Alternative Tourism and Alternative Development: nature, materialism, and culture.

As long ago as 1971 the Founex Report, prepared for the Stockholm Conference, characterized environmental problems as the "effluence of affluence" and the "pollution of poverty" (Pearson 1985:8); this evocative terminology encapsulated a battle cry for action. From the same decade came the predictions of doom from the Club of Rome with *The Limits to Growth* (Meadows et al. 1972). In spite of the torrent of scientific criticism unleashed, these are still being used in ecological arguments to portray economic growth as a cancer eating away at the earth's resources (Pepper 1987). Bandyopadhyay and Shiva accuse transnational companies, operating in the global market economy which has no built-in mechanisms to ensure ecological rehabilitation, of being in the forefront of this misuse of nature; once a mining company has exhausted the mine, or agribusiness has destroyed the grazing lands and forests, it will move elsewhere to maintain its profits (1989:53). They argue that mainstream development, in encouraging the use of hitherto unexploited resources, fails to take account of the ecological interrelatedness of the world and the way in which scarce natural resources have competing uses; often damage is done not only to nature as such and to the future productive base, but directly to people. Protests may occur against the disregard for these basic interests, as in India with the so-called ecological movements (1989:40ff). Movements by those directly affected are spreading in other countries, too, as are more generalized protest groups to highlight the costs of present day attitudes to the environment (Greenpeace, Friends of the Earth, etc.).

The alleged disregard for the environment by conventional tourism development also yields expressions of outrage. Hong expresses that mood:

Having ruined their own environment, having either used up or destroyed all that is natural, people from the advanced consumer societies are compelled to look for natural wildlife, cleaner air, lush greenery and golden beaches else-where. In other words, they look for other environments to consume. Thus armed with their bags, tourists proceed to consume the environment in the countries of the Third World—that last "unspoiled corner of earth." (1985:12)

Protest movements also arise around tourism development, wit-nessed by the recent impassioned call for international support by the Federation of Ecological Societies of the Dominican Republic to deal with the "extremely delicate situation" that has arisen as a result of eco-logically destructive tourism development, involving massive damage to such elements as forests, mangroves, marine life (FEDOMASEC 1989). Such protests have helped place these matters on the agenda of analysts and policy makers.

Materialism has also brought its own hegemony. The emergence of "modernity" and consumer society as the twin pillars of mainstream development has already been commented upon. Neo-liberals believe that the market should provide the basic organizing principles of eco-nomic activity and that the role of the state in this area should be drastically reduced. The market as it operates in reality, however, is far from "perfect." On the one hand, small numbers of powerful pro-ducers can influence market choice in their favor; on the other, large numbers of consumers are left with decreasing areas of choice and often with insufficient resources to operate in the market to their advantage. Individual acquisitiveness is at a premium; intervention by the state, notably to promote distributive justice, is limited domestically and virtually absent internationally.

This kind of development is seen as being narrowly focused on economic growth and expansion of the market; it leads to the growth of consumerism and is founded on short term commercial criteria (Bandyopadhyay and Shiva 1989:43). Many have applied similar argu-ments to tourism. A recently published Swiss doctoral dissertation can speak for them all:

The thesis is put forward that the chief beneficiaries of tourism development in the Third World are foreign capitalists and, secondly, the local economic and political elite. Tourists from abroad benefit from comparatively low prices in Third World tourist destinations, while the local population is left with modest employment opportunities, the loss of economic and political decision-making, and predominantly negative socio-cultural effects from institutionalized tour-ism. (Bachmann 1988:96)

This, as Krippendorf puts it, is because in "industrial *society*, values of being have been crowded out by values of having; possession, property, wealth, consumption, egoism are ranked above community, tolerance, contentment, modesty, meaning, honesty." The economy dominates and "man and the environment are at the service of the economy" (1986:520–21).

Krippendorf and Bachmann also extend their censure to the socio-cultural effects of tourism and the "loss of culture," and in this they echo the more general anguish about the effects of modernity and industrialism as cultural homogenizers. The keynote address of the Jordanian Crown Prince to a conference in Morocco picks up many of the doubts about development as modernization and Westernization. "Progress" has come to be identified with improvement in quantitative indicators; these concern mainly economic processes, seldom social, hardly ever cultural—and if they do, then it is simply to "measure" such matters as the number of museums operating or books published. As Prince Hassan pointed out, however, culture is more: a system of values and norms which give order and meaning to a society. Planners, however, simply cannot deal with what people want out of "development" and even less with why they want it (the meaning of development, again). And as the planners treat "our peoples as simple numbers, they respond as numbers, multiply like numbers, increase their consumption like numbers" (author's translation) (Ibn Talal 1989:24).

Others have examined this cultural impact of mainstream development on Less Developed Countries through the lens of dependency theory. Erisman, for example, argues in a discussion of the West Indies that cultural dependency exists when those values, norms, and rules are conditioned by or reflect those in an external culture, leading to a relationship of domination and subordination between the cultural center and the cultural periphery. Cultural dependency results in the "incorporation of exogenous norms and values into a nation's socialization process, which can then be said to be penetrated," so that eventually the main stimuli for cultural development come from the outside and people lose their desire to maintain a cultural identity separate from that of the dominant nation (Erisman 1983:342). In a more ideological and outraged vein Nyoni writes that ideas coming from outside the community are expressions of "imposed universalism" which "destroy local initiatives and self-reliance" through "self-colonization and elitism" of local elites, which "are heavily influenced and dominated by foreign and unworkable ideas" (Nyoni 1987:53).

Loss of culture is also explored with respect to the commoditization of relationships, when things and activities that were hitherto outside it are brought into the sphere of market transactions through exchange values (Cohen 1988a). This is often said to be the result of tourism, but in fact it usually arises primarily out of those broader processes promoted by mainstream development (de Kadt 1979:64). The already mentioned debates over authenticity are also relevant. Though these have been pursued above all in relation to tourism development, those opposing mainstream development may also allude to these questions. Thus we read in an already quoted article in IFDA Dossier, one of the main outlets for *engagé* discussions of Alternative Development is that the market economy defines people as poor who do not participate very much in the market and do not consume the products of consumer society—that is, if they eat "self-grown nutritious millets" instead of junk food or if they wear "indigenously designed handmade garments of natural fiber" rather than clothes made of manmade fibers. "The culturally conceived poverty based on non-western modes of consumption is often mistaken to be misery" (Bandyopadhyay and Shiva 1989:43).

This quote represents the polar opposite to the often thoughtless sense of social and cultural superiority of those who stand for mainstream development because in its anger with cultural domination it appears to play down the very real poverty of hundreds of millions in the Third World. These neither eat their insufficient diet of "self-grown nutritious millets" nor own just one set of simple "indigenously designed [?!] handmade garments of natural fiber" out of their own volition, and they would gladly exchange these for basic needs of the modern variety if they were available. There are, however, signs that more balanced approaches are winning adherents both in the scientific community and in the political arena.

VI. Sustainability as an Organizing Concept for Policy

We have already seen how the Brundtland Commission's report has helped to place the issue of sustainability closer to the center of the political agenda. This has drawn renewed attention to three areas in which the approaches, and reproaches, of Alternative Development can help to modify analysis and action without a "revolution" in social and economic organization: resource use and renewability, the issue of scale, and the equitable distribution of benefits (including to future generations). The following discussion also suggests that making sustainability the focus of Alternative Tourism may possibly be the most productive way forward. It would not, of course, address the more tourist-oriented and normative issues often raised, but it would narrow the discussion to some of the central issues for the host economy, society, and culture. In policy terms, making tourism sustainable would involve not just encouraging the development of "an alternative to" conventional tourism (though this could be part of it), but above all would force conventional tourism development to take greater notice of the three areas mentioned above.

First, we turn to the issue of resource use and renewability. The notion of sustainable development has been promoted largely from the rich countries of the North. Reducing pollution, carbon dioxide emissions, or the destruction of forests for the sake of "Our Common Future" is all very well for those whose unsustainable actions over decades have underpinned their high standard of living. But what about the poor countries? Their need is continuing economic growth, for which they require many of the natural and environmental resources that are under stress. Where continued exploitation of these without concern for sustainability has occurred, as in Amazonia, it has brought out the Northern television crews and galvanized the North's politicians.

For Less Developed Countries, then, a crucial aspect of sustainability is the maintenance of the productivity of resources. One relatively easy means would be to seek a sustained increase in recovery and recycling. The use and further development of new technologies, in which the materials of production or its polluting effects are decreased, can also help achieve this (Pearson 1985:9ff). Because the latter is an option that can be pursued without greatly affecting existing vested interests, it is attractive to some of the more advanced Less Developed Countries such as Brazil; this concept was also promoted by the Brundtland Commission (Brundtland 1987:217ff).

More generally, as John Pigram argues elsewhere in this volume (Chapter 4), environmental degradation can result from many small increases in environmental neglect, none of which is catastrophic in itself. Conversely, sustainability can be safeguarded by the avoidance of such cumulative negative threshold effects.

Tourism development again raises similar questions to development in general. Pigram sees Alternative Tourism as an exercise in sustainable resource management, where "safe minimum standards" would ensure that the threshold of irreversibility would not be crossed. Wilkinson (1989) discusses the possible negative environmental impacts of tourism development on small island environments. Each such development raises different and specific issues, for example, the dangers of damaging coral reefs, beach sand loss, or the contamination of coastal waters. Sometimes, especially in self-contained and very small natural environments, it is clearly essential for the maintenance of the value of the "asset" to protect its ecological *raison d'être*, and so the enterprise itself has strong reasons to do so. But often these costs will not be "calculated" by the users unless an external authority forces them to do so, usually by means of taxation or other incentives and disincentives. What is clear, however, is that such issues are now being more widely discussed and that the analytical tools for moving in this direction are becoming available.

One such analytical tool is the concept of carrying capacity, which has been available to tourism planners for many years. Tourist carrying capacity is the number of tourists that can be accommodated without creating negative environmental effects. It links questions of resource use and renewability to the issue of scale, to which we now turn.

The proponents of Alternative Development, as has been discussed, are anxious to see a scaling down in virtually all areas of economic, social, and political activity—in production, distribution, consumption, government, and administration (Ekins 1986, 1988). Brundtland, who addresses United Nation agencies, governments, and multinationals rather than "the people" as such, says virtually nothing on this issue. In discussions of tourism development, however, the question of scale has been an issue for many years (de Kadt 1979:26), and recent writings have kept it in the limelight (Richter 1989).

Four issues may be mentioned. First, how to deal with tourist carrying capacity in general. While there are obvious ecological advantages to keeping the number of tourists down, attention is also being paid to measures that can both increase tourist carrying capacity and improve the capacity to protect the environment (Wilkinson 1989:161ff).

Second, there is the matter of the promotion of tourism in less massive form. This can involve, as has been done in Bhutan, concentrating tourism development efforts on facilities for a small number of rich tourists (Smith 1981; Richter and Richter 1985:213). This option, however, raises questions of the environmental impact (e.g., energy and water) generated by facilities for the wealthy: "luxury tourism tends to require more imports, to be more capital-intensive, to be more dependent on outside control of capital, to encourage more of a sense of conspicuous consumption, and to result in a greater sense of relative deprivation than more modest facilities" (Richter 1989:183). Conversely, of course, smaller operations not aimed solely at wealthy outsiders may be more within the reach of the local middle classes—also for non-resident use.

Scale can also be dealt with by dispersion, fostering the development of tourism in a larger number of smaller places. While this will incorporate development areas hitherto unaffected by tourism, the effects can be more easily monitored and controlled, especially from an ecological point of view. An example is the plan of the Indian Government envisaging the creation of a number of regional travel circuits. These were to cover a total of 441 small centers to cater for budget and low income tourists interested in traveling "off the beaten track" (Gonsalves 1984:6). More spontaneous developments can also follow this lead. A notable example is that of farm tourism in Europe, to which Pearce refers with much insight elsewhere in this volume.

Third, there is the question of organizing for smaller scale operations. Multinationals are successful precisely because they reap economies of scale and "aggregation" through massive integrated operations, as discussed below. If scaling down is to be effective, new institutions and organizations will be required (also true in the wider areas of Alternative Development) (Friberg 1988). In tourism development the questions relate especially to the setting up of cooperative arrangements between small scale enterprises and the strengthening of local planning and regulatory capacities; this also is discussed later.

Finally, a word should be said about socialist systems and the question of scale. Command economies, where investment decisions are made centrally and where all significant productive resources are owned by the state, typically promote large scale tourism development. Hotels, built by state building enterprises or foreign contractors, are large and relatively standardized and usually owned and run by the government tourism para-statal. Moreover, in such economies the legal system prohibits capitalist accumulation and only permits the employment of a very small number of workers by private concerns. Prior to 1989, this was the pattern over most of Eastern Europe, and continues to be in Third World socialist states such as China, Cuba, and Mozambique.

Yet even before recent changes which have resulted from economic and political reforms, this was never the whole picture. The earliest of the "reformers," Yugoslavia, has shown the way in this respect at least over the last 25 years. While statistics are unlikely to be wholly accurate, in 1987 private establishments such as boarding houses and restaurants made up almost 60 percent of all such establishments and employed, in addition to the owners, 10 percent of the employees in this sector. The private boarding houses provided 34 percent of all beds available, which accounted for almost one-fifth of the bed-nights (Yugoslavia 1988: tables 119, 124, 125). These are impressive figures. Hungary and Poland are now also following this road.

The general point to note is that anti-capitalist provisions in economic legislation have often left room for limited family enterprise. As political and economic conditions became more favorable to the latter, or more unfavorable to the public sector, more workers or farmers became small scale entrepreneurs and ventured into the tourism sector. Nevertheless, economic legislation has continued to constrain essential aspects of these enterprises, for example, the number of workers that may legally be employed. Consequently, growth occurred in breadth (the number of establishments) but not in depth (their size). The result was a large, or growing, sector of very small establishments side by side with the large hotels and restaurants run by the state, and very little in between.

Another ongoing area of concern is the equitable distribution of benefits. Alternative Development has always emphasized the necessity to focus on basic human needs, but its frame of reference has often been the advanced consumer societies. The implications of its no-growth or low-growth prescriptions for the poor in Less Developed Countries have been given rather less attention. Most people in the Third World are still struggling to meet the minimum material conditions of a "decent" human existence. Distributive justice in many Less Developed Countries cannot be achieved by development policies which ignore that fact; if there is no cake, there is nothing to distribute. The poor, wrenched out of their isolation by the transistor radio and the bicycle, do not want to be told to discard their aspirations as consumers—nor, incidentally, do the elites, who wish to emulate the life styles of their counterparts in the rich North.

The Brundtland Commission, with strong representation from the South, has corrected that bias. Brundtland has been accused of not facing up to some of the conflicts its proposals are likely to engender and of having a rather "bland" view of sustainable development (Brookfield 1988:129). But the Commission has not fallen into the basic-needs-via-no-growth trap. "We see . . . the possibility for a new era of economic growth . . . . And we believe such growth to be absolutely essential to relieve the great poverty that is deepening in much of the developing world" (Brundtland 1987:1). So the Commission takes a position that is "reformist" of the present productive, socioeconomic, political, and international systems; and it raises the issue of equity wherever this seems relevant. Distributive justice is thus deemed henceforth to include consideration of the needs of future generations (Brundtland 1987:43).

In the critique of conventional tourism development, the issue of equity also plays a role. For example, in a recent overview article on the sociocultural impacts of tourism, Dogan argues that tourism has aggravated income inequalities. He stresses the need to differentiate between various host population groups (notably between those who are better off, who get more out of tourism) and the poor, whose lifestyle and culture are less like those of tourists and who stand to gain fewer benefits from tourism. He also draws attention to another distinction, that between those who are younger, who tend to be more susceptible to modern consumerism and the older people, who are more traditional in their way of life. The impacts of tourism development differ between such different groups, and policy makers have to take account of likely outcomes in this respect (Dogan 1989:225f). The lessons of European farm tourism have some relevance to this issue, too, as Pearce notes in this volume.

VII. Modifying the Analytical Tools

The congruence of mainstream economic (development) theory and conventional economic development policies has been referred to a number of times. The emergence of Alternative Development has led to a critique of the standard tools used in (economic) analysis and the development of new concepts and approaches more appropriate to a policy concerned with sustainability. This is also visible in tourism studies. Two aspects will be examined: the refinement of certain tools of conventional economic analysis, and the beginnings of the formulation of different methodologies and theories.

Cost-benefit analysis and associated methodologies are the main targets of those who would refashion the tools of economics rather than "start from scratch." Cost-benefit and cost-effectiveness analysis are micro-analytical tools which set out to give guidance on investment choices, often as between different types of (investment) projects. These methods deal with what happens within projects, or productive units; outside positive or negative impacts, commonly referred to as externalities, are not considered. Projects or enterprises can "externalize" costs; this means "the shifting of costs to third parties, or onto society, future generations, and nature" (Simonis 1989:61).

In general, the weakness of many economic and business calculations has been that they do not take ecological issues sufficiently into account, that there are neither enough built-in "signals" nor institutionalized incentives and disincentives to warn decision makers away from environmentally damaging courses of action. The same is true of the distributive effects of economic activity, and when industry damages nature it often also damages the livelihoods of poor people who, especially in Less Developed Countries, are particularly dependent on nature.

Productive enterprises cannot be expected to take account of such externalities when they calculate their costs. On the contrary, normal business practice motivated by profit maximization will attempt to "externalize" the relevant costs, thereby, for example, causing pollution. Governments, however, can force them to internalize such externalities and can shift the costs back to the problem-causing economic units through regulation or taxation. By that means the state alters the price and cost signals on waste prevention, energy conservation, and the like taken into account by firms in their costings. Changing the legal and cost balance (the principle that the polluter, or even better the likely polluter, pays) could also help bring about a shift from ex-post to ex-ante solutions, from emphasizing cure to emphasizing prevention (Simonis 1989:62f).

Exactly the same considerations apply to the tourism industry. In tourism development, too, the cost of protecting the environment needs to be treated as an "internality," that is, as a cost of doing business. And, of course, the longer the time perspective of the developer, the easier it is to absorb such costs, as in the construction of a sewage treatment plant instead of using a sea outfall (Wilkinson 1989:161ff).

Government agencies themselves, however, can and should incorporate ecological effects in their broader cost-benefit calculations. They should modify the methodology itself so that it will take into account, as a matter of course, the costs and benefits of proposed actions for the environment. Impact assessments do try to achieve this, at best also for other non-material (e.g., cultural) effects; and the Brundtland Commission discusses a whole array of institutional changes, as well as some new tools for analysis, that are relevant in this respect (Brundtland 1987:Ch. 12). This approach also needs to be followed by tourism planners.

Can changes in emphasis and perspective such as these direct us toward a new economics? The proponents of Alternative Development and Alternative Tourism continue to devote most of their time and writing to policy issues and to the advocacy needed to place these at the center of attention. Yet more interest is now also being shown in the theoretical underpinning of sustainable policies, and hence in the reformulation of economics itself (Ekins 1986). It is argued that the "nature" component in sustainability is neglected by economics; environmental questions are not taken into account in models or measurement.

The question of measurement has considerable importance. This is graphically captured in a quote which Brookfield lifted from a paper written by Repetto for the World Bank's Sustainability Issues in Agricultural Development: "a country could exhaust its aquifers, cut down its forests, erode its soils, and hunt its wildlife and fisheries to extinction, but measured income would rise steadily as these assets disappeared" (Brookfield 1988:132). Traditional economic accounting, which produces that standard international "comparator" of GNP, omits essential elements. National accounting is incomplete on flows (notably non-marketed, directly consumed environmental services), while stocks (such as the surface area under forests) are left out of the picture altogether. So "measured GNP can increase as a new industry starts production, but if associated air and water pollution are serious, the total welfare derived . . . may actually decrease." The tools of economic measurement need to take account of the fact that sustainable development "is essentially an asset management problem" (Pearson 1985:14).

The economics of enterprise, particularly under a capitalist system of production, is oriented to profitability and the expansion of markets; hence growth is a favored outcome, monitored in terms of measurable output, physical quantities, or money equivalents. In nature, however, growth is not the driving force. Rather, nature appears to strive for stability (equilibrium, homeostasis), and it can be argued that ecological stability is the main precondition for sustainability (Simonis 1989:60). Economic policy would take account of this basic fact by moving from the simple maximization of flows (growth) to paying more attention to increasing efficiency and maintaining substance. This would require a redefinition of the concept of GNP by including ecological measures, so that account could be taken of the different effects (positive, neutral, or negative) on the environment of different components of growth as measured by output.

The incorporation of environmental measures in standard national accounting would not solve the problem of "valuing" irreplaceable resources, as in the case of a wilderness region lost because of a hydroelectric development. But at least it would draw attention to the issues and force those responsible to make their value judgments explicit. That would also be relevant to weighing the immediate consumption needs of the poor in Less Developed Countries against the long term demands of future generations, which is itself an extremely difficult issue (Pearson 1985:13f).

Finally, there are those such as Bandyopadhyay and Shiva (1989) who would give economics an even more fundamental reorientation. Conventional economics deals, they argue, with market economies (or, one might add, command economies). Its models and theories, however, have no relevance to the operation of two quite separate and equally important "economies": the economy of survival, and the economy of natural processes (i.e., what happens in nature) to which the economy of survival is linked.

The market economy and the dominant form of economics employed in its analysis have been concerned with the use of resources for commodity production and capital accumulation. The resource needs of the people outside the commodity economy, the subsistence farmers and pastoralists who make up the majority in so many of the poorer Less Developed Countries, are quite different. In their survival economy, satisfaction of basic needs is the organizing principle for natural resource use. In such economies there are normally built-in checks on overexploitation unless crisis, such as has been seen in Sub-Saharan Africa over the last decade, sweeps traditional safeguards away, leading to deforestation and similar phenomena (Chambers 1988). Herein lies the link to the economy of natural processes, the third type, the economics of which analyzes the processes by which resources are regenerated in nature, as in the production of humus by forests, the regeneration of water resources, or the evolution of genetic products (Bandyopadhyay and Shiva 1989).

Bandyopadhyay and Shiva deepen the basic Alternative Development charge laid at the door of conventional economics—that it externalizes costs. They point out that the market economy has neither substantive nor analytical links with the natural or survival economies. Therefore it is not perceived that resource-intensive development, seen as positive within the market economy based on profits and accumulation, actually damages both nature and poor people. Unfortunately, they neither tell us what the economics of nature and survival would look like nor what tools need to be developed. One may suspect that professional economists would have many good reasons for being skeptical of their approach, and that the approach would be particularly vulnerable to the criticism of neither understanding nor taking sufficient account of the findings of science (Brookfield 1988). Nevertheless, it does provide food for thought and a starting point for others, concerning both Alternative Development and the development of more sustainable forms of tourism.

Thus, we have attempted to document the emergence of more analytical approaches to Alternative Development and Alternative Tourism. To end this part of the discussion a few words will be said about related changes in the political discourse of Alternative Development:

The world view of Another Development is likely to remain that of a minority, in part because most of its adherents adopt an uncompromising all-or-nothing stand which tends to alienate even those who could afford to adopt its back-to-nature lifestyle. . . . The ideas of Another Development are likely to remain on the fringe, crushed between its somewhat dogmatic puritanism and the wish or need of most people (especially the poor in the Third World) to partake of the "fleshpots of Egypt." (de Kadt 1985:11f)

These lines written only a few years ago, would no longer be accurate. The rather cranky image of the "alternative movement" is slowly dissolving, and its approach is no longer based solely on moral indignation and utopic blueprints. Moreover, Green political parties have begun to make an impact in Europe. Of course their programs are not yet fully worked out and many differences of view persist in their ranks, notably between the "greener" and the "redder" Greens. The latter accuse the former of too much reliance on trying to change people's views. As Marxists, they believe views change through action; they generally accuse the non-Marxist Greens of a lack of realism, particularly as to what would be needed to bring off their bold and essentially revolutionary challenge to the mainstream capitalist system. They hence argue for a "vigorous dialectic" between the new ideas and the creation of new economic and social structures "by practical—even revolutionary—collective political action" (Pepper 1987:338).

Yet the Greens have had a major influence on the Brundtland Commission and have jolted many of the established political parties into paying at least lip service to the issues of the environment and sustainability. In addition, as they can begin to aspire at least to participation in practical power, their self-image is no longer quite that of a group doomed to continue crying in the wilderness. Some serious thinking about realistic courses of action is being done by their political leaders as well as by intellectuals identified with them. Mats Friberg, for example, recognizes that the Greens will not be able to achieve their full set of goals and that some goals will have to be given up, especially those that would "threaten corporate actors." But he does believe that a "counter-cultural strategy of building a new society from the bottom up" could be put into practice. This would take much time to have an effect. (Friberg has studied earlier social movements in Europe, and the "distance" gained from such historical work gives him a sense of perspective.) Given perhaps fifty years to grow, the result could be a dual economy with the continuation of large scale bureaucracy and industry on the one hand and the growth of self-governing local communities and informal sector enterprises on the other (Friberg 1988:38).

There is no way of knowing whether, or when, this prediction will come true. We do know two things, however. First, that the future never quite follows any predicted course. Second, that the road toward more sustainable development policies, globally or nationally, will not be easy or smooth. Because of the widespread ramifications of sustainable development policies there will be many obstacles to their implementation. But, as the next section attempts to show, there are opportunities, too.

VIII. Worrying About Policy Implementation— Constraints

The difficulties of policy implementation are greatly underestimated. Too often policy is made, but the instruments for its management have not been put in place. If moves toward a more sustainable tourism development pattern are to be successful, attention will need to be paid to institution building in the spheres of policy management and implementation.

Various constraints and opportunities are discussed in some detail in the balance of this analysis, but attention should first be drawn to the fact that not all policies have identical implications for implementation. Certain policies that operate at the macro-level, even though they may encounter resistance before adoption, "can be accomplished with minimal development of new institutional capabilities to support implementation" (Korten 1987:151). Examples include adjusting exchange rates, removing subsidies, raising interest rates, or freeing trade restrictions. In contrast, micro-policy reforms depend on complex institutional changes that are difficult to implement. While there may be much less initial opposition to the new ideas than with macro changes, implementation is very hard. In a similar vein Harvey, who deals with problems of structural adjustment in Africa, notes the difficulties of "sacking civil servants and marketing board employees, removing the power and patronage of those who appointed them, and cutting the costs and raising the prices of other forms of parastatal" (Harvey 1988:70).

Comparable considerations apply to policies for sustainability. For example, once accepted, an increase in the tax on fossil fuels to raise the cost of contributing to the greenhouse effect (internalizing the externalities) can be implemented relatively easily, while monitoring polluting emissions by industry or hotels is more difficult. Creating viable organizations to help smaller national or local enterprises make an economic success of Alternative Tourism is a difficult task. Changing the ingrained habits of the consumer society's consumers on the one hand, and the "instincts" of any private enterprise to "get around" obstacles to the promotion of its particular products on the other, are likely to be very hard indeed. The following paragraphs examine some of the specific difficulties likely to be encountered when attempting to implement policies for sustainability.

Those who benefit from existing arrangements prefer to see them continued; and social, political, and economic institutions reflect such "vested interests." Sociologists examine social classes, political scientists study interest groups and parties, and economists look at the strain toward monopoly (which is the concentration of control over resources, and decisions relating to them, in the hands of minorities) (Brett 1987:35).

Recent work has emphasized that the state itself can be the instrument of private interests (Dearlove 1987). This is also the case in tourism, as James Elliott has shown for Thailand. While the balance of power between different parts of the state apparatus allows the private sector room to manoeuvre, as discussed below, Elliott also points to the importance and power of the bureaucracy: its permanence, stability, internal cohesion, and knowledge of the administrative system. The bureaucracy does not take initiatives but uses its power negatively, defending the status quo. It protects its own position, the "main aim being self survival and departmental growth, including more jobs" (Elliott 1983). As the Thai bureaucracy needs resources for survival, it has been opposed to the abolition of the high taxes on hotel (16.5%) and restaurant (8.25%) bills, a step considered desirable for the further promotion of tourism.

So it comes as something of a surprise to read Richter's early views of the policy process in tourism development. She may be right in her assertion that little conflict is apparent in the initial stages, but to suggest that in tourism policy there are "substantial rewards and few interests to placate or offend" (1983:318) is surely incorrect for most situations. Those interests are especially apparent with respect to the transnational system, but a move to greater sustainability would also hurt many national and local established interests.

Tourism also responds to the demands of people for what Hirsch has called "positional goods," goods and services that give status because they are inherently scarce. Ironically, long distance budget travelers (those paragons of Alternative Tourism) seek such exclusivity, which tends to be destroyed by its very success as wider groups learn of the new destinations and small scale local businesses expand or are displaced by conventional tourism enterprises (Riley 1988:322). Where a tourism destination has become an exclusive status symbol for the very rich (Theuns 1989:194), recreating their favored environment at considerable cost, strong vested interests in the status quo within the industry are reinforced by those of their customers.

Among those organizations with vested interests in the status quo, transnational enterprises are particularly powerful. Their resources are often greater than those of the governments in the countries where they operate; they employ high-powered experts to advise them on the most profitable operating arrangements within existing legal and regulatory frameworks. During the late 1960s and 1970s they were widely criticized for their role in the international economy; the scandals over the use of unsafe drugs, over the promotion of artificial baby milk, and over transfer pricing (subsidiaries charging their head office enormous prices for goods or services in order to repatriate profits) represented the low water mark (Vaitsos 1974). More recently the controversies have died down. The political climate everywhere has moved back toward market forces and private enterprise; the worst practices of transnationals appear to have been eliminated, while Less Developed Countries' governments have become rather more adept at framing the necessary laws or regulations and at imposing relevant and collect-able taxes. Even so, forcing more sustainable policies onto transna-tional corporations will demand considerable skill as well as collabora-tion among governments of Less Developed Countries (Pearson 1985).

Many researchers have emphasized the power of transnationals in the tourism industry. Erisman, writing about mass tourism in the West Indies, shows how the industry there is primarily run by and serves the interests of American corporations and their customers, through mar-keting networks in the United States. Already in the early 1980s, these networks were becoming increasingly vertically integrated, formally or informally, with the airlines standing at the center. The three most lucrative components of tourism are handled by these networks: mar-keting and the procurement of customers; international transporta-tion; and food and lodging (Erisman 1983:347).

More recently, Wilkinson has argued that micro-states which become involved in tourism find themselves enmeshed in a global system over which they cannot exercise control. They become the targets for "ex-ogenous decision-making," as "many decisions governing their lives, even those dealing with local matters, are made elsewhere by other countries, multinational companies, or airlines" (Wilkinson 1989:158). Richter draws virtually the same conclusion and writes that in Less Developed Countries with few material and human resources "almost the entire infrastructure for tourism will be built with foreign goods, controlled by foreigners, and used by foreigners and . . . all too often profits will not remain in the country" (Richter 1989:181).

The decisions of the large international airlines are particularly crucial for small states in the realm of conventional tourism. Only by being on a regular flight route can a destination's associated services, notably accommodation, be included in the computerized networks now virtually indispensable for bookings through travel agents and tour operators. So the effective start-up decision often rests with an airline, or with the foreign donor who helps finance the building of an international airport (Wilkinson 1989:159).

The importance of those computerized networks and the power they give to those at their center has also recently been stressed by Auliana Poon. She notes that computerized reservation systems, run by the largest airlines or by consortia of a few of these, are now used by about 90 percent of the travel agents in the United States and the United Kingdom. They constitute a total information system offering, in addi-tion to hotel reservations, such services as car rentals, champagne and flowers, information about destinations, or bus and train connections. Experience in the Caribbean has shown that "without links to [these] international marketing and distribution networks, hotel bed-nights cannot be sold" (Poon 1988b:540). The momentum of this system is enormous, the interests involved truly global.

As to the extent that Alternative Tourism is regarded as no more than the tourism of "alternative tourists," being bypassed by these systems may not matter so much. But this is not a tenable position if, in contrast, encouraging Alternative Tourism is seen as a wider move toward tourism with "sustainable characteristics." It should be self-evident that any such policy must come to terms with the reality of transnational electronic power. The development of sophisticated electronic sub-networks that join together a limited number of smaller facilities may be a more viable proposition than attempting to "buck the trend."

Implementation is also confounded by fragmentation of government responsibilities. The idea of sustainable policies is likely to have a growing influence on international organizations and United Nations agencies, as well as on the declared policies of many Northern governments. Brundtland will be heard. Yet as her Commission's Report emphasized, a few well-sounding declarations are but the first step on the road to sustainable development. Implementing the fine phrases demands enforcement. The responsibility for the different aspects of environmental and distributive policies is, however, dispersed throughout the government machine.

Sectoral organizations tend to pursue sectoral objectives and to treat their impacts on other sectors as side effects, taken into account only if compelled to do so. Hence impacts on forests rarely worry those involved in public policy or business activities in the fields of energy, industrial development, crop husbandry, or foreign trade. Many of the environmental problems that confront us have their roots in this sectoral fragmentation of responsibility. Sustainable development requires that such fragmentation be overcome. (Brundtland 1987:63)

The complexity of modern government and administration, where authority must be delegated in order to be exercised effectively, is one cause of this problem. But there are others. Because those working in sectoral agencies, such as ministries and other official organizations, get few rewards for working with outsiders, intersectoral collaboration is at a discount. In each sector one particular professional and disciplinary group tends to be dominant. Cooperation between such professional groups is limited because the different nature of their original training leads to different perceptions of what problems are important in the world (Theuns 1989:196). This is true even in contiguous sectors such as health, nutrition, and agriculture, where intersectoral collaboration has encountered many obstacles for such reasons (de Kadt 1989:507ff).

This sectoral fragmentation in the public administration is reinforced by compartmentalized working links between civil servants and enterprises in the sectors their departments are supposed to regulate. Ministries of agriculture deal with farmers, ministries of industry with industrialists, tourism departments with businesses in the tourism sector, and so on. Farmers, industrialists, and hoteliers soon form specialized lobbies; their viewpoints and interests come to influence the thinking of the bureaucrats in "their" sector. Sociocultural factors, such as "soft states," patron-client networks, clan politics, and "endemic corruption," may make this worse (Roberts 1987:3).

These sectoral dynamics of government and administration provide the backdrop to any effort at implementing more sustainable development and tourism development policies. While different from country to country and from culture to culture, they are deeply entrenched everywhere. They are reinforced by the specialized multilateral agencies which usually have links with one ministry alone, such as the World Health Organization in the health sector, United Nations Industrial Development Organization for industry, FAO in agriculture. Advice on tourism development comes from the World Tourism Organization, which is "concerned quite naturally with developing tourism and not with using tourism as a vehicle for development" (Richter 1989:180). Superministries, or highly centralized forms of government, may mitigate these problems but cannot overcome them completely. Constraints which need to be bypassed as much as possible are likely to remain.

IX. Achieving Policy Implementation—Opportunities

While it is compelling to recognize constraints for what they are, it is important not to exaggerate them and to be aware of opportunities and room for maneuvering. For example, certain aspects of the functioning of state and public administration have been revealed as obstacles to the achievement of more sustainable development policies. But in other respects it is only the state which can provide the conditions for movement toward greater sustainability.

In most countries tourism development will always center on private enterprise. While current conventional wisdom stresses the benefits of the market, the pendulum shows signs of beginning to swing back from recent extreme positions. As Butler argues in this volume, in the absence of control and external responsibility the free play of the market will almost inevitably lead to overreaching capacity limits, and hence a lack of sustainability. It is likely that in general more attention will again be paid to the imperfections of the market and to those specific interventions which can correct the tendencies to disequilibrium and monopoly power, both in the private and the state sectors (Brett 1987:34).

Interventions by the state are also essential with regard to the problem of externalities discussed earlier. By disregarding the costs of negative effects they may have on others or on nature, productive units in and out of the tourist industry are better able to maximize their profits. So the state, or rather development policy makers and planners, must force productive units to take account of such effects. They do this by building appropriate cost and price signals into the framework within which productive units operate, by creating incentives and disincentives, and by straightforward regulation. Insofar as maintaining ecological stability is essential to sustainability, this institutional framework also needs to safeguard the reproduction of natural resources (Brookfield 1988:134).

In the sphere of tourism, governments have long exercised controls in a number of areas, most fundamentally, of course, in the conditions on which tourists are admitted to a country and on the rate at which their currencies will be exchanged. Governments have leverage to influence the development of tourism in specific areas or particular ways: they set the conditions of investment and access, determine what concessions will be given to foreign enterprises, and they can legislate about access to land, such as, for example, by not allowing straight purchase, but only long term leases. In general, they can and do include tourism in their development plans (Richter 1984), and they often play a major role in providing infrastructure for tourism development.

This general capacity can also be focused on creating the conditions for sustainability. It helps if sustainability, as a general issue, is high on the agenda of government policy as this can draw attention to sensitive issues such as restrictions on physical development or the effects on local populations. As they can for conventional tourism, governments can create an appropriate incentive structure for sustainable tourism. Transnationals, if left to operate according to their own agendas, will prefer large scale developments and accommodations provided in mega-hotels; they will usually not be sensitive to ecological or local issues and will not be concerned that their projects yield benefits for the host country's development in general and for the poor in particular. Such issues are more likely to be addressed by the state if tourism planning is integrated with development planning in general. This is, of course, more difficult in small countries with a slender government apparatus and a scarcity of professional staff (Wilkinson 1989:168ff).

Wilkinson also suggests that Alternative Tourism development, insofar as it comprises small scale facilities which are likely to be low rise, cottage style, and energy efficient, may require rather less government involvement than the conventional variety. Infrastructure demands should be less extensive, and with respect to regulation and incentive structures a more "passive" attitude toward this sort of development may be warranted (1989:168ff). However, Alternative Tourism development will require substantial institutional innovation (and hence certain kinds of state involvement) if it is to be successful. Some of this innovation may have to be aimed at methods of increasing participation and decentralization.

From the historical perspective which Mats Friberg brings to bear on his analysis of the emergence of Green political movements in Europe, he sees the next phase as a deepening of earlier achievements (citizenship, democracy, social justice, and equity) by means of a further transformation of the state and the extension of participation through civic organizations (Friberg 1988:43). Participation has, indeed, become one of the rallying cries of development ideology of the 1980s. It is heard in sundry contexts, from discussions of the informal sector in production (de Soto 1986) to generalized blueprints for better health services. Non-governmental organizations (NGOs) have benefited from this new interest, attracting government development grants for carrying out small scale projects together with people at the grass roots. The role of NGOs in development has shot into prominence (Drabek 1987), and they are seen as possible agents of "empowerment" of local communities vis-à-vis those who do, or may in future, dominate (Elliott 1987:66).

Similar views are expressed with respect to tourism. Wilkinson's paper, which focuses on the factors influencing the chances of tourism development with "alternative" characteristics in micro-states, ends with a clarion call for community participation in the development of local tourism (Wilkinson 1989:172). Earlier he quotes Murphy, who holds the view that tourism development can be positive if the needs of the local community are placed before the goals of the tourism industry. Tourism should be seen as a local resource, and its management "for the common good and future generations should become the goal and criterion by which the industry is judged" (Murphy 1985:37, in Wilkinson 1989:171).

Yet such calls for community participation gloss over the well-known tendency for local elites to "appropriate" the organs of participation for their own benefit. Many studies have demonstrated that those who are locally influential and wealthy will become the spokespersons for communities unless specific measures are taken to counter this pattern; this is so whether one examines local political structures or such less formal arrangements as community organizations and NGO-sponsored associations (Elliott 1987; Apthorpe and Conyers 1982).

As regards participation in decision making on tourism development, there is a further problem. Communities have coped with problems in areas such as agriculture or health from time immemorial and, therefore, have a store of traditional experience and knowledge which can be the starting point of their participation in such areas (de Kadt 1989:509). But local experience with tourism is wholly lacking, and people are largely at the mercy of the opinions of those who are presented to them, or who present themselves, as "experts." As Richter points out in her discussion of tourism development in the United States, this places the "developers" at an advantage; yet their expertise may well be that of an interested party. In Less Developed Countries, too, advice is often provided by the "wrong" people (Richter 1983:320). Perhaps specialized tourism related NGOs from the North, or international NGOs involved in tourism such as the already mentioned Ecumenical Coalition on Third World Tourism (Holden 1984), could help in this respect and fulfill the "monitoring" function suggested by Richter (1989:196ff).

A similar situation of unfamiliarity with relevant issues prevails within the public administration, where awareness of tourism issues is limited, even in so highly developed a country as the United States. In view of the shortage of public servants knowledgeable on tourism issues, public administrations in the U.S. all too often turn to the hardly disinterested travel industry for advice (Richter 1983:329). Such problems are exacerbated by the fact that many decisions about tourism development are made at lower levels of government and administration, where the range of expertise is usually more limited and the competence of senior public servants less solid, especially with respect to the broader questions of ecological and social sustainability. Hence there is a need to consider seriously what institutional and organizational changes are required if policies for more sustainable tourism development are to be put into place.

Perhaps the most formidable task on the road to sustainable development, and tourism development, is that of building the institutions needed for policy implementation. Earlier we saw how the Brundtland Commission, too, regards this as the greatest challenge.

There are no quick fixes in this domain. Public administrations do not respond easily or quickly to new situations. And devising workable organizations that interface between the public and private sectors is also fraught with problems. The variety of marketing, advisory, and support services available to European farm tourism enterprises, to which Pearce refers in this volume, emerged gradually over a fairly long period of "natural growth," itself helped by the large domestic markets for this kind of Alternative Tourism. When these conditions do not prevail, devising such institutions is far from easy. We are then in the sphere of micro-policy (Korten 1987); for this to be effectively implemented, knowledge of processes of learning and change is required and a real understanding of the interests involved is needed. This refers not only to those "vested interests" who might oppose the policy shift but also to those who are the potential beneficiaries of the changes, and hence potential allies in the process.

Recent developments in the organization of industrial production provide some useful pointers to the kind of innovations that might help achieve institutional support for Alternative Development and Alternative Tourism. Much has been written on "flexible specialization," the system pioneered in Japan and made famous in Europe through the fashion business of Bennetton, which enables enterprises to respond with much greater agility to changes in the market. Poon refers to that literature in her interesting paper on the relevance of these new forms of organization to Caribbean tourism (Poon 1988c).

Some of the characteristics which have been identified in earlier sections as coherent with sustainable tourism development, notably that of smaller scale, also figure in the discussion of flexible specialization. If more tourists were to take their holidays in "sustainable tourism environments," their handling in smaller batches would become a major organizational issue. Poon shows that smallness by itself would not promise success for tourism enterprises under these conditions, notably because of the inexorable march of computerization discussed above. She emphasizes, however, the very great importance of networks: "For small firms, networks and systems have become their fundamental survival route" (Poon 1988c:20). Best, Murray, and Pezzini have made the same point, showing how the small manufacturers of Italy innovating with flexible specialization, in clothing, furniture, and so on, have been successful thanks to the creation of networks of mutual support. Particularly important have been the cooperative organizations which provide services—in design, or marketing—for all, which no one enterprise could have afforded by itself (Best, Murray, and Pezzini 1989).

Sometimes simple institutional innovations are worth exploring, such as producing a serious local "Good Food Guide," as in the United Kingdom where there is a highly respected and widely used guide produced by the Consumers' Association. This approach, which is also being tried in Cyprus, helps tourists find good traditional eating places—a bit of Alternative Tourism in the face of much standardized international catering—while at the same time strengthening the local economy. Developments such as these have often also involved innovative interface organizations between local industry and local or regional government; this contains further lessons for institution building for sustainability.

X. Conclusions

We have come to the end of a long road. We have seen how the somewhat strident advocacy of Alternative Development and Alternative Tourism, by movements on the political fringe and more often based on moral indignation than on sound scientific arguments, has made way for a broader concern for sustainability underpinned by a growing body of scientific and analytical work.

Of course, in many ways conventional and alternative development paths not only diverge but go in opposite directions. Yet this analysis has tried to demonstrate that in many respects it is better to regard those opposites as continua; policies can push countries along those continua in either direction. This suggests that policy makers can, indeed, promote sustainability by constantly striving to make the conventional more sustainable.

This is also true for tourism. Most Less Developed Countries cannot hope to create acceptable living conditions for the majority of their people without continued economic growth and for many of them, especially the large number of smaller tropical mini- and micro-states, tourism represents one of the few apparently viable routes for such growth (Wilkinson 1989:160f). Policy makers can only proceed from what already exists in this respect, and that is a powerful and still growing, highly integrated, international tourism industry. "Alternative" forms will presumably continue to evolve spontaneously, as Valene Smith notes in this volume, almost inevitably "riding piggy-back" on the more cost-effective forms of the conventional, integrated international tourism industry. How to coax that behemoth into less destructive behavior is surely the main task ahead.

*   *   *

Steven Treagust gave me considerable and valuable help with the bibliographical research for this paper.

I am also grateful to my colleagues Robin Murray and John Toye for their comments on the earlier draft.

Chapter 4
Alternative Tourism: Tourism and Sustainable Resource Management

John J. Pigram

I. Tourism and Environment

Since the publication of the World Conservation Strategy in 1980, many countries have begun working toward the goal of sustainable resource management. The broad strategy, initially developed on a global level, has been translated on a national basis in nations like Australia and Canada and on a finer scale at diverse levels of government administration. Increasingly, sustainable management of resources is being accepted as the logical way to match the needs of conservation and development.

The new era of environmental concern ushered in by the World Conservation Strategy is of immediate relevance to tourism. The environment, considered here in its broadest sense as encompassing socioeconomic and cultural phenomena as well as biophysical elements, represents not merely a constraint for tourism development but a resource and an opportunity. Ideally, satisfying tourism settings grow out of complementary natural features and compatible social processes. At the same time, modern tourism amply demonstrates the capacity of human beings to manipulate and modify the environment for better or for worse. Yet the consequences are not easily predictable. Tourism certainly can contribute to environmental degradation and be self-destructive; it also has the potential to bring about significant enhancement of the environment. With tourism-induced change, an important issue is that of irreversibility, which, in turn, is a function of the characteristics of tourism, the resilience of the resource base, the spatial and temporal pattern of impacts, and the scope for compensatory managerial response.

Clearly, several modes of expression of the tourism-environment

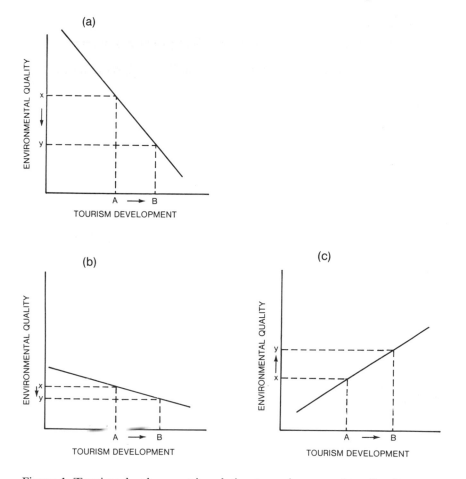

Figure 1. Tourism development in relation to environmental quality. Source: J. Pigram, *Outdoor Recreation and Resource Management* (London: Croom Helm, 1983), p. 210. Used by permission.

relationship are possible (Figure 1). The nexus is better explored in terms of the nature, scale, and pace of environmental manipulation acceptable, and whether some forms of tourism are more or less appropriate to particular environmental settings.

The realization that more than one form or manifestation of tourism is possible has prompted consideration of alternative typologies seen as achievable and desirable depending upon the circumstances. As is noted by Pearce in this volume, the term "Alternative Tourism" has been adopted to denote options or strategies considered preferable to mass tourism. Various other descriptors can be found in the literature to allude to environmentally compatible tourism. Examples include "green tourism" (Jones 1987), "nature-oriented tourism" (Durst and Ingram 1988), "soft tourism" (Mader 1988), and "defensive tourism" (Krippendorf 1982, 1987a).

Positive elements of a strategy for Alternative Tourism typically include:

- development within each locality of a special sense of place, reflected in architectural character and development style, sensitive to its unique heritage and environment;
- preservation, protection, and enhancement of the quality of resources which are the basis of tourism;
- fostering development of additional visitor attractions with roots in their own locale and developed in ways which complement local attributes;
- development of visitor services which enhance the local heritage and environment; and
- endorsement of growth when and where it improves things, not where it is destructive or exceeds the carrying capacity of the natural environment or the limits of the social environment, beyond which the quality of community life is adversely affected. (Cox 1985:6–7)

II. Policy Rationale and Endorsement

Part of the rationale for pursuing a policy of Alternative Tourism can be found in the uncertainty associated with the environmental impacts of some forms of tourism development. Prediction is made difficult because of spatial and temporal discontinuities between cause and effect. Environmental degradation is rarely catastrophic, but typified more by cumulative threshold effects. Small amounts of pollution, for example, may have a negligible impact in the short term and in the immediate environment. Beyond a certain level, however, adverse effects can rapidly occur, and perhaps in areas not directly associated with the source of pollutants.

As noted earlier, one argument for Alternative Tourism rests on the concept of irreversibility (Burns, Damania, and Heathcote 1988). Many resource management decisions call for a trade-off between mutually exclusive alternatives and, in some cases, may involve the loss of valued options which can only be restored, if at all, at prohibitively high cost. Such lost options are called irreversibilities (Krutilla and Fisher 1975).

An unfortunate concomitant of tourism development in an environmentally sensitive area is that the decision to develop may require irreversible change to certain characteristics of the area. Whereas this situation is regrettable, in the immediate sense, for current users of that environment, it also has implications for others who may wish to preserve the option of future use. This notion of "option value" is unlikely to be acknowledged in the development of facilities for mass tourism where decisions are frequently based on short term, market-determined criteria.

Again, some individuals can derive satisfaction from the assurance that a resource is being maintained intact, even though there is no intention of putting it to use. Such "existence values" make up part of the true benefits of environmental protection, but are largely ignored against the harsh commercial realities of providing for the immediate wants of the mass tourism market. Typically, development decisions fail to take full account of future social costs and benefits in favor of more pressing current demands.

Failure to take into account the validity and relevance of existence and option values means that resource development decisions, based primarily on optimal economic criteria, are myopic in the sense that they do not display appropriate concern for the well-being of present and future generations (Musgrave 1984). Moreover, there is evidence to suggest that large numbers of individuals share collective concern for valued attributes of society, to the point where they would be prepared to accept a less than optimal outcome in the interests of these distant generations. The value gained from such (sub-optimal) decisions compensates for the losses accepted and has been termed "bequest value" (Musgrave 1984).

Taken together, option value, existence value, and bequest value represent the overall worth which society bestows on the preservation of certain environmental qualities. This, in turn, underpins the growing opposition to forms of development seen as generating irreversibilities and the support for sustainable resource management strategies. In the context of tourism development, recognition of these three important values lends weight to the quest for alternative approaches to tourism where uncertainty can be accommodated and irreversibility is not in question.

Generally speaking, there is no shortage of rhetoric in support of Alternative Tourism as a desirable and essential policy option. Whereas examples of effective expression of such policies "on the ground" are harder to find, tourism plans and strategies for embracing environmentally compatible modes of tourism development have been prepared for various regions of the world, from the South Pacific to the Caribbean (Okotai 1980; Organization of American States 1984; Jackson 1986). In New Zealand, farm and ranch tours are being actively promoted as an alternative to mass tourism (Dowling 1989). Along the Australian coastline, simpler forms of tourism which permit more contact with the natural environment are being advocated (Pigram 1987; Western Australian State Planning Commission 1988). Considerations of quality of life and conservation of the natural environment and cultural heritage figure prominently in the tourism strategy put forward for Canada (Tourism Industry Association of Canada 1985). On a smaller scale, a strategy is in place for the Channel Island of Jersey which integrates resource planning for tourism development with the needs and interests of the indigenous population (Romeril 1983). Also in Britain, "Local authorities throughout England and Wales are being urged to adopt the Countryside Commission's six essential principles for green tourism—tourism that conserves rather than consumes the countryside" (Countryside Commission 1989: 2).

Among other things, the principles of endorsement for Alternative Tourism stress that tourism should draw on the character of the countryside itself, bring conservation and recreation benefits rather than imposing an extra burden, and be in keeping with the landscape and, if possible, enhance it. These principles are echoed by the Council for National Parks (1989) which has declared that tourism fit for national parks in England and Wales should be small scale, be true to the character of the park, fit the landscape, encourage sensitive use of the natural resource, and integrate into the local economy.

III. Policy Implementation

Clearly, endorsement of alternative approaches to tourism development is seen as a desirable strategy by many resource management agencies around the globe. As also discussed by de Kadt in this volume, however, the incorporation of such policy initiatives into real world decision making seems unlikely to occur spontaneously. The task of convincing developers of the good sense, both environmentally and commercially, of alternatives to mass tourism is likely to prove difficult. Reconciling ethics with economics is never easy; substantial material interests are always involved and emotive appeals to the good nature of developers are unlikely to achieve the desired outcome. It can be difficult to demonstrate conclusively the costs over time of environmental degradation, especially when set against the benefits foregone by adopting a more restrained approach to tourism development. In the absence of coercive measures, developers are more likely to ignore the longer term consequences of excluding consideration of the limitations of the resource base in favor of more immediate returns.

These considerations only serve to illustrate the gulf which commonly exists between policy formulation and implementation (Ham and Hill 1986). Worthwhile policies may be espoused and even formally adopted by management agencies, yet they encounter formidable barriers when attempts are made to translate them into action. Problems in implementation arise not so much in deciding what should be done, but in making it happen. Shortcomings in the implementation process account, in large measure, for the lack of progress toward the realization of apparently preferred policy options such as Alternative Tourism.

Policy implementation, in whatever area of social concern, is seen as a sociopolitical process (Graycar 1979). It is, essentially, a bargaining exercise meshing political and social acceptability with economic and technical feasibility and with administrative reality. Implementation of a policy option specific to the public arena, such as an adjustment to social welfare programs, is difficult enough given the need to achieve consensus between different tiers of government. With a policy of Alternative Tourism, the need for coincidence between the objectives and values of the public and private sectors makes the implementation process much more complex.

Several writers have explored the dimensions of the policy implementation process in an effort to identify the forces at work and the conditions which have to be satisfied for the process to generate the desired outcome. All attempts to establish new attitudes or institutions within society produce tensions. Smith (1973) makes the point that it is the context within which such policies are to be implemented which is of fundamental importance. Conflicts and resistance can emerge because of the nature and complexity of the policy, the way it is perceived by the target groups and the implementing organizations, and the environmental conditions—physical, sociocultural, political, and economic—which prevail.

Setting a policy of Alternative Tourism against these contextual parameters goes some way toward explaining the relatively poor commercial acceptance the policy has experienced in the harsh climate of decision making associated with tourism development. For some "hard-headed" developers, Alternative Tourism is perceived as a utopian ideal, of no practical consequence; for others, the policy may be seen as too "redistributive," requiring far-reaching changes in the institutions and socioeconomic considerations which currently govern tourism development.

Contextual characteristics for Alternative Tourism are also blurred because of overlap between the roles of developers in the implementation process. On the one hand, they are responsible for implementation of the policy, along with public management agencies. However, they also make up part of the target group who, with the communities affected, must change and be receptive to the demands of the policy. These roles can be mutually reinforcing in generating tensions and resistance to policy implementation.

Environmental factors are also influential in the policy implementation process. Smith (1973:205) sees these factors or conditions "as a sort of constraining corridor through which the implementation of policy must be forced." Given that the term "environmental" is inclusive of cultural and social lifestyles, implementation strategies need to take account of the circumstances in which these and other factors might act as serious constraints to a policy of Alternative Tourism.

IV. Bridging the Implementation Gap

For the implementation process to succeed, policy must first be perceived by policy makers as conceptually robust, defensible, and amenable to implementation. Second, the various interests involved in the implementation process must be convinced that the net outcome will be positive, or at least benign, in the longer term. Finally, the target groups—the communities affected—must be receptive to change and see the policy as a constructive response to their priorities.

The phenomenon of tourism is not viewed the same by all segments of society. The perspectives on tourism development of at least four groups can be identified: the tourist participant, the developer, the agencies, and the local resident (Gunn 1988). Achieving satisfaction within and among these various constituencies with a policy such as Alternative Tourism, which challenges established attitudes and modes of practice, is not easy. The case for Alternative Tourism must first be argued in conceptual terms and then considered in a functional context which will facilitate implementation of the policy at an operational level.

If it is accepted that Alternative Tourism is essentially an exercise in sustainable resource management, questions raised earlier in regard to uncertainty and irreversibility need to be reexamined. The task confronting modern tourism is to avoid forms of development which entail the risk of irreversible outcomes and a very high, though uncertain, potential to impose unacceptable costs on future generations. The concern for sustainability inherent in Alternative Tourism effectively counters these risks. In conceptual terms, Alternative Tourism is based on the notion of a "safe minimum standard" reflecting an attitude of "risk conservatism" (Musgrave 1988).

Put succinctly, a safe minimum standard is the level of resource supply accepted as the threshold of irreversibility, that is, boundaries are set which must not be exceeded if irreversibility is to be avoided. In an ecological context, a safe minimum standard would be set at the minimum population level to ensure the survival of a species. From an economic standpoint, observance of a safe minimum standard would seem appropriate where the potential losses from a particular course of action are very high and the costs (including opportunities and benefits foregone) of maintaining the status quo are relatively low.

A partial mechanism for applying the safe minimum standard approach to tourism development may be found in Kozlowski's (1985) Ultimate Environmental Threshold Model (partial because the model only incorporates key elements of the natural environment). The Ultimate Environmental Threshold is determined with reference to:

- uniqueness (the frequency and spatial differentiation of a given natural element within a region);
- fragility (the ability of the element to resist negative effects and to self-regenerate to a relatively unchanged state); and
- naturalness (how far a given environmental element has been altered from its original state).

After evaluation according to these indicators, the key elements can then be synthesized to produce a composite picture on which decisions on areas to be targeted or avoided for tourism development can be based.

A partial analogy may also be drawn with the concept of "Limits of Acceptable Change," which, increasingly, is being applied by social scientists as a key element in the management of outdoor recreation sites (Stankey et al. 1985). The concept represents a framework within which acceptable levels and types of environmental and social impacts of recreation are defined. It is important to note that the concept accepts some change in nature as the norm and that a decision to allow recreational use is a de facto decision to allow some level of impact to occur (Stankey 1989). It is a decision for management as to what constitutes an acceptable level of human-induced change (Hammitt and Cole 1987). Moreover, this decision is not determined entirely by ecological criteria. It should be related to the characteristics of the site, its capacity to support higher or lower levels of use, and the net balance between potential gains and losses from imposing limitations on use. A range of social, economic, and political considerations could be relevant to the setting of limits of acceptable change.

There are important lessons here for those who see Alternative Tourism as the panacea for all problems in tourism development in all situations. Not all tourist zones exhibit the same degree of fragility or of resilience. Some may permit only very low levels of tourist incursion; others may be able to withstand a much greater scale and intensity of development. Again, a decision to limit or encourage tourism development should make reference to human concerns and economic circumstances as well as physical parameters. "Ecological determinism" alone is no more defensible than "economic determinism."

In considering the choices open to tourism development, it should be possible to quantify the ecological, economic, and social costs and benefits of Alternative Tourism by putting values on the preservation of options for future generations or on the loss of such options to mass tourism. These options may well include intangible considerations such as a more satisfying lifestyle and quality of life and a more secure sociocultural setting for the residential community of a tourist zone.

A further note of qualification should be expressed in regard to the relevance of a risk conservative stance and the observance of a safe minimum standard for tourism development. Questions arise as to the extent to which fears about uncertainty and the preservation of future options should determine decisions of more immediate consequence. An alternative argument might assert that current decision makers do a disservice to distant generations by attempting to second-guess their future needs or tastes and the size of their resource base relative to technological advances. Certainly, risk conservatism could be taken to the point where it could stifle all innovation and discovery. If the advice of some present-day committed preservationists were to be taken literally, the tourist scene could, indeed, become a rather dull shade of green! Whereas Alternative Tourism represents the cautious path to follow, prudence should be tempered by receptiveness to initiative and a willingness to judge developmental innovations objectively from the standpoint of environmental acceptability. Even in a perfect world, there is a place for "Disneylands" and other created tourist attractions. As Musgrave (1988) puts it, in commenting generally on sustainability:

Clearly, some middle way must be sought which represents a tradeoff between fairness for the future and the need to retain flexibility in order to take advantage of new information and to respond to shifting attitudes. (Musgrave 1988:6)

This type of arrangement implies the need for decision makers to remain aware of changing attitudes and broadened information levels. Musgrave suggests that appropriate policies be determined from a set of institutions linked to a process of informed public enquiry. Undoubtedly, decision making in the tourism sphere would benefit from public input. Questions remain as to how this might best be achieved, the degree of importance to be accorded to community reaction, and how it might be balanced against professional judgment.

V. Public Participation

An impressive literature exists on public participation in decision making and, although the mechanisms for achieving useful participation are subject to further refinement, the principle is well established (if not always observed in practice). Given the scale of resource management decisions involved in tourism development, where the physical and social environment can experience substantial change, it would seem to make good sense to consult the communities likely to be affected by such decisions.

The view that tourism planning should take into account the wishes of local residents is well supported. Clark (1988) reports the findings of the Pacific Area Travel Association, based on research in several countries, which assert

that for long-term stability of the [tourism] industry, residential input and positive residential attitudes are essential [and that] local attractions [should] only be promoted when endorsed by residents. (Clark 1988:3)

Although many communities exposed to tourism might agree with an approach of "residents first, tourists second," market research in Australia has shown that the desired experiences of visitors differ little from those of local residents (Jenkins 1988). It may well be a case of "residents first, tourists first."

Emphasis on public participation also forms a fundamental component of the ecological community model for tourism planning developed by Murphy (1985). Murphy presents persuasive evidence of the importance of participatory planning in balancing the physical and commercial orientation of much tourism development in the past.

Input from concerned community groups could provide a balance to the short-term objectives of the business sector, and possibly encourage greater variation and local flavour in future projects. (Murphy 1985:171)

Community involvement in tourism planning and development is not merely good public relations; it can also play a role in facilitating the policy implementation process. Once Alternative Tourism has been endorsed as a policy to be pursued, active community pressure groups can become an effective force in assisting implementation. Conversely, implementation is likely to lapse or be only partial without a positive response from the community affected in support of change

(Howe 1983). Mader (1988) reports that, in the Third World too, citizen movements are being encouraged to search for alternative forms of tourism (as well as alternatives to tourism). Without sustained pressure from the grass roots, more environmentally compatible forms of development run the risk of not being considered seriously as alternatives to mass tourism by developers or resource management agencies.

The need for balanced input from the participating public is especially important in tourism development decision making. Input, both from the "top-down" and the "bottom-up," is seen as the way to avoid confrontation and achieve harmonious development: "our top-down planning process expressed in goals, guidelines and regulations, must be matched by a bottom-up process of involvement by local residents" (Hilts and Moull 1988:108).

Gunn (1979) stresses the necessity of identifying the full range of actors with the ability to make changes to the tourist system. At the same time, the perspectives from which these polar approaches are derived need to be appreciated. On the one hand, top-down assessments by policy makers could be seen to have the advantage of relative detachment or objectivity, especially when supported by professional expertise. This is the rationale underpinning the "experience survey" approach to obtaining citizen input (Gunn and Worms 1973). The method is based on the assumption that certain individuals ("knowledgeables") possess specialized knowledge and awareness of attitudes because of their occupational experience and position in a community. By tapping this source of information, it should be possible to obtain a good cross-section of opinion and likely citizen reaction to tourism planning initiatives. Involvement of such "knowledgeable" persons may also compensate for any suggestion that tourism policy makers may be too far removed from the consequences of policy implementation.

On the other hand, bottom-up responses from target groups (policy takers) may well be hampered by limited knowledge, apathy, misinformation, and resistance to change. Community input will be improved and given more respect by decision makers when it is shown to be well informed and aware of the tradeoffs associated with alternative forms of tourism development.

Heightened levels of awareness are relevant at several stages of the policy implementation process. Awareness of the issues and concerns, such as the risk of environmental degradation from mass tourism which prompted the formulation of a policy of Alternative Tourism, should hasten progress toward its implementation. In the same way, awareness of the constraints impeding the achievement of Alternative Tourism should help focus efforts on effective means to overcome or offset those constraints. The task remains of educating and informing the public and creating a more aware community without unduly biasing attitudes. Education appears to be one of the more promising ways in which a higher order of compatibility can be achieved between the phenomenon of tourism and the environment which nurtures it. Education and communication should encompass the several components of the tourist industry—the providers and managers, as well as the tourists themselves. At the same time, a fine line must be followed between dissemination of information on alternative policy options and promotion of biased propaganda conducive to alarm among target groups and to distortion of the outcome.

VI. Conclusions

Alternative Tourism is rapidly attaining the status of "motherhood" as a desirable objective for tourist zones, although actual examples of the practical expression of the policy are not yet commonplace. Without serious consideration of the conditions necessary for Alternative Tourism to succeed, the process of policy implementation is likely to remain flawed. In some cases, there would be instances where Alternative Tourism is pursued in inappropriate circumstances; in others, opportunities for successful implementation of such a policy may be lost because of the failure to appreciate the efforts needed to overcome the inevitable gap between policy formulation and implementation.

Alternative Tourism has the potential to become a tangible expression of sustainable resource development. Yet, without the development of effective means of translating the ideal into action, it runs the risk of remaining irrelevant and inert as a feasible policy option for the real world of tourism development.

Chapter 5
International Tourism Reconsidered: The Principle of the Alternative

Marie-Françoise Lanfant and
Nelson H. H. Graburn

"Virtue thus lies between excess and want."
Aristotle, *Nicomachean Ethics*, II, 5 (Organon.II).

I. Introduction

On the eve of the third millennium, the quest for "alternative" models is urgent; today this urgency is gaining power within the field of tourism. Many authors identify with this question. Seminars and symposia proliferate in opposing the problems of unchecked tourist growth. Alternative Tourism has become a symbol of the "Tourism of the Future."

In choosing "Theoretical Perspectives on Alternative Forms of Tourism" as the topic of its first seminar (Zakopane, 1989), the International Academy for the Study of Tourism invited academics and other scientists to consider all aspects of this theme. As social scientists, we must be concerned with Alternative Tourism in all its facets, actual or potential. It is the contention of the authors that the popularity of this new concept should itself be analyzed as a symptom.

The alliance of the two words "tourism" and "alternative" should alert us. It has a paradoxical resonance, an incongruity stimulating further enquiry. In this chapter, we intend to squeeze the meaning out of these words and to question the underpinnings of their use over the past two decades. Thus, ours is an essay in the sociology of knowledge and praxis.

II. Putting the Vocabulary Under the Microscope

The Complexity of the Phenomenon and Its Concept

At several recent meetings, we have noted the perplexing nature of the term Alternative Tourism. Whenever speakers were asked to define it, their embarrassment became clear. At the International Round Table organized by URESTI (Marly-le-Roi, 1986), Georges Cazes (a French geographer) and Linda Richter (an American political scientist) presided over the debate on the problematics of alternative tourism in local societies. Cazes was irritated by what he considered a confusing notion and Richter proposed replacing Alternative Tourism with the term "appropriate tourism." At Zakopane, the academicians concluded by condemning the "imprecise character of the term Alternative Tourism [as] ambiguous and hardly congruent with scientific work." Finally, at the World Tourism Organization Seminar on Alternative Tourism (Tamanrasset, Algeria, 1989), the participants voted to replace the term with Responsible Tourism, purposefully defined as "relating to all forms of tourism which respect the host, natural, built, and cultural environment, and the interests of all parties concerned: hosts, guests, visitors, tourist industry, government, etc."

How can we understand the success of the term Alternative Tourism in spite of all the reservations about it?

"Alternative Tourism" has a nice ring to it. It is alliterative like an advertising gimmick. It is dynamic and provides a rallying cry It sounds like an appeal: "Let's make the improbable a reality!" It connotes quality, responsibility, and respectability. It suggests a sensitivity that wins over the world. Yet, though attractive, the label is deceiving.

From the beginning there has been a problem of definition: where to draw the line between various kinds of tourism. The many meetings on Alternative Tourism have spawned a "discourse of good intentions." In this chapter we hope to reveal the ideological pressures behind the discourse. There is a danger of oversimplification of the complexities of tourism: in order to avoid the dilemma of having to decide whether to reject tourism completely or accept it unconditionally, people have latched onto the easy idea of Alternative Tourism.

Uncertain Origins

The emergence of the word "alternative" allied with tourism throws light on its *ideological* nature. The Ecumenical Coalition on Third

World Tourism (ECTWT) claims paternity. Since its establishment in Bangkok (1981), it has aimed "to explore possible models of alternative tourism in the Third World." In 1980, a precursor group of militant Christians gathered just before the World Tourism Organization Conference on Tourism in Manila to denounce economic imperialism, domination by transnational corporations, political exploitation, organized prostitution of women and children, the degradation of traditional cultures, and other ills.

The Tourism European Network (TEN) was soon formed in Stuttgart in collaboration with ECTWT and, in 1984, held a seminar on Alternative Tourism in Asia. In 1986 a similar international conference took place at Bad Boll, West Germany. This called for the different sectors—tourists, hosts, businesses—to participate in building a New Tourism Order. But there were broader forces and other groups also promoting Alternative Tourism.

Alternative Tourism: A Social Movement?

One could also link these calls for Alternative Tourism with various "Alternative Movements" that arose in Germany or the West Coast of the United States in the 1960s. These movements wanted to promote a counterculture by rejecting consumer society. Alternative Tourism, in rejecting mass tourism, is a similar radical attempt to transform social relations and is thus part of the larger movement. Is tourism a new kind of development strategy or, more powerfully, a prime force within a new strategy of international relations? A recent congress (Vancouver, 1988) was called "Tourism—A Vital Force for Peace." This issue of "alternatives" penetrates all domains, and tourism is but one entrée.

Thus one could envisage a sociology of "Alternative Tourism as a social movement": a force aimed at social change; a movement of people in the process of mobilizing ideas; a series of acts and speech diffused in many segments of social life, where the actors are not totally aware of their real motives (Boudon and Bourricaud 1982: 374–82). It is only with the hindsight of history that we can speak about a real change of strategy. One should be able to analyze the actors, the channels of communication, the ramifications, and the different forces of the movement. But the believers in Alternative Tourism belong to various social groups and the issue is still unclear.

The whole question is complex. In the 1980s everybody started to talk about Alternative Tourism, but with scattered meanings and heterogenous or contradictory interests.

Polysemy: A Range of Conflicting Meanings

Alternative Tourism encompasses a wide range of connotations: tourists characterized by particular motivations; touristic practices; a touristic product; levels of technology; solutions to planning; local, regional, national, or international politics; a strategy for development. In the last case, Alternative Tourism is the application to tourism of Alternative Development in regions where tourism has been chosen as a factor in economic development. Finally, Alternative Tourism expresses the concept of a "New order of Tourism." The multiplicity of these meanings is both a great source of confusion and a rich opportunity for in-depth study.

Profiles of Conceptualization

Questions of Method: The Construction of the Concept

We may approach the problem in two ways. There is a difference between the emergence of a practical concept and the construction of a scientific concept. The analysis must go further than surveying the various meanings and denouncing the confusion, even in order to clarify them. Listing the different uses of the term and coming up with an approximate definition is easy but insufficient. Using the methods of structural linguistics, we analyze the structure of meanings underlying the discourse of Alternative Tourism—the discourse of the tourists, professionals, politicians, scientists. We deconstruct this discourse in order to lay bare the conceptual operations from which it derives its power of persuasion. This is only a much needed preliminary step.

Adjective or Noun?

The expression Alternative Tourism can be baffling; to one businessman interviewed in the French Alps it meant "that the roads, the hotels, the whole place, is periodically filled and emptied!" The word "alternative," taken literally, engenders such images as ebb and flow, going and returning, leaving and arriving! But to the initiated, "alternative" (as in Alternative Tourism) is a special kind of qualifier. The whole phrase is an "autonomous syntagm"; the words are bound together like a single noun.

The Semantic Field

Using the methods of structural analysis, we look at the opposing pairs in which Alternative Tourism is used in speech. We find that

Alternative Tourism always has an antithesis: commercial, conventional, mass tourism. It arises as the contrary to whatever is seen as negative or bad about conventional tourism, so it is always a semantic inversion, found at all levels of discourse. For instance, some tourists are motivated to think that Alternative Tourism is individualized or selective, expressing their good taste, as opposed to mass tourism, which is seen as plebeian, organized, gregarious, and allowing little individual choice.

As lodging, Alternative Tourism refers to human scale, small and medium sized local, family, or community enterprises, well integrated into the area. Anything other than the usual concrete tourist establishments qualifies. Alternative Tourism connotes local artisanship, with wood and fine materials and typical local architecture.

As a tourist product, Alternative Tourism is expensive, sold by travel agents to a wealthy clientele or social leaders. "Cultural tourism" is the key word. Paradoxically, it also claims to be free of commercial circuits and capitalist profits. It appeals to advocates of "social tourism" and independent tourists alike.

As activity, it favors physical well-being acquired by good health habits, competitive sports, or strenuous outings. It implies intellectual and aesthetic attitudes, trips to far regions with unexplored cultural or natural treasures appealing to the socially mobile. It opposes mass tourism for its comfort and repetition of the "four S's" (sun, sand, ski, sex) of the average middle classes.

Finally, as planning, Alternative Tourism appears to express local wishes to bring together tourists and host communities and thereby enters into endogenous development policies concerned with local interests. Some claim that this "new model" of tourism will replace mass tourism as "old fashioned" or out of date. Thus for some, "alternative" is not just another kind of tourism, but aspires to become *the* tourism in the promotion of a new order.

The Principle of the Alternative

In logic, an alternative is based on a judgment that there are only two possibilities. Two contemporaneous terms are placed in mutual exclusion, with an "excluded middle," that is, no other possible course is open. It is either one or the other. Thus the promotion of Alternative Tourism relies on a series of value-laden judgments: devaluation/valuation, negation/affirmation, neutralization/idealization. Emerging from such a series of discriminating processes between the "reference tourism" and Alternative Tourism, logically Alternative Tourism becomes *the* tourism.

After analyzing many texts referring to tourism, an unending repetition of these mental processes can be noted. We idealize what we promote and reject what we disapprove of.

III. Alternative Tourism and the Challenge of International Tourism

To situate the Alternative Tourism movement, we must compare its goals with those of International Tourism. Within the discourse, Alternative Tourism can be seen as an opposite of International Tourism, which is itself multidimensional. Some major characteristics of International Tourism include the following.

The Primacy of Economics

Tourism: An International Phenomenon

International Tourism is generally defined as a particular aspect of Tourism (with a capital T), as the extension into international geographical space of a mobility originally confined within national limits in opposition to internal (or domestic) tourism.

There are, however, many ways to define international tourism. In the literature, modern international tourism is commonly linked with the Grand Tour, which began in the eighteenth century among young British aristocrats making an initiatory trip to the Continent. As other classes were emancipated in the nineteenth and early twentieth centuries, the idea was generalized as a "vacation." In this way, the ideas of tourism and vacations are interchangeable. Thus international tourism is seen as an irrepressible seasonal mobility which crosses frontiers, as "a tidal wave, a North-South invasion, or a stampede to the sun."

Seen historically, this is a one-sided view, that of the industrialized nations. But international tourism is an "international social fact" in the sociological sense. "Not all social facts are amenable to internationalization . . . there are some phenomena which reflect more precisely the characteristics of one group, people, or nation; other phenomena are seen to better advantage as *exchanges* between different peoples; they surpass national territories, . . . they live a kind of supra-national life." (Durkheim 1969:681–85, emphasis added; cf. Mauss 1969).

Tourism: The Duality of the Concept

In the 1930s, countries in the League of Nations were aware of the assets and liabilities of international travel on the balance of payments, "petty things" (Barètje 1987:51) which can amount to considerable sums. At that critical period, some governments protected their balance of payments by limiting travel abroad. The League's Economic Commission, however, took a position in favor of International Tourism, with the important argument: "It is ultimately wrong to consider domestic tourism to be something essentially different from international tourism, just as it would be to forget that the economic activity of a country is indissolubly linked to its external trade" (cited by Languar 1986).

Thus tourism is divided into international and domestic but, though linked, they refer to different networks of meaning. Domestic tourism is seen as a cultural habit increasingly widespread in industrial societies, but International Tourism has become an import/export activity reckoned in terms of international monetary exchange. Thus International Tourism is implicitly reduced to its economic and commercial aspects, which take preference over cultural aspects. Whereas domestic and national tourism are seen as inherently cultural, International Tourism is seen as prospectively economic. Needless to say the notion of Alternative Tourism bears the consequences of this cleavage.

Political Will: The Growth of International Tourist Movements

Thus tourism became first and foremost an "economic fact" for decision makers, who take this as a given in considering tourism within their overall planning. The opening of an area to foreign tourists is seen as a market phenomenon and is calculated as a matter of foreign exchange by international organizations. Countries are measured by their performance, and regions are urged to enter into this "competition." The development of tourism is seen as axiomatic.

Tourism is not just a matter of national growth, but must be conceptualized as part of international relations.

Tourists in the Global Flows: Always More!

Reading economic forecasts gives one the impression that tourism is constantly in danger of collapse. The discourse of officials is preoccupied with signs of weakness, decrease, or loss. Thus international tourism always appears to be on the brink of a crisis, one which it in fact anticipates and resists (Lanfant 1989a).

The constant growth of international tourism is not spontaneous, but reflects a supernational institutional will. In the Universal Rights of Man Charter the liberty to circulate freely in the world is fundamental. The worldwide expansion of international tourism is the subject of massive propaganda. In this regard it is noteworthy that the International Union of Official Organizations of Tourism (IUOTO), which became the World Tourism Organization in 1974, was originally founded at the Hague in 1925 as the International Union of Official Spokesmen of Touristic Propaganda.

In spite of variations during economically or politically sensitive periods, tourism has enjoyed an average growth rate of 8 percent per annum since World War II. In 1950, 25.3 million people crossed borders as international tourists. This number reached 390 million in 1988 and is projected to grow at 4 to 5 percent per annum through 2010. The World Tourism Organization forecasts that tourism will take first place among world economic activities, and no decline is in sight before 2000.

The question is not so much whether or not there is an alternative to tourism but whether major new emerging forms of tourism will remain within the frame of reference of the dominant model or break away from it.

Tourism: A Factor in Economic Development

A Point of Doctrine

International tourism makes money and the industrialized nations are the main benefactors. Yet as early as the 1960s Kurt Krapf (1961), one of the pioneers of the economic theory of tourism, advanced a then-revolutionary idea that the developing nations should also benefit from international tourism. Soon thereafter the United Nations Conference on Tourism and International Travel proclaimed, "Tourism makes a vital contribution to the economic development of Developing Nations" (United Nations 1963).

This theory came to the fore at the very time when affluent nations decided to help "needy" societies by announcing a "Decade of Development," just when many former colonies gained their political independence. It was reasoned that, though planting a luxury industry in such poor countries might appear shocking, the developing nations had few other resources, but they did have an abundance of natural and cultural riches and a cheap, underemployed workforce. Tourism, a frivolous activity, could become a useful instrument in economic development. But this doctrine contains a condensation of meanings which must be untangled to avoid the pitfalls into which the doctrine of Alternative Tourism also risks sinking.

The imposition of international tourism on the developing nations suggests not only a change of scale but a turning point. International tourism is not just an international extension of domestic tourism, nor just a major contribution to foreign exchange, but is also a "transmission belt" connecting the developed and the underdeveloped worlds. Tourism policy has become part of a global project which lumps together seemingly contradictory economic interests: the organization of vacations (an idea originating in rich countries) and the aspirations for development of economically weak societies.

Thus "free time" resulting from the exploitation of the surplus value of capital is put back into the calculation of economic productivity. Societies inexperienced with industrialization are re-oriented toward "touristification"; tourism comes to be judged by economic and political criteria within the international framework, a vector for global integration. It becomes a factor in the North-South dialogue and a component of the much-discussed New World Economic Order.

The Opening of Developing Nations to International Tourism

Since the 1960s, the developing nations have been persuaded to open themselves to international tourism, to give tourism a favored place in their economy, to welcome foreign capital, and to make fiscal concessions. Many countries have responded enthusiastically, hoping to solve their problems of endemic poverty. Between 1969 and 1979 the World Bank supported twenty-four projects in eighteen countries. Immense resort projects were started on the Costa Brava and the Costa del Sol in Spain, on the Bulgarian and Romanian shores of the Black Sea, in Tunisia, the Antilles, the Caribbean, Mexico, Thailand.

Tourist resorts form a world apart, a delimited area on the fringe of ordinary life. Tourists are grouped into a hotel or complex containing all the services necessary for maintenance and pleasure, following the needs of the notorious "4 S's." Architecturally and technically modern buildings are erected in spaces in the process of desertification or overpopulation. It sometimes happens that the local population must leave or nomads can no longer traverse the area, the land is abandoned or remodeled, or new fresh water supplies sought, all for the reception of vacationers from rich countries. Touristic mobility is an unprecedented "delocalization" movement.

Tourism, a Factor in Economic Development on a World Scale

At times of crisis, even the developed nations see tourism as a primary "export activity" worthy of subvention. In addition to the multiplier effect and offsetting foreign debts, tourism becomes one of the few remedies for never ending unemployment. According to Organization for Economic Development and Cooperation (OEDC) experts, tourism is moving from an accessory to a major and necessary economic activity.

Rich countries are adopting policies first intended for the poor, and tourism has become a development factor in post-industrial societies. Almost all nations promote tourism development as a producer of profit, leading to envy and stiff competition for foreign exchange and tourists.

Tourism in the Logic of World Integration

The Tourist Industry: Transnational Company Networks

The tourist industry's system of production is now considered one of the world's most powerful driving forces. Through mergers and concentrations, these companies have become agents of an interconnected network penetrating many sectors. The transnationals of tourism are the avant garde for strategies of capital internationalization. The system of tourist production has evolved into network-companies, models for transnational companies in the world economy (Dunning and McQueen 1983).

Decisions for whole regions or countries are made inside one company. Yet the states or communities involved may have no veto or even influence in this "Dialogue of Monopolies and Countries" (Perroux 1982). Competition is reduced by collusion, for profits grow best in homogeneous spaces. Thus culture, society, and identity become mass products when International Tourism enters a country.

These network-companies operate in an almost centralized system in which power stems from negotiations and meetings in search of consensus. This efficient organizational system, with its savoir faire and its capacity to manage behavior and technology, is what Galbraith (1967) called "technostructure." The system relies on experts who often bring identical solutions to contrasting local conditions. Growth is external to and independent of local conditions of production.

This system also aids the integration of regions and communities into the international whole. To accept international tourism is not only to welcome foreign vacationers and their currency, it means access to international planning, technology, and finance, entering the world economy and approaching world modernity. One cannot understand Alternative Tourism without this view of reality.

The Role of the State in the Promotion of International Tourism

It is often difficult to draw the line between the state and industry. By internationalizing tourism, the structure of the state is transformed by the arrival of officials trained in commercial technology and marketing at all levels of administration, an evolution obvious in France and many other countries. The training of government authorities integrates local business into higher echelons. In January 1990, meetings on local development were exhorted to "think local, act global/think global, act local " (*Le Monde* 1989:90). Thus international tourism is one domain where the public-private dichotomy is misleading.

From Sectorial Planning to Global Planning

International tourist planning has to do with the introduction of rational thought into management practices. Since the 1960s it has enlarged its range, from purely sectorial choices to the opening of the developing nations to international tourism. As tourism moved from a secondary activity to a primary force in national economies, intersectorial comparisons of profitability became crucial. In addition, as tourism is inscribed in national development plans, it is justified not only by profit, but for its contributions to political aims of development. It becomes the axis on which other sectors rely, and national intersectorial planning gives way to global planning.

At the instigation of international organizations or Western, formerly colonial, powers, Third World countries cooperate and endeavor to finance their investments within a long-range set of programs. National tourist offices depend on international data. Tourism becomes one of the vectors of internationalization and thus attempts to become a generating principle for the whole society, enabling the instruments and goals of the world economy to penetrate and weave transnational bonds.

Gearing Up a Society for Tourism: The Absorption of the Cultural into the Economic

What Is a Touristic Product?

Marketing, long an essential tool of international tourism promotion, articulates supply and demand within a market economy, and societies embracing international tourism are plunged into this international system. Unlike other industries, the "products" of the tourist industry are a pastiche of formerly heterogeneous elements amalgamated by advertising for tourist consumption. Combined symbiotically, they include services (lodging, dining, transportation, recreation), culture (folklore, festivals, heritage, monuments), and less palpable things such as hospitality, ambiance, and ethnicity. At last this "product" incorporates the society itself, its culture, its identity.

International tourism promotion, aimed at economic development, requires every location to offer something unique. By this logic, each country or region must produce and publicize its unique identity, with a "name recognition" that signifies its superiority. All over the world there is a fantastic incorporation of identifying signs into touristic products: nostalgic places, historic monuments, traditional and rural heritage, the skills of ethnic groups. Populations are solicited to attract foreign attention with their talent and creativity. Everyone plays himself or herself and acts out a performance. Widespread marketing research determines what this image should be, matching aspects of local identity with the desires of potential clients. This fabrication of identity defines the seductive attributes and crystallizes them in an advertising image such that even the locals may eventually recognize themselves in it (cf. Carpenter 1973)!

Touristic Restoration/Appropriation

In the analysis of the creation of "tourist attractions," cultural heritage is exploited as a "mineable resource." It must be "put to good use" by changing its purpose, and hence its meaning (cf. MacCannell 1976). It is restored along rational lines for commercial promotion and may end up looking like one in a series of reproductions rather than its own historic self.

In Europe, for example, historic landmarks and properties were often preserved by philanthropy derived from a sense of community pride. Now, however, every city restores its historic ramparts, church, or castle to attract tourists, and funding is solicited from art dealers, from cultural sponsors, and from the tourist arms of the state. Tourism promotion is allied with marketing, and uses the quick functional "cultural engineering" perfected in the United States. Heritage, transformed into productive capital, is renovated and the profit used to repay the cost rather than for safeguarding. Tourism therefore ensures renewal.

Goaded by European unification in 1992 and the prospect of additional millions of tourists, France is now turning itself into a vast "theme park." Compared with the new EuroDisneyland near Paris, other cities and villages will appear authentic! Castles, cathedrals, old villages, prehistoric sites, and public gardens appeal increasingly to the public. The new ecomuseums have also met with great success, as they look to older people to explain the activities and tools displayed. In disused factories, on canal towpaths, or in historic urban areas we might just meet the last person who has the skill for these obsolete phenomena or the last memories of their working past.

Resurrection/Creation out of Nothing

Much time and money is now devoted to the "remaking of memory" (Jeudy 1986) to create new marketable identities. Thus we restore, regenerate, conserve, and preserve works and events as identities for a touristic society. Things long resigned to decrepitude are resuscitated as heritage or "collectibles." The obsolescent and the obsolete once more become profitable. We extract the old from fragments of collective memory or, better still, from rare survivals still found in daily life.

Anything can become a tourist product as long as it can be given value. We invent new deposits to be mined: forgotten folklore, buildings in ruin, the sites of ancient cities. We move monuments from one place to another, change their meanings, and make new springs gush. Thus even the "natural" regional distribution of tourist attractions may become obsolete.

New Consecration

MacCannell (1976) first analyzed the process of the transformation of things into tourist products. In order to become an attraction, the phenomenon must be "baptized"; it must be named and become associated with a recognizable sign or "marker" bringing it to the attention of the tourist, guaranteeing its "uniqueness," and making it worth seeing.

To display this object, we frame it, elevate it, light it up, mount it like a jewel, and mark it off from ordinary objects. Detached from the ordinary world, it becomes "sacred" within the ritual of tourism. Its old meaning as heritage is stripped, and it is given a new one appropriate to its role within the tourist system. Thus marked, it becomes a signifier of the identity of the society for foreign visitors.

The New Setting

The requirements of commercialism join with the moral goals of international organizations: to use tourism for the promotion of mutual understanding and to maintain, preserve and respect cultural identities. This accords with modern humanistic ecumenical and universalist ideals whereby each culture is supposed to make a special contribution to "universal culture."

Through the will of these organizations, patrimony and the extant traditions of archaic societies are placed in new relationships and come to constitute a common cultural foundation for all humanity. The chosen markers represent the identity of the place and its rank within the panoply of world heritage. Thus we can see that international tourism acts as a powerful force in the universalization of culture and society (Morin 1962).

IV. The Dilemma of Tourism

The Tensions Between the Economic and the Cultural

The modern concept of tourism as a factor in economic development is pivotal and is the only way to understand the contradiction between the economic and the cultural. Though first aimed at the Developing Nations, this doctrine has recently been adopted by nearly all countries in response to internal challenges. The key document is Kurt Krapf's paper, presented to the Association Internationale d'Experts Scientifiques du Tourisme (AIEST) in 1961.

Treated as an Infant

In bringing together developing nations and consumer societies in one global vision, Krapf (1961) embraced Rostow's theory of development, by which societies are classified into five stages: (1) traditional; (2) pre-take-off; (3) take-off; (4) push to maturity; and (5) mass consumer. This theory of economic growth has encouraged rich countries to aid poor ones. It imitates child development theory and, though naive, provides criteria for the distribution of aid according to what economists call "the coefficient of capital."

Using this vocabulary, developing nations are "still in their infancy" and need to be pushed to maturity where citizens are assured a "stable consumption economy." The "immature" countries are labeled by their inability and have to accept the paternalistic aid of scientific experts in tourism. They are shown that it is "tourism or nothing." But nothing is not just nothing in this case, it is "the image of death appearing on the horizon" (Rostow 1961:84).

Economic Development? Not for Everyone

Krapf's (1961) argument conceals a paradox: "No one needs imagination to know that a developing country presents the characteristics of an economic take-off." In the terms described above countries have attained stage (2) or (3). As for "traditional society," Rostow's first stage, it is, according to Krapf (1961:22) "doomed to disappear." The economists' death sentence provokes us, for they assert that without tourism a society turns its back on development. In this theory, the gap is accentuated between those developing societies veering toward modernization and isolated traditional societies sliding back into decline. Yet "traditional society" keeps haunting the imagination. Put aside in the economic order it is stored in the symbolic order, and tomorrow it may reemerge, promoted as a touristic product. Threatened with "imminent death," "traditional society" must be conserved, as a haven of tradition and infancy, in order to sustain the argument for development (Krapf 1961). Tourism promotion often concentrates on destinations that are virgin, intact, and distant in space.

The Image of Death

Let us recall some of the debate of the 1960s about the ruinous effects of tourism on culture and environment.

Davydd Greenwood, a U.S. anthropologist studying agriculture in the community of Fuentarrabia in the Spanish Basque country in 1968–69, turned his attention to the Alarde, a lively local festival that drew many tourists. It was a Basque ceremony to celebrate the victory of their ancestors over the French in 1638. To attract more tourists, the municipality decided to perform the Alarde twice in the same day. The inhabitants not only refused to cooperate with this commercial masquerade but lost their will to participate in the event. For Greenwood (1977) "tourism killed the Alarde." (Greenwood partially retracted this severe judgment in the Epilogue to his chapter in the Second Edition of Smith 1989.)

Many similar cases probably exist. Just as the economic benefits emerge, tourism is discredited by the transformation of culture into market value, desecration of ceremonies, debasement of culture and the arts, falsification of traditions, and the loss of identity. The opposition of the economic and the cultural is revealed; here we are faced with the "dilemma of tourism."

The Dilemma of Tourism: Alternatives Under a Double Constraint

In logic, a dilemma is reasoning where the major premise contains an alternative and the minor premises lead to the same conclusion. In practice a dilemma occurs when there are two contradictory possibilities, yet the subject making the choice finds that either way leads to the same consequences.

The discourse of tourism decision making and management is rife with this figure of speech. Actors, whose interests should converge but are in fact opposed, face a dilemma: to develop or contain tourism, to restore culture or celebrate it, leads to the same result. To reject tourism is death, but to accept it is also death. "The touristic dilemma is clear: to freeze or not to freeze, to maintain boundaries or to remove them . . . the sword cuts both ways" (Jafari 1984:14).

This double-edged sword underlines the break between tourism as seen by outside agents and by the local society, placing visitors and the visited in a reciprocal extermination. For a developing nation not to choose tourism amounts to eventual death according to economists, but to choose tourism is also death according to anthropologists. To choose in favor of tourism is the outcome of a double bind, the requirement to make a choice between two impossibilities.

The figure of this dilemma is a leitmotif in the discourse on tourism: "blessing or blight," "trick or treat," "boom or doom," "panacea or a new slave trade," "mirage or strategy for the future." There is always the same disjunction between the economic and the cultural which governs the problematics, be they alternative or dominant. This is still the dilemma which underlies the argument for Alternative Tourism, wherein the word "Alternative" gains its force.

Three Examples

(1) The dilemma of tourism pertains to actual situations. The 1989 WTO Seminar on Alternative Tourism in Tamanrasset (see Preface) took place at a symbolically loaded site, which could have been the source of the love of Uranus and Gaia, in the heart of the Sahara Desert. Here at the gates of Ahaggar the difficulties are magnified because of the barrenness of the place. Yet decisions had become urgent; every year the tourists were coming in greater numbers. Algeria, which previously had no tourism policy, had decided on large scale projects, with perhaps 100,000 beds. Ahaggar was targeted as exemplifying the touristic image of the nation.

But the desert is an extremely fragile environment, with diminishing ancient water sources. Vegetation is sparse but includes unique local species. Garbage is not degradable. The desert people, adapted to the severe environment, have become guides, serving the tourists but anxious about uncontrolled growth. The experts were conscious of the risks and felt the proximity of total destruction. The government was perplexed when some seminar participants prophesied the end of the Ahaggar within twenty years if mass tourism develops.

(2) In Australia's Northern Territory, the management of the Na-

tional Parks faced another classic dilemma (Altman 1989). This is a special case applied to the Aborigines who at the turn of the century were seen as one of the most "primitive" groups on earth (Durkheim 1912/1979). Survivors of these "totemic societies" are scattered throughout the vast territory. The Australian Government has chosen the National Parks of this region as a "pole of growth," a plan also favored by the White residents of Darwin and the nearby mining camps. The area is highly valued by some for its nature resources and its primitive life. Here we must ask who speaks about the dilemma and whose dilemma it is.

For the Aborigines, the policy gives them the poignant choice of "to be or not to be." Already decimated and chased away by military maneuvers, their numbers are greatly reduced. These lands, ceded to them in the early 1960s, were temporarily retracted by the regional government without extinguishing Aboriginal rights. For the state as well as for the industry, the Aborigines provoke ambivalent attitudes. On the one hand they are inconvenient inhabitants, an obstacle to the development of the parks; on the other, they are a positive presence, certifying the original character of the place and its preservation from the ravages of civilization. From this point of view, Aborigine society is valued precisely because it is near extinction. One can weigh the tensions between international tourism promotion and a "traditional society." It is not just for economic reasons that the Aborigines are valued; they also possess unique skills, especially in hunting and fishing.

Thus we can see the dilemmas of both the parties involved. For the Aborigines to reject tourism is to remain welfare recipients. But to choose tourism and participate in it they would have to learn the industry's skills and become "servants," and thereby be evicted from their welfare status. They might be ready to say, "Anything other than Tourism!" In addition, the state risks making investments from which it would not reap a profit, as the land belongs to the Aborigines who, without spending any capital, might in twenty years become an economic power. Thus each of the participants might be tempted to reject the option of tourism. Do the problematics of the alternative find meaning in this kind of case?

(3) The Statement on Responsible Tourism propounded by the 1989 Seminar on Alternative Tourism at Tamanrasset is fraught with paradoxes. It amounts to a paradoxical injunction when it supposes symmetrical behavior between the partners involved, within the framework of relations defined as complementary. Proponents of Alternative Tourism favor the lodging of tourists in the houses of local people, some of whom respond: "When someone comes to my home because I

have invited them, I receive them as a friend. But when they are imposed on me from the outside, they are an occupier!"

Yes, tourism produces many situations where the imperative of the double bind traps the recipients of the message of development. To escape, it is not enough to reverse the terms of the alternative; one must break away from the frame of reference.

True or False Dilemma?

A Misleading Argument

In 1970 the American anthropologist P. F. McKean thought about the possible consequences of mass tourism in Bali, where it had not yet developed. The Indonesian government, following the usual plans of the World Bank, included a focus on tourism in Bali in its first Five Year Plan for Economic Development. The experts invited by the government drew up a Master Plan for Balinese Tourism with a somber prognostication: Bali risked the destruction of its well conserved traditions which would be devastated by the advent of mass tourism; the very attractions of Bali, its artistic creations, were at greatest risk.

To these experts the Balinese were a poor and isolated agricultural population. It was a "traditional society" where temple festivals, shadow puppetry, and sacred dances were integrated with village life. The experts proposed that, for the protection of the Balinese, tourists should be restricted to enclaves on the southern coast, for ordinary seaside tourism.

But the Balinese adopted a contrary policy. They wanted tourists spread throughout the island so that all villages could benefit. They came up with their own idea of "cultural tourism" and wanted to offer the tourists their best. McKean (1973: 1) agreed: "Far from destroying, ruining or spoiling the culture of Bali, I am arguing here that the advent and increase of tourists is likely to fortify and foster the arts."

Economic Development/Cultural Involution

McKean admits that by opting for cultural tourism as a means to modernization a country consents to transform its culture into a tourist product, its heritage into profit-making capital. Thus such a society undergoes what McKean calls "cultural involution." In such cases, every society must construct its future by clinging to its past. This implies that the society turn back toward its past in order to construct out of its heritage touristically recognizable symbols of identity. The society has to prove that it is truly unique.

To choose one's heritage as a symbol of identity leads to ambivalence. Should one restore it to the original state in which it was handed down by ancestors? Should one set it apart as an attraction for foreign tourists? For in this case, its restoration would follow the procedures of cultural engineering rather than of historical methods or subjective memorizing. Heritage would have to be managed by new criteria in order not only to be profitable but also to be added to the catalogue of world heritage. For this to happen, though, is to pass out of genuine cultural filiation.

Here is a potential source of tension.

V. A Change of Course

Since the 1960s the euphoric promises of tourism—return to nature, the noble savage, the peaceful co-existence of peoples—have been called into question by a long list of acts which have aroused indignation:

- violent expropriation and occupation of territory, pollution and destruction of forests, landscapes, and coasts;
- dominating financial interests, provoked bankruptcies, real estate speculation, the puffery of "straw men";
- tourist ghettos, private squads of armed guards, expulsion of locals and marginals, segregated residential ethnic reserves;
- violation of sacred places, appropriation of arts and crafts, manipulation of collective memories and heritage;
- indecent behavior, organized prostitution of women, adolescents, young children.

These aggressive accusations worry the authorities who try to stifle them, but their numbers continue to mount. The attacks come from many directions: from the tourists who scorn each other, from host populations whose hostility is organized in their own interests, from some sectors of the governments involved, and from experts employed by the World Bank to research the impacts of tourism. By the 1970s these converging critics could not be avoided, and tourism developers realized that the time for impact evaluations had arrived.

Rising competition, increasing marginal costs, the burden of tourism and the degradation of the environment shook the faith of the tourism experts: "Tourism can destroy tourism; tourism as a user of resources can be a resource destroyer and, through destroying the resources which give rise to it, make resource-based tourism short-lived" (Travis 1982:257).

Evolution of the Official Discourse

Let us examine how experts and international organizations responded to these criticisms, partially explaining the rise of "alternative" solutions, following this evolution through seminars and meetings because there the ghost of the dilemma mentioned above underlies many of the attempted solutions.

Actually, organizations like the World Bank, the World Tourism Organization (WTO), and UNESCO were from the start attentive to the results of their efforts. From Washington to Tamanrasset by way of Manila, one can see the same guiding thread.

Washington 1976

In 1976 the joint World Bank-UNESCO seminar on The Social and Cultural Impact of Tourism responded to concerns about the economic functions of tourism in the Third World and their sociocultural effects (de Kadt 1979). This highlighted the double cleavage between the local host societies and the foreign economic powers, and the growing antinomy between the economic and the cultural.

Analyses since that era have worried about surmounting these dilemmas which permeate the social fact of tourism. How can the local and international join together again; how can we surmount the split between the economic and the cultural? These are key questions in the analysis of the problematics of the alternative.

Manila 1980

The World Tourism Organization World Conference on Tourism held in Manila (1981) was a major event in changing directions, as can be seen in both the papers and the recommendations. The latter contained two convergent themes: (1) an insistence on the perpetual advance of tourism through the growth of "national tourism" in the better-off countries and, in contrast to the earlier WTO focus on "international tourism," the promotion of these "national tourisms"; and (2) raising the awareness of nations and organizations of the spiritual values of tourism. "Tourism . . . a vital force for peace . . . a moral and intellectual basis for mutual understanding and the interdependence of nations . . . suitable for the foundation of a new economic order which will narrow the gap between the developed countries and the underdeveloped . . . a means to promote the lessening of international tensions and to develop a spirit of friendly cooperation, with respect for human rights . . . within the equality of societies and nations (WTO 1981:5).

This was a vast ideological movement toward a new conception of tourism, surpassing the still important economic factors by linking nations with the noblest aspects of "tourism in the service of humanity" in the social, educational, political and cultural arenas. The WTO was attempting to reverse the prior order of causality by asserting that tourism is "primarily a cultural phenomenon." This is highly meaningful if we bear in mind that up to this point international tourism was seen as an economic phenomenon and domestic tourism as a cultural problem.

Tamanrasset 1989

In light of this change of course, the aims of the Seminar on Alternative Tourism organized nine years later by the WTO in Tamanrasset became clearer. One can thus understand how the evidence of the social and cultural impacts of tourism from the 1976 Washington seminar led the decision makers and government representatives to first take into account the social and cultural dimensions of tourism (Manila) and convincing all the parties concerned—hosts, guests, tourist industry, and governments—to respect the social and cultural resources on which the sustainable development of tourism was seen to rest (Tamanrasset). Here the organizers managed to use the mobilizing force of this concept to obtain consensus among the various parties present. The assembly, having been captivated by the words Alternative Tourism, finally chose to endorse "responsible tourism."

The problematics of the alternative were founded on the reversal of the terms opposed in the discourse. But to understand this, one must again pass through the labyrinth of economics. This is critical to the continuing research on the break between Alternative Tourism and International Tourism.

From the Problematics of the Impact to the Problematics of the Alternative

From Economic Impact to Sociocultural Impact

Since the late 1960s, World Bank experts have been sent to evaluate the effects of the introduction of tourism. At first the evaluations were purely economic—foreign exchange generated, jobs created, changes in the standard of living. But increasingly, sociocultural impacts were included alongside and later came to infiltrate the economic model. To the sociologist this is an interesting epistemological jump.

The question of sociocultural impact opens the economics to social analyses. The economist wants to integrate sociocultural data into his evaluation schemes, and therefore turns to the sociologist or anthropologist. One must understand that the goals of the process are to optimize the aims of tourism development. Economists want to quantify these elusive sociocultural factors into their cost-benefit analyses. This involves choosing "sociocultural indicators" which are then evaluated dualistically as "positive" or "negative" for the purposes of quantification. Sorting through such analyses of tourism impacts, one generally finds that economic changes are imputed to be positive and sociocultural to be negative, thereby widening the gap between the economic and the cultural.

This leads to absurdities, whereby the damage caused by economic activities is balanced by economic benefits! It is as though social costs can be compensated by monetary gains in order to produce a unified cost-benefit analysis. Thus sociocultural effects external to the economic, often judged as negative (i.e., as costs), are, by being neutralized, internalized into the calculations. This distorts the sociocultural data to accord with the norms of International Tourism, as though admitting that culture, society, and identity are not associated with the context that gave rise to them. This dichotomy is illuminated if we consider that the same economic activity of tourism could be evaluated either as a benefit (+) for the development and preservation it brings or as a cost (−) for the degradation and misappropriation of meanings it entails.

This approach was generally considered an analytical advance, even though it is reductionist in weighing sociocultural data in terms of profit, wherein heritage and everything unique about a society is mummified and exploited as a resource.

The problematics of the alternative stems in part from this operation: the decision maker must catalogue the impacts, clearly defining the positive and the negative, in order to assess tourism. Measures are thus taken which appear to lead to this result, so that one can build a model for "discerning tourism." Even here the method is still contained within the economic framework.

The Preconceptions of the Impact Studies

This question dominates the study of the effects of international tourism and is made real within the system of action where the local society—nation, region, community or ethnic group—is "targeted" by a more powerful external organization. From this point of view the impact is the target! (The word impact comes from the Latin *impingere*, "to hit a target.")

This conceptual scheme is not limited to economics; many other studies tackle tourism as an intrusion or benefit, an external variable on the one side through its side effects on the local society on the other. This type of theory leads to a reductionist concept of the host society:

- It treats the host society as a place without specific sociological and historical characteristics, undifferentiated for the purpose of a foreign rationality.
- In its relations with tourism, "the target" is seen as limited to reacting by submitting to foreign penetration, by resisting conflicts with tourists, or by the kind of violence sometimes reported in the press. As it is opening to International Tourism, a time when tourism breeds dissent in the social order, the host society is seen as deceptively unanimous.

The problematics of the impact and the underlying system of concepts prevent us from thinking about the *processes* by which local societies are integrated into the larger political field. Such "impact studies," therefore, never understand the nature of the changes in the economic and political systems or in social relations and attitudes brought about by International Tourism policy worldwide. Tourism management focuses on tourism alone but actually affects the whole society and its social structure, collective memory, and perspectives in an unfolding world.

A Real Alternative?

But a long term change in thinking has recently surfaced. Economists have recognized that the immediate returns from tourism may not do much for the development of the whole region. Methods of measurement and statistical data are viewed with suspicion. Growth models are discredited and the relevance of economics is challenged.

Anthropologists and sociologists are undertaking studies with a radically different awareness. As a result of local field research, in the 1980s there has been a shift from the problematics of the impact to the problematics of the alternative. Is this a real change in the problematics of international tourism?

During the 1970s, planners were forced to see the limitations of their general development model and to take into account the interests of local people. The first reaction was to grant to the host society its own personality, recognizing its viability. One heard more of local dominance, participation and development. Some have called this "the return of the local," not only in scientific research but in conceptions about planning (Lanfant 1987:13). In a coincidence of concerns, this has become the solution to all ills. From "an area to be promoted in the marketplace," the local society has been granted its own importance, its own potentials, with its own capacity for initiative and decision making.

Return to the Local/Return of the Local: Genitive and/or Dative?

The "return *to* the local" as an important factor in planning has been matched by the "return *of* the local" in the form of a network of grass roots movements, much as wished by the ECTWT. The local society is no longer taken as passive but as capable of accepting or rejecting the dominant model or of coming up with its own. "Local society" is no longer an advertising image aimed at a distant clientele also being manipulated by advertising, but has become one pole at the heart of a system of action in relation to a center.

The local society is no longer just an end-point in a movement from "above" but a generator of impulses which can climb back up the technological chain and modify the whole. It is no longer merely a reactionary form, but as a force in negotiation, intervention, and creativity is capable of its own initiatives, with all their paradoxes. Some would redefine tourism from local points of view, surpassing the norms of International Tourism. The idea of tourism is transformed to the point of rejecting the dominant model; according to the proponents of Alternative Tourism (Cazes 1989a; Barètje 1987), the local people must be helped to take over the tourist operation, rather than just having suitable conditions defined for them. Thus one can no longer judge tourism on the basis of specific "positive" or "negative" effects but must see the phenomenon intertwined as part of a total social fact.

The problematics of the alternative becomes complicated when it tries to rethink tourism or propose new strategies of global development from the local point of view.

Is this a reversal of perspective? It is up to the social sciences to examine this turning point and its methodological and epistemological foundations. We must keep in mind the difference between an "alternative ideology" which rethinks tourism from the local point of view or in terms of local development and the scientific approach which chooses the local society as the point of observation. The latter is concerned with constructing its object of study from field research using the inductive approach, but its foremost objective is not to increase the standing of the local community as would the Alternative Tourism movement.

It is troubling to observe these efforts to "rehabilitate" the local setting after it has been flattened or evacuated by planning and scientific thinking. In the Alternative Tourism problematic, the tourism production system, which carries on ever upward according to its own logic, seems to have been bypassed. In our opinion, one must work with the assumption that many parallel logics are being pushed without contradicting themselves.

After listening to the different debates and declarations, it seems that what is called Alternative Tourism while claiming to be the "good tourism" has not, in spite of its forceful declared opposition, broken radically with the "other tourism." Alternative Tourism, still included within the promotion and expansion of international tourism, may just be another stage. Doesn't Alternative Tourism still spur the local people to preserve their customs and traditions, and then use them as tourist products to offer on the market?

At Zakopane in August 1989, the members of the Academy considered Alternative Tourism as a means to contribute to the "sustainable development" of a society, whereas by October at the WTO meeting in Tamanrasset, Alternative Tourism had become co-opted as a way to ensure the sustainable development of tourism itself. That should give us something to think about.

*   *   *

An earlier twelve-page version of this paper was written by Dr. Lanfant in French and presented at the August 1989 meeting of the International Academy for the Study of Tourism. A later, longer version by Dr. Lanfant was translated into English by Cecily Graburn (Oberlin College) and Eva Graburn (Columbia University) with the assistance of Nelson Graburn, Molly Lee, and Isabelle Nabokov (University of California, Berkeley). After some slight corrections by Dr. Lanfant, Prof. Graburn rewrote and shortened this paper for publication; while attempting to retain some of the French "flavor," the present version has been constructed primarily for clarity to an English-speaking student and scholarly readership.

Part II
Case Studies

The Introduction to this volume calls attention to the many alternative styles of tourism which can be historically and temporally linked to a given society. Part I discusses the theoretical component, rooted in fieldwork, which serves as the foundation for the *Knowledge-based* platform in the study of tourism (Jafari 1989a). Conversely, the derived theoretical insights are essential to the analysis and explanation of contemporary issues in tourism, as represented by the five case studies which follow.

By way of perspective, tourism in the 1990s is regarded virtually worldwide as the primary tool for economic development. Significantly, even the post-industrial United States is turning more directly to tourism than heretofore as a source of foreign exchange, and expects to benefit during this coming decade from expanded employment in this service industry. The nation anticipates hosting an increasing number of foreign visitors, many of whom indicate that they especially want to visit small towns and rural areas as well as the National Parks. In addition, the declining value of the dollar against foreign currencies stimulates more domestic tourism. Rural communities, which in recent years have suffered from sagging farm output, poor lumber sales, and migration of their youth to the cities, are particularly attracted to so-called "soft" or local-level tourism which requires minimum investment in infrastructure.

Economic planners seeking revitalization of America's agricultural midwest and mountain regions in general see only four avenues for development: trash (the burying of imported refuse from major metropolitan areas); construction and operation of prisons; senior citizen complexes; and tourism. Aside from tourism, senior citizens are most often solicited because they tend to import their pension incomes and, like tourists, are a source of "new money" added to the economy. Tourism is by far the most popular tool for development because it is deemed a "clean" industry, and the facilities created for the visitor (including hotels, restaurants, and recreation) usually also benefit local residents.

Bryan Farrell is widely known for his analysis of tourism in Maui in the book *Hawaii: The Legend That Sells* (1982). In the present case study he examines the effect of new, outside, and (most recently) foreign management of an expensive resort situated in the quiet community of Hana, for a long time an isolated enclave of "old Hawaii," where seclusion and tradition prevailed.

Boracay in the Philippines was an obscure islet until it was "discovered" by tourists a decade ago and rapidly rose to fame in the avant garde tourist press as the "most beautiful beach in the world." Lacking any significant investment in crucial infrastructure, such as culinary water and sewage, the expansion of tourism is a product of tourist demand. The case study questions the sustainability of local-level tourism in relation to physical carrying capacity, local leadership, and government policy both in Boracay and in many other similar tropical islands.

According to some advocates, a major advantage of Responsible Tourism is the opportunity to "get close to the people." The case study by Graham Dann of tourist attitudes among visitors to Barbados indicates considerable variation among those polled. In particular, he notes the need to study the tourist's *pre-trip* motivations, and host preferences concerning type of tourism, before alternative tourism can be established as an effective dialogue between them.

Tourism policies and planning must inevitably be sensitive to future change. Just as Butler (1980) has been widely cited for original research on the cyclical evolution of resorts, Geoffrey Wall addresses the potential impacts of global warming on present and future tourist sites. Martinus J. Kosters also looks to the future, in recognition of the social and environmental impacts created by 100-mile-long gridlocks associated with European highways. The train seems destined for revival to a position of pre-eminence in Europe, and quite possibly also in the United States, as plans move ahead for a rapid shuttle between Los Angeles and the gambling center at Las Vegas.

Chapter 6
Tourism as an Element in Sustainable Development: Hana, Maui

Bryan Farrell

I. Introduction

While most of the articles in this book are concerned with alternative tourism, largely from the consumer's point of view, the main focus of this essay is on the possibilities of management change as a response to a philosophy arising from worldwide consideration of sustainable development. Over the past fifteen years, an encouraging degree of developmental enlightenment has emerged from meetings of international groups such as the United Nations Environment Program (1981) and the World Wildlife Fund (1988). In a nutshell, sustainable development is the integrative linking of development, environment, and society to provide signposts for the processes of change into the next century.

From this deliberative thinking have come such seminal statements of philosophy and policy as the 1972 United Nations Conference on the Human Environment, the Cocoyoc Declaration, and the World Conservation Strategy. More recently, the World Commission on Environment and Development (WCED) has been supported, not by advocacy groups, but by the General Assembly of the United Nations (WCED 1987:ix). This has sparked considerable discourse, research (e.g., Turner 1988, Clark and Munn 1986), and increasing governmental interest in policy and change. Its philosophy has touched groups as disparate as national governments, Greenpeace, the Sierra Club, the World Bank, and giant transnational corporations.

Changing viewpoints have developed at different places and at varying paces by diverse players, reflecting, in a way, a global environment and development "perestroika" in which tourism can play an important part. And like perestroika, those with much to gain are at the forefront of change and many of those with much to lose, such as the politically and economically influential, are notably tardy.

There are of course huge gaps in the understanding of sustainable development. While the World Tourism Organization (WTO) has been an essential part of the process, many otherwise bright and influential tourism developers and managers have been ignorant of changes taking place.

It is of interest that much of the initial momentum stemmed from the insistence of developing countries. Now, as the result of newer studies such as the report of the World Commission on Environment and Development (WCED), the so-called Brundtland Commission (WCED 1987), governments, task forces, and industry have been part of the move toward saner resource use and some degree of biospheric redevelopment (Regier and Baskerville 1986:75–103).

II. A General View of Sustainable Development

Numerous notions are associated with emerging sustainable development. Some are fundamental, whereas others are ephemeral or difficult to come to grips with. Some issues, like ending poverty and hunger or sharing knowledge, are so obvious as to be largely unchallengeable. But there are fundamental ideas that are more than slogans and ideas that have application to every sphere of activity in the developing and developed world; in terms of this article, such ideas include teaching, research, and the management of tourism. A consensus regarding the major fundamentals of sustainable development can be found in the Tokyo Declaration of 1987, issued after the final meeting of the WCED and after two years of hearings worldwide. Those with the greatest application to tourism follow.

Development (including tourism) is a wide-ranging activity that should never be divorced from a serious and concerned consideration of environment and society. In fact, the development system consists, at a minimum, of a mixed system of elements and linkages derived from the economy, environment, and society. For present purposes, the so-called "development triangle" represents the major elements just noted; and in theory, if not in practice, no component may be more important than any other.

Conversely, environmental systems cannot realistically exist in an operational vacuum but most co-exist with judicious economic development and address relevant needs and aspirations of society in the same mixed system. Regrettably, many environmentalists seem unaware of this fact. This once again points to the necessity, for policy makers, managers, and scholars alike, to subscribe to an integrated systemic approach.

Within this integrated approach to the development system are the three critically important and interdependent subsystems: economy, environment (conservation), and culture (including society). Taken together, the expanded system illuminates and in practical terms largely equates with the total environment, the total ecosystem, or more precisely the human environment, as an operational system. To think narrowly of the human world order in terms such as the "natural environment perturbed by human agencies" omits so much, is unrealistic and artificial, destroys an integrated approach, and by its restrictiveness all but denies sustainability in its non-fundamentalist new sense. At the other extreme, to think narrowly in terms of tourist management concerned only with tourism supply, demand, infrastructure, and consumers, in other words "the industry," is to sadly misinterpret today's realities.

To view development in the matrix of the development system does not dilute attention to the economy or natural environment; rather, it adds significantly by acknowledging previously missing elements. Under contemporary circumstances, the natural environment is being looked at much more seriously than before, but in a considerably wider context. In developing countries, it is understood that long term survival means the conservation and enhancement of the resource base in a closely knit milieu of cultural needs and economic aspirations. I term this element in this context "conservation," but conservation in its widest sense.

Poverty is considered a major element in environmental degradation in some countries (for precision in the use of the term "degradation," see Blaikie and Brookfield 1987). Attempts to prevent poverty in some places, and in others to prevent degradation from other sources and to restore degraded landscape while maintaining acceptable living conditions, require both development and redevelopment to take new and more benign directions. Large numbers of the elements of more conventional development may remain, but they may not be extended as far as previously and they might now explore new directions while others are being reassessed.

The removal of negative externalities where serious environmental and social impacts exist would normally become an expected cost of production, and higher consumer costs would be a tradeoff for a non-deteriorating, overall human environment. The use of higher priced, chemical-free meat and vegetables, perceived by numbers of tourists as already worthwhile, or higher room rates associated with lower tourist densities on environmentally sensitive land would be examples. But for the tourism operator, all would not be lost by any means. What might appear a setback in one area can be an unexpected surprise in another. Interesting tradeoffs may arise, such as specialized eco-tourism (Goldfarb 1989). Other examples include tourism protecting or reinforcing the protection of wildlife in Kenya, gorillas and chimpanzees in Zaire (World Wildlife Fund-Conservation Foundation 1988), harp seals in Labrador, wetlands in Jamaica (Bacon 1987), and rain forest in Costa Rica (Budowski 1976).

Non-haphazard and monitored growth under these circumstances, so-called "charted development" under the rubric of sustainable development, implies long term commitment. This means monitored development in which society and the environment, cultural and environmental conservation, are viewed as essential considerations, as factors of production. Past development models, often imposed from abroad or from another region, are rejected in favor of essentially indigenous national, regional, or local models compatible with on-the-spot human, economic, and social needs and aspirations. In this way, local people feel more a part of the process and can give development full attentive cooperation, other things being equal. For the time being, this is termed "cultural compatibility." The local society essentially becomes a partner of the tourist industry, not just another resource; and partnership brings with it responsibilities and obligations. As a partner, the local society must for its part see that tourism runs smoothly along agreed-to lines.

When immediate enthusiasm for one part of the development mix/ system is pushed with little regard for other components, and with no consideration for the future, disaster is often just around the corner. The East-West arms race, the development of the automobile in the United States, over-irrigation in parts of California, and over-fertilization in midwest farming in the United States, are examples of head-in-the-sand development. Tourism abounds with similar short term, take-the-money-and-run examples. There are numerous Hawaiis, Miamis, and Costa Bravas existing or in the making. This abundantly shows the need for long term planning to avoid the dire consequences of operating within too short a time frame. Furthermore, it can easily be argued that, once underway, the short term development strategy can easily develop a momentum of its own, virtually making a transfer to a sustainable long term mode non-viable.

In the past, local communities have often been overlooked in development decisions, but it has become clear that many more voices are demanding a part in decision making which will vitally affect their future. Not only do people demand better access to information and to participate in decisions based on this information, they also do not want to become developmentally more dependent than before. There is also usually an essential wish to be in a position to supply a much greater proportion of the goods, resources, services, and management talent that accompanies new development. Such things are commonly referred to as "local input." If these issues are not addressed, cultural compatibility will have been violated.

Finally, when the majority of these elements—an integrated approach, conservation, charted development, cultural compatibility, long term planning, and local input—come together in such a way that development activity firmly focuses on halting degradational processes, on restoration, and on the use of locally acceptable development strategies which appear capable of continuing indefinitely into the future without harmful side-effects, then the situation will be well on the path toward sustainable development.

Realistically, ultimate sustainability is probably not achievable. At any particular time, some groups may not be in a position, or may not be inclined, to meet the challenge. Human values constantly change, and a host of other parameters are in flux as the result of new directions or systemic surprises—natural, economic, or social. But that point is academic. The goal, sustainable development, is concrete even if some elements are elusive. Among world leaders, perceptions are now becoming strong that contemporary conditions are so bad that there appears to be no other course than to strive for the only goal which has been globally articulated despite its flaws and lack of precision. Implicit in the various notions of sustainability is that possible impacts of any strategy, new or old, should be anticipated and corrective action taken. For some, there will be a conflict here. To escape damage successfully, new action will often have to be taken by policy makers and managers while the scientific jury is still out. This is happening now as major food producers turn to chemical-free production in a response to buyer perception rather than argued, proven fact. Ceilings are put on development or densities on the assumption that, if intervention did not take place, resulting conditions would be untenable.

It is with this background that this analysis looks at tourism, and it is in such a context that more tourism scholars, policy makers, and managers should scrutinize contemporary tourism. In particular, the balance of this study examines the notion of sustainability and evaluates the extent tourism could be considered an instrument of sustainability in parts of Maui County, Hawaii.

As a geographer who works in environmental studies focusing on the relationship between culture and natural environment and as a researcher specializing in the systemic study of tourism, it is obvious to me that both interests should be brought together. This author believes the notion of sustainability is a powerful one; furthermore, enough evidence has accumulated from work in other fields to signal a direction toward which tourism policy might wisely proceed.

Most studies done within the sustainability context have been crude and preparatory, requiring refinement and appropriate methodology along with the implicit concept of integrative optimization. Some elements lend themselves more easily to study than others. The fact that some research may be difficult is not a reason for rejecting the goal, nor is the fact that the popular press and advocacy groups have already muddied the waters.

III. Sustainability in Hawaii: The Maui Example

The decade of the 1970s was one when Maui County, Hawaii, came into the spotlight through a conscious state policy of directing funds away from the main Hawaiian tourism hub of Waikiki. As a consequence, tourism development emphasis was diverted from the main island of Oahu to outer islands where it was believed a new type of planned tourism, quite different from the concentration at Waikiki, could take place.

On the tourism supply side, in the mid-1950s Maui seemed supreme among the islands just waiting for tourist development. Long, beautiful beaches, a small population needing work as sugar plantations closed and pineapple processing was curtailed, beautiful mountain and coastal scenery, great areas of agriculturally zoned waterfront property which was often of debatable agricultural worth, and proximity to a huge, affluent North American market served by cheap domestic air routes all added up to something extraordinary.

From a present-day conventional tourism viewpoint, Maui is a success story. It has 17,000 rooms in hotels and condominiums. Some of these facilities at the resorts of Kapalua, Wailea, and Ka'anapali are exquisite models of tasteful architecture and planning. But outside the resorts where hotel and tourist condominium zoning exists, tourist densities appear high, buildings are crowded, and areas such as Kahala, Kihei, and Lahaina present an unpleasant, "unplanned mess" to many, though they are perceived as areas of excitement to others. Many miles of coastline are designated agricultural and, for the time being, remain safe from development. But there seems no strong and compelling reason why Ka'anapali may not one day, perhaps before the year 2000, look like Waikiki today. When one observes what has happened in two decades, simple extrapolation brings such a conclusion with minimum reservations. The 1970s established the form, and the 1980s filled many of the gaps. Development in these two decades led to a proliferation of shopping centers, clogged the roads with rental cars, created a burgeoning local commuter population, and continued the never-waning construction traffic. The decade of the 1990s may turn out to be an almighty struggle between old and new forces.

On the western coast of Maui, where most of the tourism is, the newly arrived population lives as tourists, affluent seasonal visitors, or resident labor. They are largely white, mainland Anglo, with few or none of the behavioral characteristics of the former Japanese/Hawaiian population. Many of the original landowners, large and small, have made a killing on land sales and moved out. Those who remain and own land are often sitting on a gold mine, including even those who came later and paid what they considered at the time exorbitant prices. Few if any children of the original residents, or of those who remain there, now can ever anticipate remaining on or returning to the land of their childhood. Hawaiian enclaves like Makena must inevitably yield to the outsiders because no significant force yet opposes this trend. In 1990, a large portion of the non-white, pre-tourism families live on the eastern shore at Kahului or Wailuki, and many from those areas commute to supply labor to the western tourist side. Tourism has led to segregated population in Maui along ethnic and economic lines.

Without doubt, there is great economic activity brought by tourism and its ancillary operations. There are jobs for all; but for a significant number of employees, tourism is perceived with ambivalence and with little enthusiasm. Not everyone sees tourism to be high on the local job totem pole. New white faces from outside willingly come in to support the labor market, and further "anglicize" the multi-ethnic base. For the past two decades, there has been a constant population flow from mainland United States to Hawaii and from Honolulu to Maui.

For many newcomers, Maui is a delightful place in which to live, with numerous attractive shoreline and mountain slope residential areas. Many say tourism with an affluent clientele has reached a stage where the island can support artists and provide a much richer cultural life than previously existed. Despite conscientious county planners, one cannot see the growth halting. History partly gives the reason for this situation.

For years, local residents felt their lives were at the mercy of the great agricultural companies, and certainly earlier in the century this picture was not far off the mark with contract laborers imported from Japan or the Philippines and a large proportion of the population under the watchful eyes of paternalistic agricultural employers. Those times have gone, but local people still remember them clearly and still see today the remaining economic power of the "haole" (white) which in the past excluded them. Tourism has allowed the non-white minority residents to redress the economic disparity. By entrepreneurship, land owner-ship, property speculation, and a host of other activities, a number of local people have succeeded where predecessors failed. And, in turn, business-minded residents have frequently provided business-oriented local governments which encouraged investment and gave blessing to exaggerated development plans and such things as the inauguration of direct airline flights bringing hosts of tourists from the mainland and Japan. Now, as a reaction to the oppression of history, many are shar-ing in the economic pie.

People in Maui are not oppressed as they were during the plantation days. But some see the handwriting on the wall: the tyranny of tourism, controlled in the technical sense but so lively and aggressive that it conjures up images of a somewhat tired county dog catcher trying to control a mob of spirited, somewhat unruly, and poorly leashed dogs. Tourism has been aggressive in Maui, and there are increasing num-bers of critics and others who have reaped their own benefits and are now having doubts and second thoughts.

The economic and social gains that one may put on one side of the tourist evaluation are there for all to see. Obviously, many people have gained considerably from tourism, but there are those who feel they have lost. Among the losers are those who are pragmatists, reluctant to lose cherished values but willing to compromise, mindful of one of the imagined alternatives, a 1940s-style agricultural Maui projected into the present, absent of tourism. There are groups of small landholders contributing to a growing diversification of agriculture who, while simultaneously competing for water, push tourism from their minds and operate in areas largely free of tourists. And there are more militant Hawaiians who feel they have always lost, and who want to fight for what little of the traditional ways they feel is left. But overall, in the context of United States culture, the "American dream" em-braced by most citizens of Maui has played a very important part. To cater to tourists under the conditions of the time was inevitable, but the present shape and character of tourism was not.

For losers, the losses were great, and these losses have helped to exacerbate perceptions of present-day problems. The past overwhelm-ingly rural ambience and style were transformed. There are those Hawaiians who would rather have unsophistication, many fewer main-land values, and a life which is simple. Places where quail could be hunted are now golf courses, and shoreline landscapes have been so transformed by urban symbols and foreign implants that they are unrecognizable. While shoreline access has become legally and more technically free through planning, traditional pathways to fishing and mountain hunting are considered impaired. Heritage by birth or adoption is inexorably being whittled away. For the hardcore critic, tourism is an unnecessary evil. Many, not uncritically, concede that it is at least a necessary evil.

There are clogged roads, culture sold as a commodity, little affordable housing, limited money for infrastructure, too few funds spent on education and health, and high prices in every arena. Great gaps exist between the haves and have nots, and to live a Hawaiian style of life as perceived a half century ago, one must find a remote location and distance oneself from a thoroughly alien world. The environmentally rather than the traditionally minded see polluted air, diminished water quality, damaged reefs, drastically changed ecology, and aesthetically offensive development.

These statements are perceptions only; nevertheless every one of them has some degree of basis in fact. But every tourist area anywhere has its deeply held feelings, and its ambivalences. Perceptions about Maui are highly subjective: for every perceived cost, a countervailing perceived benefit can be readily produced.

IV. Sustainable Tourism in Maui

The general formula for one important view of sustainable development is elaborated above. Sustainability in this context is essentially an exercise in the optimization and fine tuning of all elements and sub-elements of the "development system" so that, in its operation, the system as a whole maintains direction and one or more of the elements does not "surge" or is not enhanced to the detriment and impairment of others. The variety of "impairment thresholds" will range from absolute parameters, such as those, like water quality, that must be maintained in a narrow range of limits, through various middle range decisions such as permittable building densities and shoreline setback, to those requiring subjective political decisions, such as beach access policy or architectural appropriateness. Parameters will also vary from place to place and time to time, based on current priorities and local input.

The ability to achieve a "development system" will depend on changing human perceptions. With the goal of sustainable development in mind, the best and only things that can be expected are specific but constantly reviewed formulas for particular places. Even here, there is always the possibility of contention between local, regional (county), and state, each with a different constituency and varied perspectives based on different perceptions. Optimization means getting the most out of something while compromising to accommodate group perceptions and competing issues. There should be one constant, however: maintenance of at least a degree of sustainability. The greater the degree, of course, the better. However, statewide sustainability strategies may be in tension with those of a region or locality; what is good for one level of government is not always good for the others. The following discussion touches on such issues at the regional and the local level.

No important element in the general sustainability framework of Maui is totally ignored, but some are so cursorily considered that the effect is the same. The integrative approach is not obvious in planning, development, or implementation. There are enlightened individual development plans which hope not only to accommodate legal requirements, but also trends as seen by the developer and hired consultants, and to achieve desired standards. But the criteria are largely internal to the development and predicated usually on maximizing profitability within limits and assuring economic survival. Frequently, an owner-developer thinks only in terms of several years at which time the property is to be sold for profit taking. A plan which widens the parameters is hailed as innovative. Sometimes those who attempt to expand horizons are burned by restrictive legislation or by not cooperating fully with local people of influence, the so-called "power brokers." And for development to be successful, one must be on the lookout for a legal system that is not a disincentive to innovation or sustainability. The planning department can and does act as an integrator of sorts, but this is not its primary function. Its primary function is to approve or reject applications and to pronounce and advise on development as presented to it by consultants and private planners, a number of whom got their start as planners with the county.

Major agricultural operations like Alexander and Baldwin, Amfac, Maui Land and Pineapple Company, Castle and Cooke, and Ulupalakua Ranch, had to look at both tourism and agriculture before tourist development took place. Without doubt, this activity, while initially widening the county's resource base by adding tourism as an income earner, was done for the enhancement of the landowner (despite, as it could be argued, accruing community benefit) rather than for the benefit of Maui County as a whole. County and state plans in Hawaii do a better job than in most states to relate elements of the economy to one another. State efforts to relate tourism to a number of other elements in the tourism plan could well be copied elsewhere.

In the development of Maui, however, little more than lip service has been paid to conservation, especially in relation to tourism. A major national park, Haleakala, covers much of east Maui; but for all intents and purposes, although a major attraction, it operates in a vacuum.

The structure and shape of development in Maui is controlled by the state and the county, but within those areas designated by the state for tourism, original planners working for the county were so generous and, in many respects, permissive, that there seems little that present planners are prepared to do. Plans prepared twenty or more years ago have been given the authority of a bible. Annual reviews and substantial downzoning are largely unknown concepts. The results of lavish initial provisions are such that a cap on development will not come in some areas for many years.

Planning in a major area of Maui, Kihei, was done quickly and, once approved, has been extremely difficult to revise. In this case the tyranny of a plan is in full force. The attitude seems to be: "We all know it's a bad plan, but what can we do?" The plan can always be changed, but the will to change it must exist. The plan was originally, in fact, a short range strategy to get tourism off the ground in a hurry, projected into the future by persons with virtually no experience. But Kihei is not unique. Development is, in effect, always short range. A considerable proportion of planned resort areas which community members naively thought would be in the hands of the same managers have been spun off by the original developers, and individual hotels may have passed through a series of owners, sometimes in a very short period of time or even before a hotel has opened. As a result, there is a planning process of sorts, but it is virtually all short term and the idea of a long time frame with constant review and revision is unknown.

Maui is relatively small, and in many ways the county should get high marks for local input. All community plans have steering committees; and local advisory committees are in place, but local advice may not necessarily be taken. New projects are heard publicly and developers have been known to discuss plans with the local people, but as yet there is no semblance of true "cooperative tourism" (Farrell 1986) where one or more representatives of the community join regularly with a developer group for discussion and true participation in decision making. This, among other things, would ensure that the community co-determine what will appear in the future and consequently take responsibility for what will be created.

V. Hana and Lanai

Conversation with reflective tourist industry representatives in Maui County on the subject of sustainability will ultimately direct one's attention to Hana and Lanai. Each is self-contained and is insulated from other tourist areas: Hana by forty miles of winding, sometimes one-way roads, and Lanai by a sea channel of thirty miles. Furthermore, both areas are characterized by expensive tariffs. At Hana, for instance, hotel tariffs are such that only the top five percent of a generally affluent tourist public can afford to pay.

While Hana embraces one of only a few truly Hawaiian ethnic enclaves, Lanai is mixed ethnically with a high Asian element paramount. Both communities are quite rural, unsophisticated in comparison with urban Hawaii, and each depends almost entirely on one corporate employer—Castle and Cook for Lanai and the Rosewood Corporation of Dallas, Texas for Hana.

In both locations, one company has operated a combined agricultural/tourism operation, in which being land rich is an unquestionably flexible asset. All land, even that zoned agricultural, is consciously or unconsciously perceived as a potential tourist or residential resource; and land values reflect this perception.

Three final points characterize each area. In each place there is a wide open space, with planned but flexible areas for integrated community development. Second, neither place has sensational gimmicky attractions, and other than enjoying scenery, the beach, and having superficial but nevertheless physically close contact with very friendly communities, tourist guests are left to their own devices and upscale hotel attention. This is not conventional resort tourism.

The last point, and in some ways the crucial one, is that the projects developed in these destinations, as of the late 1980s, were novel. They had been brought about by the principal owners of both corporations and reflect their philosophies towards community and tourism. Just as one hears much about alternative tourism, these areas provide the possibility of examining "alternative management" and the steps that can be taken toward sustainable tourism development. Because Lanai's tourist facilities were barely in operation as of 1989, and Hana was already reflecting the changing course of events by that time, this article focuses only on the micro case study of Hana.

VI. A Short History of Hana

Until the end of World War II, tourism was unknown in the remote area around Hana; however, the year 1945 was fateful for the general Hana region. It reflected all too well the decline of the Hawaii sugar industry, through the closing of C. Brewer and Company's Kaeleku Mill (Jokiel 1988:45) and the selling of the sugar lands in 1946 to wealthy San Franciscan Paul Fagan.

Before the sale, unemployment was high, people were drifting away, and there were the doomsayers who talked of a ghost town. But tourism saved the day. Paul Fagan built a small hotel, sold some land to easterners down the coast, and was responsible for the construction of a small airport on the Kahului side of town. Fagan was not a profit-driven individual, and he developed a clientele somewhat the same as that which the Rosewood Corporation attempted to reconstruct. Alberta de Jetley, the wife of Tony de Jetley, who managed the hotel in the 1970s, wrote that the original hotel "was an exclusive refuge for wealthy visitors from around the world [who] arrived [complete] with references" (de Jetley 1988).

These guests, loyal and wealthy, stayed long periods of time, enjoyed the low-key "total environment Hana experience," and often insisted on occupying the same rooms each time they revisited (de Jetley 1988:54). In a sense, with one short break and minor changes over time, the Hana hotel tradition established over forty years ago continued through the 1980s.

A lumber company from Delaware purchased the hotel and Fagan's cattle ranch in 1968. The hotel, then known as the Hotel Hana Ranch, saw itself as a tropical dude ranch, but the excitement and the targeted patronage did not materialize. With changed policy and under de Jetley's management, revival of the old tradition was attempted, but not without considerable struggle. By the time of de Jetley's death in 1981, there was need for a substantial infusion of funds to upgrade facilities, parts of which were almost forty years old.

During the 1970s the county's mayor, Cravalho, made it perfectly clear that in terms of development, which was rampant elsewhere on Maui, Hana, "the last Hawaiian place," would remain inviolate. While the predominantly Hawaiian community had long been considered special, a need to draw attention to the vulnerability of its cultural integrity increased as up to 2,000 cars daily, as well as tour vans with day-trippers, crawled the narrow, winding road from Kahului through Hana to the falls and cascades of Seven Pools and Ohe'o Gulch. Some people stopped in Hana for gas or refreshments, becoming a constant reminder to residents and planners of the long term threat of heightened tourism and the short term commercial potential for Hana itself if conscious encouragement were given to harnessing the existing flow. This could quickly increase, perhaps tenfold, when a highway would be built to Hana from Maui's western-shore tourist region over the relatively easy terrain of the south shore, where a jeep road already existed.

VII. The Rosewood Corporation

In the early 1980s, after battles with the community over unacceptable extension plans, the Hana Ranch Company was sold to the Rosewood

Corporation of Texas, owned by the Caroline Hunt Trust Estate. The corporation had been active in oil, gas, and real estate as well as in tourism. As of 1989, it owned two hotels in Dallas and one in Japan and managed the exclusive Bel-Air Hotel in Los Angeles. "We believe in a very small market and in very small hotels to give guests the very highest level of service" in surroundings "impeccably dignified," said Robert Zimmer, president of Rosewood Hotels (*Honolulu Advertiser,* July 25, 1989). With the $20 million purchase price and subsequent activity, the corporation bought the 4,500-acre Hana Ranch, Hana Water Resources supplying the town, Hana Water Company, Hana Maui Transport Company, Hana Land Company, Hana Pacific Inc., Zen at Hana Ranch (horticulture), Hana Ranch Ltd., and Hana Stockers Company. This indicated the scope of the operation, which employed close to 400 persons in 1989 out of a total estimated population of 2,000.

By all accounts Hana residents were more impressed by the new owners than with the old. A celebrity clientele was nothing new to the town; and to have one of the world's wealthiest women, Caroline Hunt, through her corporation, buy into their future, visit Hana, and evince great interest in the community made an impression. This, among other things, suggested long term stability without the imperative of immediate operational profitability. It seemed a good start. Financial stability and genuine long term concern for a community appeared to be necessary ingredients to win local support and, in a remote and special area like Hana, an outside company could go nowhere without the community behind it.

After an estimated $24 million of renovations on top of the initial price, the Hotel Hana Maui at the Hana Ranch, the anchor operation, was living up to most of the copywriters' rich fantasies. It was small (61 rooms, expanding to a maximum of 108), low rise, and elegant and, despite a tariff of $350 to $650 a night, the psychological barriers to local people drinking at the bar or using the restaurant were as low as could be contrived while still maintaining the stated goals of elegance and dignity.

Recreational facilities were distinctly limited but seldom missed by the discriminating guest. Although the site of the facility is not waterfront, the ocean is clearly visible; one can swim or picnic at two splendid secluded seaside beaches (Hamoa and Lehoula Beaches), trail ride ranch horses, hike, wander, reflect in lush tropical gardens, and shoot recently stocked pheasant or hunt pig or deer if proper arrangements are made.

Nearby in small Hana Ranch Center was a bank, associated development and ranch offices, and a public restaurant. Virtually all commercial land in the area was owned by Rosewood, except for a lot next to the very old Wananalua Church on which local families planned to create a Hawaiian marketplace, a necessary local, cultural-commercial expression in an area dominated by single, non-Hawaiian ownership.

Upon the purchase of the ranch, two major changes took place. It was determined from Dallas that the cattle operation should be chemical-free and run on agro-ecological lines and that its operation and that of the hotel should be intermingled so that one would mutually support the other. These were only two of a number of ideas to be put into effect, in what Rosewood Hotel's president Zimmer (1988) called a "holistic approach."

VIII. A Holistic Approach

Holistic, integrated, systemic approaches have been around for a long time, but have tended to be anathema to science and business, although good business people and scientists know that a balanced, long term operation needs such planning. Some employees cautiously used such words as "cosmic" and "flakey" to explain their perception of Rosewood philosophy. This is not surprising because the seeds of a number of worthwhile contemporary developments were sown in that decade.

In the first four years of Rosewood's presence in Hana, a loosely articulated philosophy was certainly the differential that separated Hana's approach from other tourist management. It was at the forefront of every major Hawaii newspaper or magazine article on tourism, and it became the first thing learned in conversations about "what's new on the Maui tourist scene."

Caroline Hunt, whose approval was required on all policy matters, saw, after "falling in love with Hana," that it "would fit well with Rosewood's philosophy of providing guests with unique experiences. To her, the Hotel Hana Maui was the perfect complement to Rosewood's exclusive group of small, elegant hotels and resorts designed for the affluent and discriminating traveler" (Jokiel 1988:48).

But Dallas and Hana are a world apart physically and culturally. After a couple of years of construction during which members of the Hana community asserted they were overrun by Texas construction workers who had no place to live and had filled all available buildings, causing rents to go "sky high," Rosewood publicly explained that "they would like to renew communication with the Hana community." Robert Zimmer presented a sweeping vision to the media and the community in the form of an information package, or what might be called the "Rosewood Public Policy Statement of June 1987":

Rosewood is committed to being economically prosperous and self-sustaining. We maintain that this is vital to Hana's economy and raising a family in Hana. We encourage diversified economic development and other agricultural and cultural enterprises not solely dependent on tourism, while fostering a low density population and land use. Hana needs an economic base sufficient to support spirituality, wellness and fitness. Rosewood is committed to an aesthetic rural lifestyle in the community and an environment that is clear, healthy, safe, and sustainable. . . . Hana is a living community perpetuating traditional cultural arts. . . . Preservation and appreciation of the Hawaiian traditions and archeology while blending cultures through communication and cooperation will continue to be the focus of our goals. . . . We are here to generate enthusiasm for change, good change. We are here to show our goals and objectives are the same. We are here to listen. We are here to share. HUNA KA MANA LOA. IKE AO NEI.

This statement, in a package distributed at a public meeting, also included a "characteristics balance sheet" of how Rosewood saw Hana, past and present, with its positive and negative characteristics. The new look given the hotel and the "holistic" management, together with new productivity, were seen as positives built on people, environment, and Hawaiian culture, and the latter two elements were to be preserved. In addition, the presence of a revitalized hotel, and presumably the Hawaiian market and other activities, would lead to diversified agricultural opportunities.

The negatives stated in the package were lack of affordable housing, limited educational opportunities, lack of small businesses, and minimal community activities, including recreational facilities and community services. The implication was that, in spite of all its distinctions, Hana was flawed by forces which Rosewood could stem. With the Rosewood contribution, Hana would be a much more complete place.

To counteract the negative elements, Rosewood listed its intentions to preserve historical values, to increase job opportunities, to provide opportunities for the provision of truck crops and flowers, to improve the town center and Hana Store, to provide an affordable housing subdivision, to give scholarships and provide work-study programs, and to see that there would be new space for small businesses and an open market as well as new recreational opportunities in the form of a Hana Rodeo and improved public parks. Rosewood also wished to facilitate "community service functions" through such groups as the Hana Community Association, to improve and expand water supplies, to provide co-op land use opportunities for Hana residents in agriculture and wild game raising, to work with the Bishop Museum of Honolulu in preserving the archeological record, to use such information to celebrate Hawaiian culture, and to enhance education directly. A number of other items also appeared on the agenda.

Robert Zimmer, enlisting the aid of Dr. George Kanahele, instituted Project Kina'ole, through which Hawaiian employees assessed their own potential and personal roles using traditional methodologies for communication and interrelationships brought to light and emphasized by the new focus in the state on Hawaiian values (see Kanahele 1982 and Shook 1985). Zimmer was also responsible for a grant of $50,000 to the Hana Cultural Center, $2,500 for scholarships at the high school, and $10,000 to the day care center. A number of the projects outlined at the June 1987 meeting were implemented, started, or at least, like the affordable housing subdivision, discussed and planned as of 1989. A special covenant guaranteeing residents, but not the general public, shoreline access and possibly mountain access was still being discussed after more than a year of negotiation.

The Rosewood agenda was ambitious and without doubt, in comparison with almost anywhere else in the world, innovative in scope. It penetrated every particle of the Hana fabric. Its vision was integrative, "holistic" in Zimmer's words (1988). In some ways it might have been too ambitious. One wondered where the expertise would be found to carry out the grand scheme and what, in the absence of a sole visionary on the spot and able to integrate, would be the instrument to set and maintain course and fine tune all elements so that the framework would remain self-adjusting. The concept was exciting, but at the same time some aspects were troubling if only in terms of their non-conventionality.

IX. Public Reaction

Understandably, in such a small community, reaction ranged from positive enthusiasm to skepticism. One person suggested the holistic approach appeared only after the public outcry about the impact of the construction workers for whom Rosewood had made no provision for accommodation. The fear that a deep-seated way of life could be disappearing, amplified inordinately in a small community, must have had the planners and managers rehoning their strategies and working the drawing boards overtime. Mistakes were made, damage control strategies were put in place, and new ideas were implemented as Rosewood learned by trial and error.

Such a project, so novel and unanticipated, must naturally engender defensiveness. The Maui model of what the alternative might be was just down the road. A thriving hotel, if it became such, was fine, and hundreds of jobs were welcomed, but how long could it last? Would not alleged cost overruns mean a mortgaged ranch, less benign partnerships (perhaps even with the Japanese), a sell-off of land in an area the community wanted preserved, or worst of all a sale of the newly completed operation to a conventional buyer? In other words, there was distrust in the permanence of the situation. Community ambivalence prevailed. Some wondered, "Where's the catch?"

There were others who welcomed the new "stability" (like the job security) and felt that they and their community could not do better than work for Rosewood. But employees of big companies have always been "silent majorities" in Hawaii, and one always needs to look carefully at their wants and any discontent before it becomes damagingly apparent. People did argue that by its very scale and overwhelming presence Rosewood was taking the role once assumed by the big plantation company, something people of Hawaii try to forget, even if Rosewood did have old-time plantations as part of its architectural theme. By its omnipresence, Rosewood could risk assuming the paternalistic role exhibited by the Robinsons of Ni'ihau (Stepien 1988). If so, this would certainly militate against true sustainability. Innovation is never easy.

For the Hawaiian traditionalists, gaining access to the shoreline and the mountains, to which people have "always" had access, was of pressing importance. A covenant was negotiated with local representatives who asserted that it covered the sea access only, while officers on Rosewood's development side at Dallas claimed that mountain access across ranchland was of course included in the covenant being discussed.

The contemporary reaction in Hana was as one might expect. Nothing monumental was in the immediate offing. There were those who felt that development of the affordable housing project was too slow, but this sort of criticism will always be present. The community would never be completely satisfied with Rosewood, while Rosewood in turn was sure to feel that its efforts were not adequately appreciated and that a community such as Hana might never fully understand the financing of such a project and how its priorities depend on other corporate activity outside Hawaii.

X. Sustainable or Not Sustainable?

To throw light on the idea of sustainable development, this analysis has looked at two case studies, Maui and Hana, each at a different level. In terms of the criteria noted earlier, there are few elements which point to sustainable development in Maui. For Maui in general, tourism is planned, and there are aspects of Maui's tourism that are very well planned, but this does not mean it is sustainable. In comparison with other areas of the world, Maui has much about which to be proud, though much of its development is discrete and cellular and there has been limited integration. Tourism might be maintained into the distant future, but this does not take into account the resulting quality of life, especially for Maui's residents. A situation cannot be classified as sustainable development where people must leave the area in which they were brought up because of excessively high land values; where development is slowed or brought to a halt through lack of water; where one can already see how development in two decades (Kihei and Kahana) has already impaired the activities of residents; where vast areas of native vegetation are replaced by artificial golf course landscaping for imported players; and where much local character has already disappeared.

Yet planning which determines greater waterfront setback, provides for beach access which would not otherwise be obtained, requires architectural review within historic districts, and necessitates that at least one-third of employees must carpool may not fit the definition of sustainable development. These are, however, certainly steps in the right direction, necessary to counter negative cultural forces. There is much tension in the planning process whenever individual prerogatives are placed in conflict with broader principles, and it is encouraging to see positive results, no matter how small, which have been accomplished against great odds.

Hana, though still in Maui, has been a horse of a different color. There is no doubt that Hana and its community are Maui's greatest resource for tourism. All other resources listed in the criteria can be found elsewhere in Hawaii. Only in Hana is found the unique set of features, all human, which is the essence of the community—a largely "non-haole," potentially very friendly, little-developed Hawaiian community. The local people made it; it is theirs. Rosewood capitalized on that fact, while providing most of the economic base for its existence. A friendly community is the crux, and friendship cannot be bought but must be earned by visitors and corporate interests alike. On their own, a deluxe hotel and full employment for community residents, though noteworthy, do not constitute reciprocation for the use of such glorious resources so serendipitously assembled by the community and by nature. They need constant fine tuning by those in positions of responsibility, such as Rosewood, and reciprocal enthusiastic cooperation on the part of the community and the employees. To have a unique situation acceptable to all sides, sustained in perpetuity, requires constant work by all parties. With the Maui model of conventional tourism always at hand, it is evident that even enlightened tourism may not be sustainable. By the late 1980s, the goals set for Rosewood were still not clearly formulated in the minds of many of the participants. Until all parties understand the objectives and the rules to play by, sustainable development cannot be achieved.

Rosewood had done many admirable things which probably would to some degree meet the test in all elements of sustainability. However, even Rosewood, though masters in the tourism business, were relative neophytes at sustainable development.

Sustainable development, once firmly established, could continue its rewards in theory at least, but its actual sustainability over time would still be vulnerable. If decision makers at such a company were to change, would the philosophy be so deeply embedded that it would no longer depend on one person, or a few persons? And would others within management be competent to continue on the path?

It is important to remember that tourism is part of a business process. There is always the bottom line, and in cases like Hana some type of financial failure could injure the community or the company in charge of its operations. There is no legal or even moral obligation to continue in the direction initially chosen; the company could slip back into high-class conventionality. It can only be hoped that the company would realize the importance of its pioneering contribution and that the same wisdom would take the operation into a more advanced stage of integrated development. The company can learn, the community can develop understanding, and government bodies can pay more than lip service to sustainable development, yet it is still inherently difficult for these three entities to integrate their activities as much as they should to achieve a greater likelihood of sustainable development over changing economic, social, and environmental conditions.

A postscript to this case study is in order. In 1989 Rosewood sold its holdings to a company of foreign and local investors who intended to create a golf resort mainly for Japanese clients. What will emerge from this change in ownership is certainly difficult to predict. When this sale occurred, it was clear that the community were confused, though the leaders were still aware of the need for sustainable development. The situation highlights the weakness of having the philosophical inspiration for innovation in the hands of just one person, in this case, Robert Zimmer. It also highlights the fact that a corporation can fall back at any time on conventional short term profit objectives. It also points to the need, in a situation like Hana, for a more formal contractual agreement between developer, community, and government bodies. If the community can exercise its legal rights in such a fashion, such changes should only result in temporary setbacks.

Chapter 7
Boracay, Philippines: A Case Study in "Alternative" Tourism

Valene L. Smith

"Alternative" Tourism, a jargon term of the late 1980s, was quickly adopted by popular travel writers such as Frommer (1988) and some travel brokers because it constitutes a new sales market. It is compatible with eco-tourism, a travel concept that is emerging as a popular advertising phrase of the 1990s. As promoted, Alternative Tourism promises tourists something "different": a social experience, a relief from the crowds of mega-resorts and, for some, an opportunity to learn first-hand about lifestyles different from their own. NANET (North American Network), sponsored by the North American Coordinating Center for Responsible Tourism in San Anselmo, California has actively advocated what are termed socially responsible tours offered by their members. As already documented elsewhere in this volume, however, alternative tourism per se has been academically discarded but the demand for small scale tourism persists.

Cazes (1989b) identifies tourers who seek out these variants to mainstream tourism as "trendy," "participatory," and "elitist." For example, in Mexico one finds affluent young American urbanites "roughing it" on a short vacation, traveling by public bus and overnighting in small native-owned inns or pensions. Word of mouth and avant garde guidebooks provide limited data on bus connections and hostelries. Back home in their corporate offices and comfortable condominiums, these returned travelers transform such adventures into good cocktail hour stories. As of 1990 their numbers were not yet great, but the proposed La Ruta Maya and "archaeotourism" (Daltabuit and Pi-Sunyer 1990) as popularized by *National Geographic* (Garrett 1989) portends for North America a probable expansion of this type of travel into Belize and Costa Rica. Some among them may become the Western hemisphere equivalent of what Riley (1988:313) has accurately described as "international long-term budget travelers," a group whose average member

prefers to travel alone, is educated, European, middle class, single, obsessively concerned with budgeting his/her money, and at a juncture in life. Many are recent college graduates, delaying the transition into the responsibilities associated with adulthood in western society, or taking a leave between jobs. Their status is achieved on the road by experiencing hardship and non-touristic experiences, and by "getting the best value."

Advocates of responsible tourism are quick to sanction their one-to-one interaction in a host community because their travel style presumably mitigates some of the much-criticized aspects of mass tourism: overcrowding, pollution, the sir-servitude syndrome, economic leakage, and multinational control. However, fieldwork by the author on the island of Boracay, Philippines in January 1987 suggests that unplanned development of tourism on a small island can create such massive physical and social problems that a tourist industry based on "alternative tourism" may not be sustainable. The following case study points out the implications that might be global in extent.

I. Boracay: The Physical Setting

The islet of Boracay (Figure 1) lies some 200 air miles south of Manila, accessible only by small aircraft to short runways at Tablas and Kalibo on adjoining islands and by scheduled jet service to Roxas City, some four hours' drive away. The island is only 4.2 miles long by 1.7 miles at its widest point and attains a maximum elevation of 930 feet. An engineering study (Helber et al. 1984) describes the island core as dominantly limestone. Erosion has produced sands of talc-like fineness which form White Sand Beach (Figure 2) and the additional small, crescent-shaped cove beaches which lie between dramatically eroded headlands on other sides of the island. The climate is subtropical and warm year-round, but tourist use is somewhat seasonal due to prevailing winds. The numbers of foreign visitors peak during the Northern hemisphere's winter, when White Sand Beach is sheltered by the island from the dry monsoon winds out of Asia. Boracay has a smaller summer patronage during the rainy season, June to September.

Boracay has been occupied for generations by families who practiced subsistence farming and fishing, which traditionally supported an island population of some 3,000. The island's interior is arable, although soils and drainage are both marginal, and crops were limited to small padi rice and fish farms. Most households have vegetable gardens and chickens. The fishing industry has declined in importance because

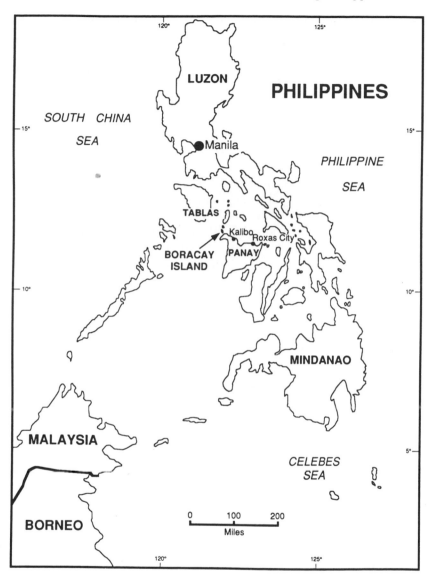

Figure 1. Location map, Philippines.

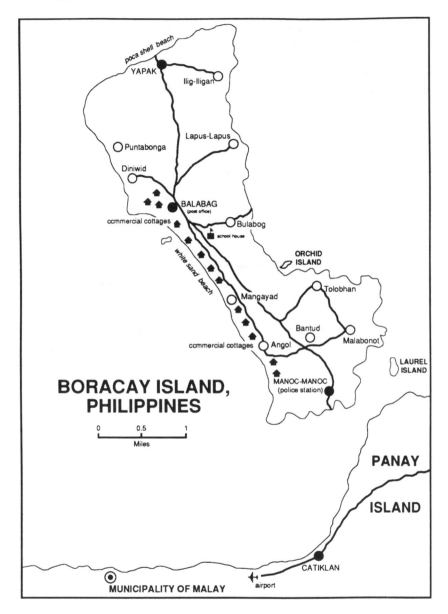

Figure 2. Map of Boracay Island, Philippines.

dynamiting fish in past decades destroyed most of the local corals. The sloping beaches provide no harbor; there is no fishing fleet nor are fish traps set in the arrow-shaped pattern typical of other Philippines shores. Individuals fish from small boats for home consumption and now also sell some of their catch to local cafés.

The sale of copra once provided limited cash income, but that industry has failed, and the faltering economy of Boracay parallels that of the nation as a whole. Of deep concern to local families is the lack of wage employment for a younger generation who crave the material benefits of Westernization. Upward mobility and cash income have encouraged out-migration; such individuals return to Boracay only occasionally, thereby weakening traditional family ties. Thus Boracay has drifted into social and economic stagnation—an island deemed by Filipinos as a very pleasant place to live (in contrast to the slums of Manila) but with little hope for financial betterment.

Only the police, the postmaster, and school teachers have permanent paid employment. The elementary school (grades 1 through 4) was established in the 1930s, intermediate classes (grades 5 and 6) were added in 1953, and a high school was started in 1971. In 1987, elementary enrollment was 287 students, with nine teachers in eight classrooms. In 1987, with the peso valued at 20 per U.S. dollar, the monthly government-paid salary per grade school teacher was 1,337 pesos (US$67). In addition, students were expected to pay the Parent-Teacher Association 5 pesos per month as a contribution for their Boy and Girl Scouts activities. According to the principal, most teachers had established some kind of cottage industry in their homes because "the salaries had shrunk due to the inflation generated by tourism" (Tumaob 1988).

The high school is public but not state supported. Only seventy percent of the teacher's salary is government provided, and tuition is 20 pesos per month for the ten-month school year (some parents pay in kind, as 100 bananas are valued at 25 pesos). In 1987, the high school numbered 282 students. Classes met from 7:30 to 11:30 A.M. and from 1:30 to 5:30 P.M., thus enabling many students to work at family-owned restaurants and snack bars during the lunch break as well as in the evenings. The high school was minimally funded by USAID in conjunction with Aklan Agricultural College through a Foundation for Youth Development in the Philippines (FYDP), where students had asked for courses on dressmaking and T-shirt printing to develop saleable souvenirs for the tourist trade. The principal also hoped to offer more courses in carpentry (especially for furniture manufacturing) and business management courses. She particularly wanted to institute more training to make agriculture profitable, as many farm plots had been recently abandoned while their owners worked in tourism, creating a shortage of fruits and vegetables on the island. Unfortunately, the FYDP monies only covered personnel salaries, and no funds were available to buy sewing machines and cloth or for plant seeds.

The small population is broadly dispersed across the island. Of the three commercial centers (Figure 2), Balabag is largest because of its central location, post office, schools, and (as of 1990, closed) health clinic. One small general store stocks staples and an open-air café functions as the informal social center. Footpaths link the small landholdings, each with its thatched cottage farm home, to the small cross-road supply centers with their tiny open markets and soft drink stands. At Manoc, the one-person police (military) post maintains radio connection with Panay Island and the 500-person municipality of Malay, with its government offices and magistrate, who was also serving as mayor. Being an island people, most Boracayans use their boats and travel to Catiklan and Malay occasionally to attend cinema and to bring back outside news. All residents are bilingual and literate in both English and Tagalog, reflecting the widely recognized long term Western and European orientation for education that characterizes the Philippines.

The regional center of Malay also has a twenty-bed Baptist Hospital (with an emergency overflow wing to handle an additional twenty patients). For the resident Filipino population, the chronic ailments (in ranked order) are gastric enteritis, tuberculosis, amoebic dysentery, bronchial pneumonia, and neonate malnutrition, with vehicular accidents and botulism also of recurring importance. In 1982, Tumbun or "red tide" sickened hundreds of local residents with fish poisoning, and in 1983 an outbreak of cholera claimed ten victims. Since the advent of tourism, the hospital has treated mostly foreign men, especially Germans, and gastro-enteritis is again the most common complaint, followed by gonorrhea, syphilis, and herpes. Malaria is not endemic to the area but occurs among foreign ers who contracted it elsewhere, and the hospital also treats substance abuse, especially "mushrooms." Foreign women patients are seldom seen.

II. The Advent of Tourism

In October 1978, consistent with a developing national tourism policy, the island of Boracay was declared a Tourist Preserve by then-president Ferdinand Marcos, and jurisdiction for its development was vested in the Philippines Tourism Authority (PTA). Land along the beachfront was valued at about US$1 per square meter.

A Cottage Owners' Association was formed with PTA assistance

Figure 3. Beach Road amidst coconut trees, with White Sands Beach to the right.

in 1979 and established interim development standards, including a thirty meter setback from the sea for all tourist enterprises. Thus waving palm trees screened the houses and road and preserved the tropical ambience (Figure 3). Powered vehicles were to be barred except for one or two necessary government service trucks, and boats and bicycles could serve visitor transportation needs. The By-Laws restricted membership to Filipino cottage owners, and elected leaders were to cooperate with the government and PTA in tourism developments. The annual membership fee was set at 25 pesos.

Modern tourism began in Boracay in the early 1980s, initiated quietly and unintentionally by overseas expatriates. Americans and Europeans employed in the Philippines who had heard of the island and its beauty were attracted there for short vacations. Word spread quickly to other expatriates living in the Philippines, and then to their conationals resident in Hong Kong, Tokyo, Singapore, and Seoul. Boracay was close enough for a quick and very inexpensive family vacation. The beach was pristine, the villagers friendly, and English was spoken. A family could bring some luxury groceries, Filipino beer is excellent, the soda waters are safe, and the thatched bungalow cottages provide adequate shelter. Annual repeat visitors began to multiply. Soon young footloose or vacationing Europeans began to trickle in,

TABLE 1 Arrivals at Boracay, 1983–1986 (total and foreign visitors)[a]

| Month | 1983[b] | | 1984 | | 1985 | | 1986 | |
	Total	Foreign	Total[c]	Foreign	Total	Foreign	Total	Foreign
January			1415	682	2608	986	2720	934
February			715	430	1215	729	1155	608
March			1029	522	1784	912	3376	745
April			2673	454	3612	606	4714	616
May			3025	336	1340	324	5109	382
June			1290	210	1043	245	1234	432
July			630	321	466	186	1083	519
August			465	282	604	280	862	504
September			519	174	601	290	709	466
October	480		673	331	1064	306	1364	577
November	558		630	306	1841	450	2003	1131
December	762		1213	956	1062	989	2615	1648
Total			14277	5004	17240	6303	26944	8563

[a]Non-foreign arrivals include fishermen visiting family, military, government personnel
[b]Registration began October 1983.
[c]Data not reported separately

lured by descriptions of low cost living and the crystal clear water for snorkeling and windsurfing. A good thatched cottage could be rented for US$5–$8 per night; a satisfying meal was less than US$1; and beer was ten cents per bottle!

In late 1983 the Philippines Tourism Authority opened a small Boracay office to assist tourists with accommodations and to collect statistics. During the last three months of that year foreign visitors numbered 1,110 (Table 1). The foreign tourist arrivals reported for early January 1984 averaged twenty persons per day with an average stay of at least one week. Although the then-existent infrastructure was severely strained, the statistics indicated a tremendous economic potential for the island if tourist facilities were properly developed. The Manila headquarters of PTA immediately commissioned a Honolulu-based engineering firm to prepare a resort plan, finalized by June. Extensive in scope, the study outlined a total development plan which, if augmented, could "physically support an ultimate visitor unit or room count of between 1,700 and 1,900 units, with a maximum projected nightly visitor population of some 3,700 to 4,200 persons. This level of development will require a corresponding daily employee count of between 2,400 and 2,600 persons," most of whom could be housed on the island (Helber 1984:11). The total ultimate permanent population for Boracay was projected between 4,400 to 4,600.

The Helber plan (1984:9) for resort development sought to preserve the "inherent qualities to attract and sustain international tourism" as follows:

To retain the island's present ambience and strong sense of a tropical Philippine island environment;

To preserve the island's profound scenic qualities as expressed in its white sand beaches, clear waters, dominant coconut palm groves, rugged headlands and rural development character;

To maintain a socially viable balance of tourism and permanent communities and to foster a cross cultural exchange between visitors and island residents;

To establish a maximum level of development so as not to deplete the island's scenic, natural and cultural resources; and

To establish a high standard for all tourist facilities which express the unique character of the island's tropical environment.

The concept then detailed five principal use or activity zones. A Tourist Village Zone along the West Beach would contain clusters of accommodations for economy-minded and younger action-oriented visitors. At the north end of the island, an Integrated Resort Zone would contain two or three quality resort hotels, a 10-acre stable complex, a par-72 18-hole championship golf course, and numerous comparable amenities. The third component was the Traditional Barangays Areas for employee residences "in which it is hoped that strong Filipino community lifestyle can be maintained" (Helber 1984:10). The fourth area, a Community Facility Zone, would contain schools, marketplace, recreational core, and farm lands including fish farming. The final zone was Open Space Reserves to preserve quietude and separation, where existent structures might remain but no new construction would be permitted.

III. The Development of Tourism

From the engineering team, Boracay residents began to grasp the potentials of their future. The Helber study was careful, however, to assess the challenges ahead conservatively: in June 1984, Boracay could support about 350 visitors per night during peak times, housed in "backyard" cottages and restaurants, and their presence had not as yet adversely affected the island's carrying capacity. However, the report specifically states it was prepared on the "assumption that adequate water sources, waste disposal systems and other infrastructure services can be provided to the island" (Helber 1984:11).

Months passed and nothing governmental occurred to implement the plan; nonetheless, tourist arrivals increased (Table 1). To meet

Figure 4. Thatched "stands" along Beach Road, hastily constructed to serve tourists in violation of 30-meter setback prescribed by Cottage Owners' Association.

housing demands, beachfront property owners rapidly constructed more thatched cottages. Soon, individuals who owned no land in this tourist zone set up temporary "stands" at the edge of the sand, where they had tourist access, to sell soft drinks, beads, T-shirts, and other souvenirs. For many years, the major access "road" was the beach walk from Diniwid through Balabag to Angol, paralleling White Sand Beach (Figure 3). Because there are no trucks or cars on the island, this footpath was eight feet wide and occasionally used by oxcarts transporting coconuts and other heavy items. It also served as a buffer, protecting homes from wave action and high winds. These new "stands" now stood between the road and the beach and were both an infringement on property rights and an eyesore (Figure 4).

Meanwhile, some incoming foreign visitors (Table 2) also recognized the profit potential and remained to go into business. Deed restrictions prohibited the outright sale of land to foreigners, but it was not difficult to find Filipino individuals who were eager to benefit by a "partnership" with a foreigner, especially if the latter had investment capital and business expertise. In January 1987 a Swiss operated the bakery, a

TABLE 2 Foreign Visitor Arrivals at Boracay, 1984–1986 (by selected nationalities)

Nationality	Jan	Feb	Mar	Apr	May	Jun	Jul	Aug	Sep	Oct	Nov	Dec
1984												
USA	83	43	86	54	55	15	44	25	20	21	25	126
Australian	39	11	25	14	22	9	50	9	14	27	13	65
French	25	17	23	17	20	26	20	38	18	18	14	70
German	188	131	125	113	89	8	47	65	30	74	98	173
Japanese	7	3	22	11	9	10	16	18	4	8	4	18
Swedish	43	30	23	21	18	10	16	7	18	34	30	90
Swiss	133	86	64	64	44	22	32	33	16	44	48	142
1985												
USA	79	53	69	143	40	32	60	21	37	47	52	121
Australian	61	38	49	32	35	28	15	12	29	24	36	41
French	33	27	45	29	18	9	6	28	98	26	27	56
German	256	196	243	99	68	42	18	53	71	62	52	190
Japanese	13	15	20	23	4	7	6	24	8	6	23	112
Swedish	75	49	59	30	16	5	11	13	8	16	31	64
Swiss	190	100	120	78	57	29	21	24	28	31	47	134
1986												
USA	81	40	87	79	61	75	96	57	68	104	136	249
Australian	35	28	35	46	31	46	46	37	59	33	97	91
French	67	51	46	74	23	12	49	49	29	28	65	105
German	232	132	191	106	61	59	53	65	61	111	221	373
Japanese	29	20	0	18	11	7	27	57	12	20	24	97
Swedish	63	40	35	37	24	15	15	20	20	45	122	133
Swiss	149	98	122	97	53	66	53	48	40	38	132	151

Source: Philippine Tourism Authority, Boracay

Frenchman and his common-law Filipino wife owned a thriving restaurant, his co-nationals operated the Sports Centre that rented windsurfing and snorkeling equipment, an American was importing appliances to outfit "his" bungalow court as the most modern, and a popular floating restaurant-bar built atop a large triple catamaran was German owned. At the time of the fieldwork, Boracay was served by 630 businesses; of the five new businesses opened in December 1986, all were foreign owned.

The tourist numbers continued to increase but an effective tourist industry to benefit local residents was *not* being developed. The Helber study observes:

another concern is that while the present low key and inexpensive backyard-type tourism has a certain charm and appeal, it does not contribute significantly to the economic development of the region nor does it recognize the significant potential of the island. Ideally, the scale and feel of the island's present tourism can be maintained, but the standard and variety of facilities can be expanded and the associated visitor spending increased so that the industry becomes self-sufficient and contributes in a positive way to the economic well-being of the area. (Helber 1984:10)

IV. Boracay's "Alternative" Tourists

The newcomers arriving in 1985 and later were different from the predominantly family groups who first "discovered" Boracay's tourism attractions. Boracay had become a prime destination for the "international long term budget traveler" described earlier. Termed "backpackers" by the Boracayans, these young, single men had learned of the island by word of mouth from individuals met on beaches in Ceylon and Thailand as well as from books issued by avant garde publishing houses including Fourth Estate (Figure 5), Lonely Planet, and Moon Publications (of Chico, California). Even in this author's home town of 50,000 people, the evening paper carried a nearly full-page pictorial with the following description of Boracay, headlined as a "Gringo Express":

word of mouth and guide tips propel Australian, European, and a few North American travelers toward the delights of this 3 kilometer-long, white sand beach; plentiful single travelers, many bars and discos, all water sports, scores of beach huts for 40 pesos ($2) per night, and markets and restaurants every 30 meters where rice, eggs, crackers, fruit and a newspaper will set you back all of a buck.
It's a beautiful, bacchanalian (except in a typhoon), and bargain-basement beach—even when the headlines portend trouble on the streets of Manila. (*Chico Enterprise-Record,* March 8, 1987, 4C)

In 1987, access to Boracay was from the island of Panay via the small town of Caticlan which has a short grass runway for nineteen-passenger Twin Otter and smaller charter planes; one-way fare on scheduled carriers was US$52.00. At the twenty-foot dock, passengers and baggage would be loaded into fifteen- to twenty-foot sailboats (some also have outboard engines) for the approximate half-hour crossing, which can be smooth or varying degrees of rough to impossible, depending upon wind and surf conditions. Boracay landings were "wet," as passengers disembarked to wade ashore carrying their luggage. All supplies came to the island via these same boats, which would be beached, empty, at night along the shore. Few individuals arrived with advance reservations because Boracay has no telephone service. Most newcomers had been "tipped off" by a friend about the names and locations of various cottage complexes and best eateries, and they

Beach bar on Boracay, the Philippines. Photo: Nick Hanna

The world's best beaches

Research for the *BMW Tropical Beach Handbook* took Nick Hanna and two researchers to well over 200 tropical beaches and islands. We asked him to list his favourites:

1. **Boracay, Philippines:** People often ask which is the best beach in the world and the reply is invariably Boracay. It really has everything you could possibly desire for tropical beach life.

2. **Nananu-I-Ra, Fiji:** Perfect island hideaway for beachbums on a budget, just offshore from Viti Levu, Fiji's main island.

3. **Hanuama Bay, Oahu, Hawaii:** Superb snorkelling amongst thousands of tropical fish in a marine national park within easy reach of Waikiki and Honolulu.

4. **Rantu Abang, Malaysia:** Well-known turtle watching beach on Malaysia's east coast where giant leatherback turtles come ashore to lay their eggs from May through to September.

5. **Cape Tribulation, Queensland, Australia:** The meeting point of rainforests and coral reefs in a (so far) unspoilt wilderness.

6. **Koh Phangan, Thailand:** The next step for those who find neighbouring Koh Samui already too commercialised.

7. **La Digue, Seychelles:** Fabulous, unspoiled beaches within easy reach of reasonably-priced guesthouses.

8. **Na'ama Bay, South Sinai, Egypt:** The desert-type beach is unattractive but Na'ama Bay lays claim to the nearest coral reefs for snorkelling and diving to Europe.

9. **Anse Chastanet, St. Lucia:** Well-run diving resort hidden away in a secluded corner of this lush, mountainous island.

10. **Negril, Jamaica:** Sheer indulgence, Rasta culture and reggae on seven miles of beach. Good value, good fun.

The *BMW Tropical Beach Handbook* is published by Fourth Estate (£12.95). Buy it and you can enter a competition to win a tropical beach holiday worth £2,500.

Figure 5. Advertisement for Boracay among "world's best beaches."

would go in search of quarters. Because most guests are surf-minded, proximity to the beach was the overriding consideration.

The various thatched cottages (numbering 737 housing units in January 1987) are very similar in price and amenities and rented for about US$15 per night. All were equipped with cold running water, flush toilets, cots with linens provided, mosquito netting, wooden table, chair, mirror, and daily maid service. The travelers themselves have set these standards by virtue of being willing to pay for them. Most Filipinos in rural villages (including local business owners in Boracay) sleep on raised wooden floors or mat-covered dirt floors and use outhouses. In 1987 Boracay had no electricity, no central water or sewage system, no waste or garbage center, no resident police, no fire department, and no health clinic. Visitors had therefore set the lifestyle and, contrary to local intent, it was visitor demand that introduced diesel generators to power the discos with tape decks, refrigerators to chill beer, and neon lights. Most villagers despised the associated noise and air pollution as well as the late night loud laughter, which the chickens and dogs frequently protested noisily.

For most visitors the day would begin with a late breakfast, then a full afternoon on the water and beach followed by rounds of cocktails, a late dinner, and dancing well into the night. Female singles were conspicuously rare, and single men often brought "girl friends" from Manila's notorious Ermita district or even from Thailand or Ceylon. The imported prostitutes constituted a special problem as, in January 1987, approximately one hundred were stranded in Boracay, having been abandoned there without funds to return home when their erstwhile friends departed to other destinations.

V. The Physical Impacts of Uncontrolled Tourism

The Helber study correctly anticipated the water shortage and sanitation problems which worsened with increased visitor usage. A World Tourism Organization ecological study (Ganapin 1985) also commissioned by the PTA further emphasized water problems in relation to land use. Along the densely populated White Sands Beach, the ground water table is barely four feet, and private-individuals-turned-innkeepers simply hand-dug shallow wells into the sandy soil, attached a hand pump, and drew up the water. Toilet wastes had traditionally been buried, but with visitor demand for flush toilets and wash basins the "engineering" was a downpipe which carried the wastes into the sand, often within six to ten feet of the "well." In 1987, at our lodging, a diesel pump raised the water fifteen feet to a tank which provided gravity flow to the bathroom (Figure 6). At ground level where the pump

Figure 6. Hand pump raised water to tank for gravity flow to service toilet and shower in rental cottage. Groundwater table is 4 feet; toilet downpipe is less than 6 feet from well.

attached to the pipe, one could see into the sandy basin and smell the contaminated water. Hotel and restaurant owners assured their clientele the water was "safe," or that it was "boiled," even "bottled." Most visitors were aware of the problem and solved it by drinking beer; however, the use of polluted water for dishwashing was evident. Surface run-off from showers, laundry, and dishwashing formed rivulets and drained fifty to one hundred feet into the sea (Figure 7). Trash and garbage accumulated along the road and near buildings; some proprietors raked it into piles that were all too often scattered by on-shore winds or foraging dogs.

Some landowners built hillside cottages to advertise Ocean View rooms (Figure 8). The combination of removing forest growth and inadequate structural foundations accelerated erosion. Access paths were muddy and slippery, and the structures were visible eyesores which violated the Cottage Owners' Association zoning restrictions.

Physical visitor impact during the three years from the inception of record keeping to the time of this field study had been essentially all

Figure 7. Bridge constructed by school students over a drainage ditch of contaminated water, draining directly into the beachfront sea.

negative. The political turmoil which accompanied the overthrow of President Marcos, and creation of a new constitutional government under Cora Aquino, precluded much attention or allocation of funds to remote Boracay. It is to the great credit of the PTA that they recognized the potentials of tourism (and attendant problems) early in the decade and earnestly sought developmental guidelines. As of 1991, remedial action seems unlikely because of the great expense. Culinary water is of highest priority and would be obtainable via pipeline from the nearby island of Panay but at a cost of millions of pesos. A sewage treatment plant and landfill are also urgent requirements. In March 1991 an electric power line linked Boracay with Panay to provide for more lights, refrigeration, electric stoves, and ceiling fans.

VI. The Sociocultural Impacts of "Alternative" Tourism

The sociocultural impacts are multiple but not as visible as the physical problems of water and sewage. The three-hundred-year history of Western influence in the Philippines supports a strong emphasis on education. Ninety-five percent of the children attend primary school;

Figure 8. Hillside cottages built for "ocean view."

adult literacy is 88 percent. Even in Boracay, virtually every adult has traveled away from the island, has visited or worked in major cities, and is quite urban in outlook. This is not an island of illiterate, ignorant peasants. Nevertheless, the introduction of the tourist business into rural village life has dramatically changed the traditional social structure.

Local elderly informants believe their island has been settled for many generations. During this time, a network of traditional leadership has evolved and serves as the informal regulatory and power structure to maintain peace and public harmony. A personal disappointment in the fieldwork was my lack of time to investigate the pretourism social network, for the data were still available. A principal informant in this regard was a well-educated and personable young woman, Judith, who served as the salaried resident representative of the Philippines Tourism Authority. Not a native of Boracay, she had none of the historic family ties with the island that would enable her to know which individuals were the recognized decision makers and their linkages to other families. As a Filipino, however, Judith fully recognized the importance of the exiting social matrix and that her institutional role would be enhanced if only she had the time and experience personally to unravel the inherent power structures and identify decision makers. In accord with Nash in his concluding chapter of this volume, there is a process in tourism development of which an important element is locus of power in *local decision making*—a topic that has not yet been addressed in field work.

As might be expected, individuals who owned White Sands Beach frontage suddenly found their property had increased in value to 350 pesos per square meter, and old houses were being sold for as much as 40,000 pesos. Inland families were eager to find ways to enter tourism. Lacking beach access, they built stands between the path and the beach to sell soft drinks and shell jewelry (Figure 4). Their "boutiques," complete with treadle sewing machines, could produce a made-to-order colorful shirt or beach shorts for US$3.50. Straw hats cost US$1. Cottage Owners' Association members were furious at this violation of their restrictions and appealed to Judith at the PTA office for protection, to no avail. The only avenue of correction lay in a letter to PTA in Manila. Judith *did* remind the stand owners of the thirty-meter setback; but since they were not members of the Association, they had not participated in the relevant discussion nor agreed to the restriction. This issue, small as it may seem to outsiders, was sufficient to sever long term alliances and fracture the social web. As Dogan (1989:226) clearly shows, a redistribution of political power generates hostility and resentment.

For the most part the tourist presence was viewed in positive terms. The guests spent money, stayed in their own milieu, and interacted with each other. Perhaps because of the guests' interest in sport, in 1987 Boracay was not a major drug center like Thailand; no one talked of AIDS (Cohen 1988b) nor was sex tourism apparent (Perpinan 1984). Most young women in Boracay were employed in the family businesses that catered to tourists and did not need to turn to prostitution for survival. Some women did fraternize with male tourists, hoping to cultivate a permanent union (marriage) which would assure them upward mobility outside the Philippines. In addition to the late night noise, complaints included the negative role model of youthful idleness and hedonism paraded daily before the envious eyes of Boracay male teenagers, the offensive nude bathing, and the tourism-induced minor increase in petty theft. One direct attack in 1986 against a boat bringing tourists to the island had resulted in the loss of money and watches. Local authorities knew the perpetrators had been attracted to Boracay for the purpose of theft, and the criminals had been incarcerated as a "lesson" to others. Thereafter, the military permanently assigned offshore an aged and lumbering patrol boat, which locals looked upon with some derision as an ineffective deterrent to what the military referred to as "piracy."

In an effort to assess community attitudes concerning the impact of

TABLE 3 Locally Perceived Effects of Tourism in Boracay

Question	Average evaluation by respondents
Is Tourism a Positive *element in Quality of Life in Boracay?*	
Does Tourism provide more economic opportunity for you?	8
Does Tourism provide more upward social mobility?	6
Do Tourism earnings help maintain family bonds?	6
Does Tourism provide more *local* amenities for you to enjoy? (essentially a negative answer)	2
Does Tourism enhance your sense of well-being and enjoyment of living?	8
Do you enjoy the contacts with outsiders (tourists)	5
Has Tourism improved your health or education standards?	2
Is Tourism a Negative *element in Quality of Life in Boracay?*	
Does waiting on tourists make you feel inferior to them?	2
Is the presence of liquor/drugs a problem to Boracay?	3
Is prostitution and crime a problem in Boracay?	4
Does the presence of tourists destroy your privacy?	2
Are you concerned about environmental pollution here?	6
Is Boracay becoming too dependent on tourist income?	0
Has the presence of tourists meant loss of control over your daily activities?	1

Source: Author's survey questionnaire.

tourism, some thirty Filipino residents of Boracay were queried in the course of other data-gathering. In what was not intended to be a statistically significant survey, the individuals were informally asked, "How do you feel about tourism in relation to the quality of life in Boracay?" In conversation, we set a value on their assessment, with 0 to mean of no importance and 10 to mean of great importance. In summary there was general concurrence among all participants, irrespective of their role in tourism as fishermen, boat operators, cottage owners, stand operators, school teacher, and so forth. These results are summarized in Table 3.

Overall, Boracayans *like* and *want* tourism for social as well as economic reasons. Income generated directly into family enterprises has given many participating women considerable social independence as well as cash resources. Several women were among the most articulate leaders in the Cottage Owners' Association and were involved in letter-writing campaigns to PTA in Manila. In the traditional society, men had gone fishing and taken their catch to sell in larger communities while women stayed home to tend hearth and garden. The new presence of outsiders has broadened the worldview. Local employment also has meant that family members could remain on the island (and few Boracayans truly want to *live* in Manila). The lack of electricity precluded families buying non-essential gadgetry, and the new money was being used for permanent purposes, particularly higher education for a better future.

An element of excitement accompanied the development of tourism in Boracay. The presence of outsiders is highly flattering, especially since several small cafés and lodges had hung on their walls framed pictures containing clippings from newspapers in Frankfurt, Zurich, and Stockholm that describe their business in a paragraph or two. Some even had their photos in the clippings! However, for some and especially the women, excitement paled with the long hours of routine laundry, bed-making, cooking, and waiting on the public. Parents worked to get ahead, but teenagers wanted wages to be able to join the foreign visitors in the coffee houses. Family solidarity was being strained.

VII. Tourism on Boracay—A Sustainable, Viable Industry?

The insights of the engineering and ecologic studies of Boracay presented earlier suggest that cottage or "backpacker" tourism is not sustainable with 8,563 foreign visitors per year, most of whom stay at least a week and many a month or more. When would cholera occur again, and tourists depart not to return?

Privatization of the tourism industry is a stated goal of the Philippines Tourism Authority in its efforts to maximize local control, employment, and cash flow within a developing tourist community. However the government faces dilemmas:

- If tourism growth is unrestrained, the essential attractiveness of the island will be damaged, perhaps permanently.
- If limits on new construction are established, who will administer and enforce them?
- The likelihood of massive government investment for infrastructure is remote, given the national economic malaise.
- The amount of private investment required to develop both the necessary infrastructure and a resort hotel, per the Helber study, seems excessive given the limited projected guest capacity and an uncertain political future.

If the long term budget travelers forsake Boracay because of overuse and pollution, is there another potential tourist group who would come to occupy the beachfront cottages? Hanna (1989) may rank Boracay the ultimate beach, but this writer can name many other locations with greater attractiveness as well as investment and long term potential. To date most Asians who have the requisite leisure, discretionary income, and social sanctions to become tourists have not been oriented toward beach vacations. Filipinos who can afford to travel usually follow their Spanish or American governmental fore-bears, and vacation in Madrid or visit relatives in the United States. Values within their national culture favor urban sojourns, theater, nightclubs, and shopping, or they cruise.

Economically, visitors to Boracay are providing local residents with newfound wealth. However, Cohen (1982) found in Phuket, Thailand, that craft tourism generated so little real profit (above costs for im-ported food, water, etc.) that tourism authorities were even then dis-couraging it. Boracay may prove to be another such example. No reliable data were available to measure population growth due to the return of family members from elsewhere and from the in-migration of non-Boracay Filipinos who recognized wage opportunities, working for alien entrepreneurs. The presence of employed Filipinos from other islands, however, caused some Boracayans to express concern that they were in fact "losing control" of their industry. Moreover, the combined population pressures from tourism and internal growth do significantly contribute to inflation, especially with the increasing ne-cessity to import food and water. Mounting prices may deter travelers and redirect their goals elsewhere. "Backpacker" tourism by the long haul budget traveler may not sustain a viable travel industry.

VIII. Boracay in Theoretical Perspective

Boracay corresponds to what Ciaccio (1982) identifies as an off-shore island of a metropolitan nation, such as Italy's Eolian Islands, Britain's Channel Islands, and the French départements of St. Pierre and Mi-quelon. Their small size, their remoteness from the national capital (where economic division of tax money takes place), their limited resource base (including energy), their high transportation costs, to-gether with their lack of infrastructure, lead to an archaic socioeco-nomic structure. Ciaccio compares them to Third World outposts.

Tourism in Boracay should be critically examined in light of what Wilkinson (1989) discusses as strategies for tourism in microstates. His literature review on the "inevitability" of tourism for island communities, given their small size and lack of resources, is current and germane. In this instance, the Philippines government did sponsor two engineering studies and a cultural impact analysis as feasibility assessments, principally because they considered Boracay to be a pilot project in small scale tourism development. The University of the Philippines already has a well-established, research oriented Institute of Tourism as well as one of the best industry training programs in Asia. The PTA is therefore sensitive to what Tuchman (1984) terms the "folly" of tourism development which may destroy viable economic alternatives that are more productive in the long run. Currently, severe economic constraints limit decisive action in managing the Boracay area.

In contrast to Britton (1989) whose tourist-flow models correlate with dependency theory to show that tourism is channeled by foreign ownership and government for *their* benefit [emphasis mine], the Boracay study illustrates that the tourists themselves were the industry developers, and not the government or an international air carrier.

A major issue in Boracay is physical and sociocultural carrying capacity, a topic already addressed in this volume by Pearce and Pigram. Water contamination and sewage control are problems common to many "low islands" and coral atolls, with an immediate parallel in Belize (Pearce 1984; Smith 1989). It is the probable expansion of tourism by long term budget travelers in Meso-America and elsewhere that places the problems of Boracay in global perspective.

IX. Alternatives to Tourism

In 1987 Boracay natives were already independently involved in "integrated development" (Wilkinson 1989:170). Artisans who make and sell clothes at stands on Boracay have now had sufficient contact with tourists to understand that such items could also be sold in Manila, or even exported. Boracay could now develop a small cottage industry.

Agricultural diversification is another option. During my field stay on the island, farm advisors from Aklan Agricultural College were experimenting locally with new crops including sweet oranges, mangos, pineapples, eggplants, and tomatoes. Funded by a United States Aid for International Development grant, the project had two goals: to provide marketable foodstuffs for local consumption (and especially to serve the expanding tourist needs), and for economic diversity in the event tourism declined. The principal advisor was enthusiastic about the potential for a sustained poultry industry, for eggs and broilers could yield profits of up to 35 percent and would be marketable as far away as metropolitan Manila.

Boracay is one of seven thousand Philippines islands, many equally small with lovely beaches and a hospitable and needy population. One reason for PTA interest in developing a soundly based tourist economy here is the realization that other islands might also become tourist hosts, with similar small cottage resorts to alleviate local unemployment. However, with so many new destinations available to them, both in the Philippines and elsewhere in the Pacific, there are few compelling reasons for the beach crowd to remain at Boracay. This type of "backpacker" population may readily move on in search of the unspoilt, leaving in their wake both pollution and a sadly disappointed host population for whom the cash benefits have been short term.

Chapter 8
Predisposition Toward Alternative Forms of Tourism Among Tourists Visiting Barbados: Some Preliminary Observations

Graham Dann

I. Introduction

For many island microstates of the Third World bereft of natural resources and struggling for a slice of the developmental cake, tourism has become something of a cargo cult. For them, there are seemingly no alternatives to the panacea of tourism beyond those of destitution, debt, and despair. Moreover, within tourism itself, there appear to be no viable options to replace the well-tried bliss formula of sea, sand, and sun, neatly packaged by the tour operators of the North for metropolitan consumption. Those of the South thus find themselves dependent on both the goose and the golden egg.

There are, however, ominous signs on the horizon that the proverbial goose may not be willing or able to continue laying and that the eggs have begun to deteriorate in quality from the free-range to the battery variety. Just as tourism has escalated from the individual and adventurous wanderings of the classes to the more ubiquitous and collective sedentary patterns of the masses, so too have corresponding restrictions come to be placed on untrammeled growth. Some of these limits are physical; others are more psychological or sociocultural in nature. Few are self-imposed.

The Anglophobe Caribbean is no exception to this necessarily oversimplified and broad scenario. From colonization in the seventeenth century until the achievement of independence some two or three decades ago, its major resource base was mono-crop agricultural and all that is implied for such exclusive investment in the frail ecosystem. During this period, the majority black population, recruited via the infamous Middle Passage as slaves, together with their emancipated descendants, were scarcely affected by sporadic ship-borne visitors from the Mother Country, whose travelers' tales appeared disparaging and at times quite racist, whenever they did not feature exploits with the expatriate host plantocracy (Dann and Potter 1989).

However, with a growing spirit of local autonomy, shifts in the balance of power, changes in patterns of trade, and the advent of modern aviation, many of these tropical paradises were swiftly "discovered"; and within a few years a trickle of predominantly North American vacationers had increased rapidly to become a stream, and then a flood. Small family-run establishments and social clubs soon gave way to high-rise multinational chain operations. Mass tourism had come to stay.

Of course, not all Caribbean territories experienced the same rate of change; indeed, some are only just beginning to chart their seemingly inevitable courses. Yet commentators in their various ways all appear to agree that, whatever the stages of Caribbean tourism, they do tend to form a definite pattern, similar to that outlined by Butler (1980). Wilkinson (1988), for instance, argues that microstates given over to tourism usually experience initial rapid growth which in turn is often transformed either into steady growth or fluctuation. McElroy and de Albuquerque (1989) refer to these stages as "styles" of tourism when they distinguish low impact emerging areas from high impact mass market destinations, at the same time allowing for an intermediate period of transition. They additionally assemble a battery of socioeconomic indicators associated with each of these styles of tourism development.

While those countries in early stages or styles have scope for experimentation, based on the lessons learned from their more mature neighbors, what is problematic for them and their observers, as well as the residents of such destinations, is the final stage of the evolutionary model, for, as this approaches, the greatest difficulties will be experienced in relation to the environment, carrying capacity, and sustainable development. In many senses such territories face a very real dilemma, particularly where much of the prime beachfront property is already occupied by large hotels (and casinos). Since, in most cases, these have traditionally evolved from private homes, pensions, and small hotels to international luxury establishments (Kariel 1989), it is difficult to see how they can throw the process into reverse and arrive at the status quo ante (cf. Butler in this volume). Given also that the majority of these complexes are located on small islands with limited coastlines and that they are often already located close to residential areas, an enclave solution, as for instance in Cancun, Mexico, is also not possible. Besides, as English (1986) has noted, long haul visitors, on which much of the Caribbean depends, are unlikely to find enclaves attractive.

Small island resort areas thus appear to face two alternatives if they wish to continue along the tourist path. One is to expand; the other is to mark time. The former often involves either encroachment on remaining coastal areas of natural beauty, such as national parks or sites which were presumably responsible for attracting tourists in the first place, or else moving inward to lands primarily designated for agriculture or housing, thereby increasing real estate prices, ruining the environment, or disrupting patterns of employment. The latter amounts to a refurbishing or upgrading of hotel properties, which often runs the risk of being tasteless and out of step with surrounding vernacular architecture. More fundamentally, however, a bricks-and-mortar solution may fail to take into account changing attitudes of holiday makers. Whereas Richard Butler, in his article in this volume (Chapter 2), may be justified in believing that mass tourists are probably quite content with the hotel, swimming pool, and beachfront facilities, Dalen (1989) has recently argued that there have been changes in tourist values from those of comfort and rationality to those of individuality, self-realization, and community. If the latter picture is correct, some visitors at least will no longer be content simply to remain on the hotel compound, despite its new and clean appearance.

Sensing the non-viability of the foregoing approaches, four other suggestions have been put forward as alternatives to the alternatives. The first and most drastic seeks an alternative to tourism itself by replacing it with self-development through the diversification of other resources. Since Caribbean tourism is said to engender the same kind of dependency as slavery (Harrigan 1974) and to suffer the worst forms of exploitation under contemporary capitalism (Perez 1974), it should either be socialized or abandoned (the hotel plant presumably being given over to communal housing). This radical option is attractive to those critics who maintain that sociocultural costs outweigh the economic benefits associated with tourism. In the Caribbean, this view has also been partially responsible for an ideology opposed to the introduction of tourism (until very recently the position of Guyana), or at least for its postponement until either other areas of national development have been sufficiently promoted, or as a means of last resort, and then with a number of provisos (the position of Cuba). A more moderate version of this perspective argues that tourism should only be introduced or expanded if adequate safeguards are taken to protect the fragile economies, environments, and cultures of the host island societies, and even then tourism should stem from the will of the people (Caribbean Ecumenical Consultation for Development n.d.).

While this position is appealing for its simplicity, it has been largely overtaken by events and fails to come to terms with current political reality. The majority of Anglophobe Caribbean island states have either reached the stage where tourism has become the major pillar of their economies and prime foreign exchange earner (e.g., Barbados, the Bahamas) or are fast approaching that threshold (e.g., Antigua, St. Lucia). To ask these countries to revert to an earlier stage in their development and to take a substantial cut in per-capita income and standard of living is highly unrealistic. At the same time, all territories, to a greater or lesser extent, are heavily dependent on aid and trade from the United States, and it is this economic dependency which is reflected in their pro-capitalist, and hence pro-tourism, regimes, despite occasional rhetoric to the contrary.

The second solution, put forward by Wilkinson (1989), recognizes the inevitability of tourism for Caribbean microstates, together with the economic, social, and political ramifications for these small island territories. He further agrees with Harrigan (1974) that mass tourism, control by multinationals, and the presence of large scale facilities, are very much predicated on macrostate emulation, microstate reality imperception, external domination, and exogenous decision making. However, Wilkinson maintains that these characteristics in themselves are insufficient reason for the perpetuation of the "folly" which has come to be associated with tourism growth. Instead he argues that environmental quality, tourist carrying capacity, and adverse economic and sociocultural impacts can be controlled, *provided* that tourism becomes integrated with all other sectors and local development. In his words:

Countries should not regard tourism planning in the same way as industrial planning, but rather in the broader context of national planning or development, involving resources, energy, education, transportation, agriculture, social planning, etc. Countries that do not begin to plan in this way may pay the price of having to deal with continuing fluctuations and frustrations at best, or economic disaster at worst. (Wilkinson 1988:24)

Thus, he believes the way forward is to reach the stage of cooperative tourism where one will be able to speak of a "community tourism product." As examples of modest success he points to the British Virgin Islands, Anguilla, Cayman, and Turks and Caicos, where small hotels and guest houses have shown far steadier growth of tourism revenue than their large-facility counterparts in other islands. At the same time, he lauds Barbados for dealing with its fluctuating fortunes through a process of economic diversification while exerting environmental and other controls on its existing tourism industry.

Certainly there is much merit in Wilkinson's ideas, including his various suggestions for environmental control, which are perhaps the strongest and most practical of his proposals. The key theme of integrated tourism development becomes somewhat utopian, however, in a Caribbean context, or in any other context, with an accompanying quotation from de Kadt (1979) to the effect that such a policy had not been implemented in any known tourist destination. The reality of the situation is that few Caribbean territories have any tourism policy beyond that of unlimited growth, and many of their sporadic development plans are often idealistic. Even the Barbados case, for which Wilkinson shows so much admiration, has failed quite dismally in enforcing a national policy of centralization at the expense of community and local government. Consequently, it is difficult to see in less well-advanced Caribbean territories how and with what results a poorly articulated tourism policy could be integrated with an even more woeful development plan. Nevertheless, this author would be the first to agree with Wilkinson that initial failure is insufficient reason for not pursuing an ideal.

The third alternative, favored by McElroy and de Albuquerque (1989), comes after their rejection of the perpetuation of mass marketing (along with various strategies to deal with crowding and congestion), since they argue that

the weight of recent evidence suggests that achieving an environmentally compatible high-impact style is exceedingly difficult and risky at best, given the overgrowth dynamic of international tourism interests. (McElroy and de Albuquerque 1989:13)

Instead, they propose a two-pronged plan. The first part of the plan is to target specialist vacation groups, such as naturalists and divers, "that prefer long stays and new cultural and nature based experiences." The second, and more fundamental, is to "make a serious policy commitment to increase net visitor expenditure (rather than maximize arrivals) by reducing off-island income leakages and encouraging longer stays." As the means of implementation, they suggest tax incentives for the use of local labor and materials, opening up scenery and historical sites by low impact access routes, and preserving archeological and cultural sites in preference to new accommodation construction. They conclude by demonstrating that gross tourist expenditures and tourist-induced GNP can actually increase even though the number of arrivals falls, provided their recommendations are put into effect.

Again, the McElroy and de Albuquerque proposals are in many ways attractive, given the scenario they outline of tourism styles and their implications for small island states. Indeed, some countries in the region, such as Dominica and Trinidad and Tobago (the latter after much debate), have already begun to promote themselves as nature tourism resorts in the hope that they will not fall into the same environmental traps as their more developed neighbors. Perhaps for this reason the suggestions of McElroy and de Albuquerque are more appropriate for the initial low density, long stay style of destination, once the unexamined problem of control over the contents of promotional literature has been overcome. However, as regards the high-density mass market resorts, their recommendations appear to come a trifle too late. Even though the point is taken that cultural and historical sites could be brought into greater prominence as a form of increasingly popular "heritage tourism," there is still the problem of what to do with the already excessive existing hotel plant. Certainly if one Barbadian pressure group, known as "windows to the sea," had its way, much of the infrastructure could be razed to the ground, thereby affording visitors and locals alike physical and psychological access to the ocean and its surrounding beauty.

Finally, there are the suggestions of Auliana Poon. For her, the key to regional tourism should be examined not so much in relation to stages or styles but rather with respect to demand. She argues that, by taking into consideration changes in consumer preferences (Poon 1988c, 1990), prospects for the future lie in innovation, information technologies, and flexible specialization (Poon 1987, 1988a, 1990). In order to strengthen their claim, she investigates corresponding changes in management style in both Jamaica and St. Lucia (Poon 1989). Here she discovers that, where hotels have become all-inclusive in order to match new trends in market segmentation, not only do they become more profitable than their co-existing traditional counterparts, but in some cases they also result in higher rates of tourist satisfaction. She further outlines the merits and disadvantages of her all-computerized establishments for those who supply ancillary services, as well as for hotel employees and guests, and concludes that the former substantially outweigh the latter.

Poon's proposals are particularly interesting since they relate predominantly to complexes with at least 150 rooms, a position reached by many of the more mature Caribbean destinations. While they also appear to heighten greater contact with hotel staff and less with the local population, Poon does not endorse the Club Med variety of all-inclusivity, which is said to deny local participation and to be of little benefit to the host economy. At the same time, among Poon's recommendations one finds support for the view that a limited territorial circumscription of tourists is probably less damaging to the surrounding society than penetration by outsiders, a position taken by Cohen (1989a). However, the chief merit of Poon's contribution seems to be that the key to alternatives rests as much with the guests as with the host community.

Surprisingly, or perhaps alarmingly, such a realization is not matched by parallel empirical research. As de Kadt points out in this volume (Chapter 3), much of the discourse on alternative tourism is fairly high on rhetoric and ideology but correspondingly low on the sort of empirically based proposals put forward by Poon. Butler too feels that the inverted snobbery of middle class academics writing on alternative tourism would be very much improved by introducing a "people" component into the discussion.

Yet in the Caribbean, with few exceptions, little has been done by way of researching the various initiatives instanced by Pearce in this volume, in such places as St. Vincent, Puerto Rico, Guadeloupe, Tobago, and Belize, or indeed anywhere else in the region.

Sensing this void and the need to emphasize the visitor component of the equation, the present writer decided to extrapolate data from a much wider study of tourists visiting Barbados in 1989. To complete the picture with resident attitudes, a number of related questions were included in a sociocultural impact study of the same island, together with three others, in the following year (United Nations Economic Commission for Latin America and the Caribbean, forthcoming).

II. The Barbados Study

The predisposition toward alternative forms of tourism among tourists visiting Barbados is based on the initial analysis of an interview-based survey of 535 tourists visiting Barbados during February 1989. Due to the unavailability of a reliable listing of visitors, quota sampling was adopted. This permitted stratification of the target group by proportionately projecting the non-cruise ship arrival statistics from the previous year according to age, sex, country of residence, and type of accommodation. After selecting respondents in these respective categories, interviewers were further instructed to exclude from the inquiry members of the same family and those first time visitors who had been on the island three days or less.

While the main thrust of the investigation focused on tourist motivation and satisfaction, a number of other areas were also explored including spatial perception, knowledge of local culture, reaction to

TABLE 1 Responses to the Question, "Have You Ever Been Inside a Barbadian Home?"

Category	Frequency	Percent
1. Never been, don't want to	26	4.9
2. Never been, unsure if want to	40	7.5
3. Never been, would like to	297	55.5
4. Been, negative experience	10	1.9
5. Been, neutral experience	89	16.6
6. Been, positive experience	73	13.6
Total	535	100.0

promotional material, quality of life, and the authenticity of touristic experiences. Among these miscellaneous avenues of inquiry were some questions which sought to examine attitudes and behavior towards members of the host society.

One item in particular attempted to discover the willingness or otherwise of tourists to accept a form of tourism which differed from that based on the traditional multinational resort hotel to which many had grown accustomed. This surrogate measure of predisposition toward an alternative tourism to that which had been adopted by governments throughout the Caribbean since the inception of mass tourism in the 1960s concentrated visitors' attention on the issue of visiting Barbadian homes. Arguably, since willingness to fraternize with the natives at such a socially proximate level would be a necessary condition for a radical departure from the status quo, respondents were asked in a filtered question whether they had actually entered a local residence. If the response was negative, they were subsequently asked whether or not they would like to undergo such an experience. On the other hand, those replying in the affirmative were quizzed as to the nature of the event. Their various descriptions were later classified by content analysis as being predominantly negative, neutral, or positive. The full breakdown of the responses is given in Table 1.

A glance at Table 1 quickly reveals that, while most had not ventured inside the doors of a local abode, over half of the respondents were quite ready to do so. Of the 32.1 percent who claimed that they had made such a visit, the majority described the experience in positive or neutral terms.

Before exploring the quantitative association of this variable with others, however, it is useful to examine from a qualitative standpoint what exactly the interviewees were saying. To this matter we now turn.

Qualitative Analysis—Negative Experiences

As can be seen from Table 1, predominantly negative experiences were highlighted by only ten respondents. In all cases they were from metropolitan countries; half were from the United Kingdom, the former colonial power.

Six of the observations focused on the poor living conditions of the local inhabitants which were considered to be "very basic" or "unrefined." One fifty-five-year-old Canadian woman elaborated her description in terms of the giant cockroaches, both dead and alive, which she saw about the place. She further noted that "the boards had spaces—you could look out to the streets." Her reaction could be summarized as one of shock. In two instances, the "look of poverty" and the "poor amenities" evoked respective respondent sentiments of sadness and sorrow. In another, a sense of outrage was expressed at the small size of the accommodation. When compared to the United States, its corresponding lack of comfort was attributed to low levels of local pay and the associated exploitation of nationals.

Finally, while two related their negative idiosyncratic experiences in terms of hostile dogs and absence of ventilation, the other negative respondents emphasized overcrowding. One in particular expressed concern about the irresponsibility of Barbadian men. She asked rhetorically: "Where do they put all those children? Where is the father?"

If, after entering local homes, a positive experience represents a favorable response toward alternative forms of tourism, then a negative experience can be taken as an unfavorable predisposition. Consequently, it is worthwhile to explore very briefly various features of the foregoing experiences in order to highlight the actual and potential barriers to such experimentation.

In the first place, tourism from the Metropole to Third World countries tends to highlight asymmetry in relation to affluence. While this characteristic can attract visitors to poor developing countries and give them a sense of power over the local population, in others it can lead to feelings which range from disgust and contempt to pity and indignation. Second, the shock which may be experienced is more often than not "culture shock." Here it is all the more salient, since it represents the clash between a WASP (White Anglo-Saxon Protestant) "culture of materialism" and a Black "culture of poverty." Third, while tourism oscillates between motivational forces of novelty and familiarity, the *strangerhood* associated with the former, particularly in cases of perceived deprivation, tends to militate against forms of tourism other than the enclave mass variety.

Qualitative Analysis—Neutral Experiences

Neutral experiences, which accounted for the majority of replies, expressed little or no emotional reaction beyond that of mild bewilderment or surprise. The accent was far more on the features or setting of the house than on its residents. Although situations were sometimes different, they were still reckoned to be normal and comparable with those back home. Quasi-meaningless or cliché epithets such as "nice" and "typical" were in abundance. In one or two cases respondents admitted difficulty in describing their experiences.

The need for a comparative yardstick (incidentally a strategy often employed by writers of travelogues) was evident in many of the replies, particularly among visitors from outside the region. The following examples illustrate such a viewpoint:

"Very much like the South East Blacks in the United States in terms of taste, behavior and food" (41-year-old female, USA)

"Much like a middle class home in the United States" (33-year-old male, USA)

"There was no second floor. Everything was on one floor. It was different from the usual homes in Toronto" (40-year-old female, Canada)

"It was well built, though small in comparison to those back home" (64-year-old male, USA)

"It was just like back home. It had a comfortable atmosphere" (69-year-old male, Canada)

"No different from home. No difference in lifestyle except the lady was a very religious lady" (46-year-old male, Canada)

In one instance the condition of the house was compared by a middle-aged American male to those in a variety of travel destinations. The Barbadian home was said to be much better than those he had found in Mexico, Panama, Costa Rica, Colombia, Ecuador, Thailand, and China.

Although some differences were noted, these were not perceived as negative or barriers to communication by extra-regional tourists. Among visitors from other Caribbean islands, such differences were negligible. Thus:

"It reminded me of Trinidad" (24-year-old male, Trinidad)

"Just like home" (20-year-old female, Guadeloupe)

"It reminded me of home" (27-year-old male, Trinidad)

Absence of a comparative mental measuring device tended to result in a feeling of strangeness or amazement which, while not positive, was not negative either. Hence a male visitor from Sweden described his experience as "odd," while a retired woman from Canada expressed surprise at finding a chattel house so absolutely spotless.

Three comments in this response category briefly touched upon the issue of race. In each case a potentially problematic situation was apparently canceled out by a more positive experience. Interestingly, all featured young Canadians staying in relatively modest tourist establishments:

"I felt welcomed, but the owner appeared to be unsettled with having me. At first he was concerned about what his neighbors would have said" (30-year-old male)

"It was enlightening but the *residents* felt strange to have white visitors in their home" (emphasis added: 31-year-old female)

"I went to visit. We had met the year before. Some said that there were two white people outside. A cute nice experience" (31-year-old female)

Qualitative Analysis—Positive Experiences

The emphasis now became much more people directed and was placed on feelings of belonging and being accepted. Residents were described as being "warm," "kind," or "friendly," and the atmosphere was correspondingly felt to be "welcome" or "homey."

The theme of "homeliness" somehow stood in contrast to the description of a *house*, with or without a direct comparison to those "back home":

"It was a nice house with a homely atmosphere" (55-year-old male, UK)

"I felt at home" (30-year-old male, Antigua; 24-year-old female, Antigua)

"A friendly homely atmosphere. I felt very comfortable. The people were receptive" (25-year-old female, Bahamas)

and, with the addition of the nostalgia factor:

"I felt at home. It brought back memories of my father's house" (38-year-old male, Tortola)

Even though the majority of these descriptions were from Caribbean nationals, it was left to a retired Canadian woman to articulate more fully the theme and nuances of home:

"A feeling of acceptance: at *home*. Back *home* people do not invite you into their *homes*, unless you are friends" (emphasis added)

The word "welcome" featured in several accounts:

"One of comfort and welcome" (50-year-old female, USA)
"I felt relaxed and welcomed" (18-year-old male, UK)
"I felt welcomed" (77-year-old female, Switzerland)
"Welcoming atmosphere" (65-year-old male, UK)

While most of these feelings were spontaneous, as in:

"I was welcomed immediately" (31-year-old female, USA)

some initial strangeness was also admitted:

"I felt strange at first, but it was interesting. I felt welcomed and quite comfortable after a short while" (23-year-old male, Canada)

"Warmth" and a "warm atmosphere" were also fairly commonplace in respondents' descriptions:

"Warmth" (79-year-old female, USA)
"A warm feeling of welcome" (50-year-old male, USA)
"Friendly and warm within" (55-year-old male, Canada)
"A warm lived-in house" (21-year-old male, Canada)

It was this feeling which was said to be *impressive*, an epithet frequently employed in positive experiences:

"I was impressed with the warmth of the people" (48-year-old female, UK)

Two other attractive qualities were noted by a handful of interviewees, "pride" (in the better sense of the word) and the behavior of children. The former (which is associated with the Barbadian national motto of "Pride and Industry"), was thus observed:

"their cooking smells great and tastes just as good. . . . They really take a pride in their homes" (47-year-old male, Northern Ireland)
"though modest, they take a pride in what they do to the home" (39-year-old male, Guyana)

The latter was noted by two more respondents:

"What a nice home she had, and how mannerly the children are" (78-
year-old female, UK)
"Closeness with the family. The children were well mannered and not
disobedient" (32-year-old male, USA)

The introduction of "the family" became a central theme in a final
selection of respondent descriptions. This time, however, the accent
was placed on the visitor's feeling a part of that same host family:

"I was treated as part of the family" (56-year-old female, Canada)
"The reception was as good as with people you know all your life
(although it was the first time with these people)" (34-year-old fe-
male, Canada)
"I just felt at home. I felt as if we were all one family" (30-year-old male,
Trinidad)

However, one description in particular not only epitomized such
feelings of belonging, but did so in relation to the touristic theme of
self-perceived royalty:

"I felt just like a king since they had prepared a beautiful lunch. I
couldn't have asked for them to be more friendly. I have been to that
home three or four times now. It is an open house to me. They treat
me as part of the family. It gives me a beautiful feeling" (52-year-old
male, Canada)

This last statement arguably represents predisposition to alternative
forms of tourism par excellence.

Qualitative Analysis—Other Responses

While the nature or quality of the experience of entering local homes
may provide some idea as to the desirability or undesirability of similar
experiences under alternative forms of tourism, the same type of
argument cannot be extended to those without that type of experience.
Instead, in the latter case, it was suggested that predisposition toward alternative forms of tourism could be gauged by hypothetical
responses indicating a willingness to undergo such an experience.

In this final subsection, however, a cautionary note should be added
to the proceedings, particularly since hypothetical questions have a
way of yielding replies which may be similarly unrealistic. Fortunately

(as will soon be seen) in the present investigation hypothetical responses could be associated with other attitudinal and behavioral variables in order to gauge consistency. Additionally, however, and more by way of serendipity, a number of interviewees who had not entered Barbadian homes but who were either unsure or wished to do so, nevertheless supplied unsolicited further comments, thereby providing a fuller contextualization of their positions on the matter. For this reason, it is perhaps a worthwhile exercise to examine briefly some of this supplementary material.

Among those who declared that they were *unsure* as to whether they would like to visit a local home, one encountered the following remarks:

"I wouldn't mind, but this time I'm looking to relax. I'm not that curious. Maybe I should be" (68-year-old male, USA)

This was a response from a retired, though fairly affluent, tourist patronizing a luxury hotel. Although he was quite content to spend the duration of his holiday on the nearby beach or by the poolside, there was still an awareness of the curiosity motive, one which appeared to be nudging his conscience, and a potential which could perhaps be activated by appropriate promotional discourse.

Another guest who stated that he was unsure was staying at a similar five-star establishment. This seventy-eight-year-old Canadian male indicated that if he were in Barbados for a month instead of just a few days then he might well reconsider the matter more favorably. For him, the barrier seemed to be one of time constraint rather than an issue such as value for money, thus suggesting that priorities can be altered to prevailing circumstances.

Further light could also be shed on those who qualified their willingness to enter local homes. A sixty-eight-year-old male retiree from the United Kingdom, for instance, made the distinction between tour representatives and local people. While both were Barbadian, the former were usually white and the latter were predominantly black. Whereas he was quite prepared to meet families of the latter, he was not willing to mix any further with the former. The point is an interesting one because it has very much to do with the touristic perception of authenticity, particularly as it relates to interracial encounters. In expressing his preferences, the individual in question was acting in a direction contrary to the language of social control employed in tourism promotional material in which fraternizing with the natives is not normally encouraged.

Another visitor, this time a sixty-three-year-old male from the United States, added a condition to his willingness to enter local homes which had the effect of further complicating the issue. He stressed that, while he was quite prepared to visit somebody whom he knew, he would be quite reluctant to enter the home of a total stranger.

An additional proviso was supplied by a forty-year-old female visitor from Canada, who emphasized a condition of reciprocity in the arrangement. As far as she was concerned:

"I would like to go into a Barbadian's home, but she must also come into my home."

Interestingly, the lady in question spoke of her hypothetical encounter in terms of the same sex variety and on a one-to-one basis.

Finally, a thirty-six-year-old male from the United States not only agreed with the idea but admitted that he had "fantasized about it." Such a freely given confession, although unique to this set of responses, nevertheless underlines the connection between motivation and social action, together with the well-known associations between pre-trip and on-trip behavior. It additionally suggests that these linkages should be explored in an examination of predisposition toward alternative forms of tourism. At the same time, the supplying of various conditions by respondents indicates that further research in this area should take into account distinctions made by tourists themselves. With this limitation understood, we are now in a position to examine the variable quantitatively.

III. Home Visits—Association with Other Variables

Since one wished to obtain an attitudinal continuum ranging from negative to positive appraisals of the situation, it was decided to group categories 1, 2, and 4 from Table 1 as the lower limit, to leave category 3 as a midpoint, and to group categories 5 and 6 as the upper limit. This scheme had the added advantage of arranging the replies from a hypothetical situation to one based on experience. A series of cross-tabulations was then calculated in order to gauge the degree of association with the independent and some other allied variables. Table 2 records the significant relationships.

A few comments are both relevant and necessary to each of the significantly related variables.

Country of Residence

For this variable, visitors were classified according to domicile rather than country of birth; in most cases the distinction evaporated. An

TABLE 2 Cross-Tabulation of Variables with Entry to Local Homes

Variable	Significant chi-square	d.f.	Level of significance
Sex	—	—	n.s.
Age	—	—	n.s.
Country of residence	27.98	6	0.001
Type of hotel accommodation	45.88	6	0.001
Number of visits to Barbados	80.71	6	0.001
Occupation	—	—	n.s.
Change of job	—	—	n.s.
Education	—	—	n.s.
Traveling companions	24.02	4	0.001
Marital status	—	—	n.s.
Religion	—	—	n.s.
Persons wished to meet (pre-trip)	28.63	4	0.001
Persons wished to meet (on-trip)	13.30	4	0.01
Number of friends	—	—	n.s.
Whether met locals	—	—	n.s.
Travel can help achieve self-identity	9.03	2	0.02
With whom identity achieved	—	—	n.s.
Motive for travel to meet a new set of people	16.86	6	0.01

attempt was also made to place these national groupings on a descending scale according to average per capita income, ranging from the United States and Canada to the United Kingdom, Europe, elsewhere, and the Caribbean. The direction of the relationship revealed that those hailing from North America were less inclined to enter Barbadian homes than visitors from other climes. It is unclear from this variable alone, however, whether such reluctance was due to differences in culture or relative affluence.

Type of Hotel Accommodation

This variable sought to clarify the foregoing dilemma by using the category of hotel as an indicator of income, given the inaccuracy and unwillingness often associated with establishing income levels in sample surveys. Hotels were thus classified in descending order from A to D by calculating average winter season double-occupancy room rates from figures provided by the Barbados Board of Tourism. After noting their favorable attitudes toward their hosts, the fifteen visitors who were actually staying in local homes were deleted from the analysis of this variable. As anticipated, it transpired that, among the remaining 520 cases, those who were in less conspicuously affluent accommodations had either entered or were quite willing to enter Barbadian homes. Here, in addition to the income differential being less pronounced between themselves and local residents when compared with those visitors patronizing more luxurious establishments, the actual style of accommodation and physical proximity to the host population may well have contributed to their favorable predisposition.

Number of Visits to Barbados

Predisposition to enter the dwelling of a stranger is more often than not predicated on the degree of strangeness anticipated. It was not surprising, therefore, to find repeaters to Barbados were correspondingly quite prepared to mix with their hosts in this way. While there were even differences in attitude between those first timers who had been on the island less than a week and those who had been there for a longer period, the greatest variation occurred between those who had visited on just one or two previous occasions and those who had been three or more times before. In the last instance some 52.5 percent had entered a Barbadian home and had referred to the experience in neutral or positive terms. The corresponding mean figure for the sample as a whole was 29.9 percent.

Traveling Companions

When this question was originally formulated, a geometric coding scheme had been employed to cater to the various combinations of traveling companions and whether or not they included spouse, children, relatives, friends, and companions of the same or opposite sex. In any event, the data could be reworked to yield three major categories: traveling on one's own, traveling with spouse, or traveling with somebody other than spouse. When they were subsequently cross-tabulated with the dependent variable under discussion, it emerged that those most predisposed to enter Barbadian homes were those who were traveling unaccompanied, followed by those who were traveling with a person or persons other than their marital partner. Seemingly, therefore, the presence of spouse places additional constraints on enjoying a vacation in a manner which includes possibilities other than those associated with the traditional holiday experience.

Persons Wished to Meet (pre-trip)

In this situation, respondents were placed in a hypothetical position and asked whom they hoped to meet in Barbados prior to their making the actual trip. Replies ranged in degree of openness to the host community from no one at all to fellow travelers, fellow travelers and locals, and locals only. Needless to say, as one ascended the scale, there was a significant and growing association with predisposition to enter local homes.

Persons Wished to Meet (on-trip)

This time interviewees were presented with a real on-trip situation. Whereas the association was still in the predicted direction, however, it was less pronounced. Furthermore a far greater proportion of visitors were placing themselves in the locals and fellow travelers category, with corresponding reductions in the none and locals only categories, in comparison to the pre-trip question. While the implications of such a change of heart are not fully clear at this stage of the proceedings, one may venture to suggest that the reality of the on-trip sharing of accommodation with fellow guests must have had the spin-off effect of increasing the camaraderie among guests. At the same time there was a corresponding diminution of interest in fraternizing with members of the host community.

Travel as an Aid to Self-Identity

Several interviewees confessed that this was the most difficult question which they had faced, since in some cases they had never given the matter any thought. Others, however, recognized the validity of the query. After some consideration, approximately two-thirds of the respondents felt that on balance travel did not create a sense of self-identity. They either claimed that they knew themselves already or else discovered themselves in a home environment through introspection or through contact with others. The remainder, however, believed that a break from the routine home setting provided the necessary milieu for self-discovery, whether by reflection, interaction with fellow travelers, or mixing with members of the host community. A cross-tabulation revealed that this minority was more disposed to entering local homes.

Motivation for Travel to Meet a New Set of People

At one stage of the interview, respondents were given the opportunity to provide their own travel motives in an unprompted fashion. Later on in the inquiry they were presented with a list of motives in prompted format and asked to rate their importance on an ascending scale from 1 to 10. Meeting a new set of people was the motive considered closest to the predisposition to enter the homes of locals. As expected, those giving the highest scores on this variable were also the most inclined to enter Barbadian homes, if they had not already done so.

Non-Significant Associations

Having examined the significant associations, a brief word is necessary in relation to those variables which failed to attain the preset 0.05 level of significance. While the *sex* ratio is practically on par for visitors to Barbados, no discernible trend was noted with respect to predispositional gender differences. *Age,* on the other hand, which was classified into five groups, while not in itself a predictor of willingness to enter local homes, was nevertheless subsequently found by correlation analysis to relate to those variables which did significantly affect the dependent variable. With this variable, the trend was for younger persons to display more favorable attitudes.

Occupation and *change of job* in turn were linked with age, to the extent that younger individuals tended to have better jobs and also to change them more often than those more advanced in years. In that sense, they were also indirectly associated with favorable attitudes towards entering local homes. *Education* was likewise positively associated with occupation, though inversely related to type of accommodation, itself linked with predisposition to entry.

Marital status and *religion* only just failed to attain significance. The former was highly associated with age, the latter less so, thereby stressing a greater proportion of single non-religiously affiliated visitors among the young. A subsequent breakdown between the two major religious groupings revealed a slight tendency for Protestants to favor mixing with their hosts when compared with their Catholic counterparts.

The *number of friends* a person had in the home environment was positively associated with age. However, its inverse relationship with traveling companions suggested that those with fewer friends were more likely to travel on their own, and this in turn made them more disposed to accept the invitation to enter the home of a host. As far as actually *having met locals* was concerned, since 98.1 percent of the sample claimed to have done so, the variable lacked sufficient discriminatory power for analysis and was consequently deleted.

Finally, it had been originally hypothesized that those who indicated that they *achieved self-identity by interacting with others* would be more disposed to enter the homes of others than those who believed they attained this state through more introspective methods. Whereas this hunch was not in fact validated, significant indirect linkages were established between this variable and youthfulness, the pre-trip desire to meet hosts, the quest for identity itself, and the motive to meet a new set of people. All these variables in turn led to predisposition to enter local homes.

IV. Profile of Tourists Most Disposed to Entering Homes of Hosts

When all the previous information was reassembled, the statistical profile presented in Table 3 emerged from the correlation matrix as representing those most disposed to entering Barbadian homes.

The presentation in the table employs four levels of logical and temporal sequencing, arranged as follows:

Level 1   inherited characteristics: age and nationality
Level 2   characteristics acquired through socialization: via school, church, peer group, and spouse
Level 3   pre-trip attitudes: people-oriented aspirations and motives
Level 4   on-trip attitudes and behavior: accommodation, number of visits, travel companions, and desire to meet locals

Moreover, every variable contributes directly or indirectly to an explanation of the predisposition to enter the homes of locals. Where the linkages are indirect via intervening variables, the level of the latter is included in parentheses. Here the intervening variables are of the same or a higher level because the highlighted variable is being treated as independent. At the same time, however, they may be considered dependent on lower levels, as with, for example, the association of age with higher level variables. For simplicity's sake, these lower level linkages are presented only once.

Thus, even at this preliminary stage, a fairly clear picture emerges of the salient characteristics of those predisposed to enter the homes of locals and hence by extension open to various alternative forms of tourism. As the analysis progresses, it will be possible via path analysis to transform the correlation coefficients to beta coefficients, that is, to control simultaneously for the interactive effects of variables at different levels and to determine their respective influences in terms of strength and direction.

V. Conclusion

Since the foregoing discussion has highlighted a number of visitor characteristics and attitudes mainly present at the *pre-trip* stage of the

TABLE 3 Profile of Tourists Most Disposed to Entering Homes of Hosts

Level	Characteristic	Association	Via variable(s)	Significant correlation
1	Young persons	indirect	country of residence (1)	−0.19
			marital status (2)	0.47
			number of friends (2)	0.10
			religion (2)	0.14
			travel and self-identity (3)	−0.13
			identity through others (3)	−0.13
			type of accommodation (4)	−0.11
			number of visits (4)	0.30
			travel companions (4)	−0.18
1	From non-North	direct	—	0.22
	American	indirect	marital status (2)	−0.12
	countries		education (2)	−0.25
			motive to meet a new set of people (3)	0.10
			type of accommodation (4)	0.31
			travel companions (4)	−0.12
2	With few friends	indirect	education (2)	−0.12
			identity through others (3)	0.14
			travel companions (4)	−0.11
2	Single	indirect	motive to meet a new set of people (3)	−0.15
			type of accommodation (4)	−0.18
			travel companions (4)	−0.23
2	Well-educated	indirect	travel and self-identity (3)	0.10
			type of accommodation (4)	−0.12
3	To meet locals (pre-trip)	direct	—	0.18
		indirect	motive to meet a new set of people (3)	0.30
			identity through others (3)	0.13
			type of accommodation (4)	0.14
			to meet locals (on-trip) (4)	0.37
3	Travel can	direct	—	0.14
	provide self-	indirect	identity through others (3)	0.33
	identity		type of accommodation (4)	0.12
3	Identity through others	indirect	motive to meet a new set of people (3)	0.15
3	Motive to meet a	direct	—	0.17
	new set of	indirect	type of accommodation (4)	0.21
	people		to meet locals (on-trip) (4)	0.10
4	Lower category	direct	—	0.28
	accommodation	indirect	number of visits (4)	0.14
4	Number of visits	direct	—	0.35
4	To meet locals (on-trip)	direct	—	0.12

tourism experience, clearly it is necessary for researchers to examine more thoroughly the dynamics of this situation before they can begin to make recommendations to policy makers, advertisers, and industry officials. It has emerged, for instance, that tourist motivation plays a key role in understanding an openness toward alternative forms of tourism. If this is people centered and other directed, it is quite likely that such an attitudinal cluster will have behavioral ramifications. The same applies to those aspirations which include the desire to meet members of the host population and the belief that self-identity is achieved through interaction with others.

Yet, if alternative forms of tourism are to develop, it is required that discussions also be initiated with hosts in order to establish the sort of tourism they wish. Tourists in turn can be invited to submit their reactions and ideas. Eventually both parties can engage in dialogue so as to yield an agreement which is mutually beneficial.

The data from this study have only looked at one side of this dual process. In a preliminary fashion, they have highlighted that tourists, even in a traditional setting, may be thinking along alternative lines. The realization that these same independently minded tourists are predominantly young, unattached, and well educated clearly offers promise for the future. Yet whatever this entails will be quite unattainable unless the hosts are also brought into the picture. Only then will a consensus be possible as to the exact nature of these alternative forms of tourism. That is surely the basic condition before such alternatives can become viable.

Chapter 9
Tourism by Train: Its Role in Alternative Tourism

Martinus J. Kosters

I. Introduction

Much of the discussion surrounding Alternative Tourism concerns itself with problems of mass tourism and Third World Countries and with the issues of congestion, pollution, and misuse of society's resources that result from masses of tourists trying to enjoy their leisure time in environments away from, and different than, their places of residence. Similar challenges for tourism appear in industrialized countries as well, and these perhaps more often are related to over-crowding: too many people wanting to travel to, and enjoy, the same destinations at the same times of year. Nowhere are these challenges greater than in the affluent and densely populated countries of Western Europe. And no single factor is closer to the center of these challenges than modes of transportation for tourists.

Though presently relatively unimportant as a transportation mode for tourists in Europe, the train, which has existed for nearly two centuries, still fascinates and attracts many passengers and aficionados today. The train was instrumental in the creation of mass tourism when, in the mid-nineteenth century, James Cook became the first tour operator, chartering trains for tour groups in England and on the continent. Although the train has improved as a means of transportation over the years, in this century its previously dominant role has been seriously undermined by the automobile, the bus, and later the airplane. As a result, its relative position as transportation has considerably diminished.

Today the train still plays an important role in society, but its role as a passenger carrier has clearly declined in industrialized countries. In the United States, trains are considered a second-rate means of passenger transportation. In Western Europe, trains hold a valuable market share of passenger traffic primarily because of policies of protectionism and subsidization by the respective governments. In the countries of Eastern Europe, because of lower income levels, the train remains an essential transport medium.

In Europe, the train still has a role in tourism, although a modest one. In Western Europe it draws a market share of under 5 percent in tourist transportation. The automobile holds a tourist market share of about 80 percent, though this varies somewhat from country to country. Trains lost much of their previous tourist clientele during the last few decades and have failed to attract large numbers of new clients to replace them. It seems that, for many potential travelers, trains are perceived as an inferior form of tourist transportation, although there are now excellent fast trains, night trains with good cabins and beds, special sleeper trains for passengers traveling by automobile which are also suited to carry automobiles on board at night, express trains to important tourist destinations, and the inception of more international high-speed trains.

Considering the strategic role of railways in Europe, respective governments or private sector interests have shown an ongoing willingness to invest in new developments, such as with the Channel Tunnel project beneath the British Channel between France and Great Britain. There are plans for railways on a trans-European scale with new tracks for high-speed trains, parts of which have already been constructed in France and Germany. Some national railway companies are investing in new, fast, and comfortable trains, as with the French TGV (*Train à Grande Vitesse*).

The train cannot be overlooked in the future of European tourism because the infrastructure of motorways is and will continue to be insufficient for the increasing demands for transport. Motorway vehicular traffic also has destructive effects on nature, such as by contributing to killing trees and entire forests in nearly all European countries. (Exhaust fumes of road traffic are not the sole reason; industrial pollution and some agriculture techniques also share the blame in this matter.) In addition, air transportation in Europe is confronted with growing congestion problems in major airports and air corridors throughout the continent.

In densely populated Europe, therefore, the train should and likely will return as a valuable and more important means of transportation. Train transport is less damaging to the environment and less injurious to nature and mankind than the alternatives. The position of railways will likely be improved not only inside specific countries but also on a European scale. Therefore, it is worthwhile to consider the future of the train with regard to its future role in tourism and its potential contributions to "alternative tourism." The important policy issue is: will trains remain a relatively insignificant transportation mode for mainstream tourism, or will they form an important alternative means of tourist transportation which will reduce some of the externalities associated with automobile and airplane based mass tourism?

II. Mobility

Western Europe has, on a relatively small surface, a total population of nearly 320 million. Compared with North America, Western Europe is very densely populated, though there are considerable differences among countries. The same holds true for average living standards in European countries, with countries like Switzerland, Sweden, and Germany at the top and countries like Spain, Portugal, and Greece at the bottom. Mobility within each country is considerable, and the recreational share of mobility is increasing along with the countries' growing economies.

Due to the anticipated realization of the European Economic Community (EEC) of twelve Western European countries, it is to be expected that after 1992 recreational mobility will be considerably stimulated. Without significant national interior boundaries to the EEC and, as a consequence, no internal passport control, there will be more free and more frequent movement of EEC citizens among the Community. Furthermore, the effect of a strong Common Market is expected to favor the economy of a united Europe, and this will undoubtedly stimulate additional leisure-time mobility of the population.

Mobility in this respect can be described in three measurable dimensions: the total number of kilometers traveled per person per year, the total of all kinds of trips and transfers per person per year, and the total hours spent moving and traveling per person per year. Increasing mobility in this context means either an increase in one of these three dimensions, with the remaining two remaining at least stable or constant, or growth of two or all three dimensions. Research in the Netherlands has indicated that the number of kilometers is increasing nearly continuously, while the other two measures have remained more or less stable; the number of trips has increased very slowly, and the number of hours underway has stayed on the average nearly constant. People probably have biological clocks that exercise a restraining influence, preventing them from spending too many hours in transport. The tentative conclusion that could be drawn from these data is that people do not spend more time moving and/or traveling, but have realized their kilometer goals by utilizing faster means of transportation.

The consequences of these developments along with a steadily increasing number of kilometers traveled, increasing especially during leisure time, are:

1) *Heavy traffic congestion.* This occurs already on motorways to major tourist destinations, mainly on the primary north-south motorways. Particularly in France and Western Germany, it is not unusual to have one horrendous traffic jam extending 100 kilometers or more during peak tourist periods. During holiday seasons there is also considerable congestion at European airports and in the air corridors. Congestion is also increasing inside popular tourist destinations, such as along the Mediterranean coasts during summer and in the Alpine region in the snow season.
2) *Pollution effects.* New roads and motorways cut the landscape and nature to pieces, and parking lots often create visual pollution. Vehicle engines severely pollute the environment and tourist towns with exhaust fumes. Noise, also a serious type of pollution, is produced within motorways and air corridors as well as in more pastoral settings.
3) *Erosion of natural amenities.* The growth of tourism requires scenery, landscape, and nature for the increasing numbers of tourists. New tourist areas are continuously being developed to add to the existing ones. But sometimes planning systems are very poorly conceived, as can be observed in Greece and Turkey, and sometimes they are overwhelmed by visitor volumes, including those visitors' transportation needs. Dependence on traditional means of transport, such as the automobile, creates a conflict between the amenities an area has to offer and the pressures placed on the amenities by those wishing to enjoy them.

Tourism growth, therefore, often damages part of its major attraction as a side effect of the modes of transport it encourages. Particularly in densely populated Europe, this poses a serious challenge that is not easily resolved. In Europe, where abut 80 percent of holiday travel is presently done by automobile and about 10 percent by airplane, transport mode related problems continue to mount. The train, in contrast, which is the least environmentally damaging of all major forms of tourist transport, captures only a small percent of the tourism market.

It is instructive to look at modes of mobility in the Netherlands to appreciate the potential train transport has for future tourism development. Though data analyses do not break out tourism trips, other patterns can be discerned. In spite of variation from country to country in Europe, the Netherlands experience can in may ways be considered typical.

Commuter, business, and education travel together account for about 38 percent of total mobility. These activities cause modal split problems on work days, especially in the larger towns, the cities, and agglomerates. Therefore the role of public transportation is extremely important. In the Netherlands the market share of public transportation as a percentage of all trips for these activities is respectively 13 percent, 4 percent, and 33 percent. As a percentage of all trips, trains get 6 percent of the commuter market, 2 percent of the business market, and 14 percent of education travel. Thus, educational activities form a main segment of the train market.

Leisure activities form another important cluster of mobility: visits/stays, recreation/sports, and tours/hiking together comprise 40 percent of total mobility. In these categories, public transportation realizes a market share of 13 percent, 8 percent, and 7 percent, respectively, and train transport registers market shares of 7 percent, 4 percent, and 3 percent, respectively.

In total, public transportation captures 11 percent of all mobility kilometers, and the train, a major category within public transportation, gets a total of 6 percent. Market share of the train for leisure activities is relatively modest. But with expected future decrease in labor hours and therefore more leisure time, on the one hand, and an expansion of leisure activities and opportunities which will induce increased mobility and the demand for transportation on the other, the train will likely gain market share among transportation modes in the Netherlands in the future.

Up to now about 10 percent of an average automobile's lifetime is spent in holiday usage, but at least another 10 percent to 20 percent is for other recreational uses. These percentages will increase in a more affluent society with greater leisure time and opportunities. Because of the greater congestion and pollution costs associated with the automobile, however, an important policy question will emerge as to whether governments are willing and able to influence private decision making, through incentives and disincentives, so that more people will turn to public transportation in the future (see, for example, de Kadt's discussion on internalizing externalities, Chapter 3 in this volume).

III. Tourism and Leisure

In advanced Western European countries, the leisure hours per person are increasing. New labor contracts generally show a diminishing number of working hours in the future than in the past. Instead of the traditional 40-hour week, more and more labor contracts are agreed upon with 38-hour, 36-hour, or even 32-hour weeks. Besides, the average worker receives 20 to 25 paid holidays per year, depending on age of worker and type of job. In some countries, like the Netherlands, there is a bonus system in which the worker gets an 8 percent bonus of yearly salary as additional holiday income.

As a consequence of increased leisure time and higher living standards, leisure-time mobility has surged during the last half of the twentieth century, and the growth in holidays has played an important role in this trend. In the countries of Switzerland, Sweden, Norway, Denmark, and the Netherlands, at least 70 percent of the population goes on holiday one or more times per year. (A "holiday" in this sense is a period of at least five successive days spent outside one's home town for recreational reasons.) In the Federal Republic of Germany, France, and Great Britain, participation has been a bit lower, around 60 percent; in the remaining Western European countries, it is considerably lower, about 40 percent. The inclination in Western Europe to take one or more holidays a year is stronger than elsewhere in the world. Furthermore, the frequency of scheduled holidays is higher.

Considering that the holiday participation rate in the advanced countries may soon reach a saturation level, the major increases in holiday taking may be over. Holiday growth will continue to occur in countries with relatively low current holiday participation rates, and other growth will depend on changes in the inclination to take more than one holiday per year.

Besides main holidays, in recent years there have emerged the so-called short holidays or short stays. These are periods of at least one to four successive overnight stays outside one's home town for recreational purposes. These leisure periods are likely to continue to increase in popularity in the future. In the Federal Republic of Germany and the Netherlands, where the total number of major holidays is nearly stable, there has recently been an increase in short holidays, with more than 90 percent of these spent inside the home country. In a united Europe with more and better travel facilities, an increase of short stays in neighboring countries within the EEC seems very likely.

Finally, there are, of course, day trips. With a population of 320 million, there will be billions of day trips per year. The more leisure time one has, the more day trips one will consume. These leisure activities are also mainly domestic. An important question is whether people will use the train as a means of transportation for short stays and day trips, especially if automobile transportation continues to create congestion on local motorways.

In general, the use of trains for domestic tourism is greater than for tourism abroad. The tendency in recent years, however, has been to increase holidays abroad, and the market share of trains for tourist travel decreased through the 1980s. In Belgium, Switzerland, the Federal Republic of Germany, and the Netherlands, more than 50 percent of all holidays are spent abroad. So, on the one hand, the market for leisure spending is increasing tremendously, but, on the other, the share of train-based tourist transport is still decreasing.

The main reason for the weak showing of train transport is that the automobile is more flexible transportation to nearly every destination and is much more convenient, as it takes luggage from door to door. With two or more passengers, the automobile is usually lower in price than the train and, even when not, the higher price is often compensated by the ease and comfort of traveling by automobile. And obviously, airplanes can connect tourists with new destinations, especially in faraway and distant locations.

One question that can be posed is which people are still traveling by train today? And will they represent a growing market for train travel in the future?

It is likely that the bulk of tourists traveling by train include:

- young people without a car or a driver's license;
- elderly people who do not like the hectic traffic on motorways or in foreign towns and destinations;
- people who feel much safer with public transport, because they do not have to be responsible for the organization of private transportation plans;
- people who prefer to travel in the cheapest way, and in many cases train travel is the most economical;
- train lovers, who always prefer train transportation, even when other travel facilities are cheaper or easier;
- special interest groups, such as tour operators who organize holiday travel by train, especially when trains have the advantage of going directly to major European cities; or in the winter to Alpine resorts, when snowfall may disturb road traffic and bad weather can make scheduled airline flights uncertain; and
- people who consider trains a preferred alternative for travel in their leisure time; people who like to see the landscapes, meet the locals, and smell the countryside.

Even if demand warranted it, because of the restricted number of tracks in Europe, trains could capture only a modest share of total holiday travel. Without new tracks and lines, new destinations are hard to reach by train; traditional spots are better.

Among the reasons why the railway systems have been losing market share are:

- Trains are no longer serving all the important European tourist destinations. Even when a railway company is willing to follow the new, rapidly developing market demands, it may take years before its tracks reach a new destination. Furthermore, few new railway tracks have been built in recent decades.
- The speed of trains during the 1960s and 1970s was scarcely greater than 100 years earlier, though this has improved slightly since. Furthermore, people do not like changing and waiting for trains.
- In many people's minds, trains are considered old-fashioned. A car has a lifetime of approximately ten years, an airplane fifteen years, a ferry perhaps twenty-five years, but a train reaches forty years and is often technically operational after that period. Therefore, many consumers think that trains may not be suitable for them because they belong to an earlier generation.
- Trains cannot solve the inconveniences of train changes and being unable to transport luggage door to door. A good public transportation system, with excellent terminal facilities, may lower resistance to train travel by mitigating these issues. But many new villages and suburbs still have no rail tracks.
- Although prices for traveling by train may differ from country to country in Europe, domestic trains are usually the cheapest way to travel, except for walking and cycling. However, for traveling abroad, train prices are, for the most part, less competitive.
- When a consumer has a car, why should he or she leave it and take the train instead? The majority of tourists do not even consider the train as an alternative if they own an automobile.

As a result of these factors, the train as a viable tourist transport mode has declined rapidly in the second half of the twentieth century. The train is considered by many to be old-fashioned. It may be a good means of transportation for those who like an alternative way of travel, but it is not relevant for most holiday makers. However, in spite of these factors, other forces point to the possibility that a revival of the train for tourism is likely.

IV. Modern Railways

Railway infrastructure must last for centuries, as history in Europe has taught us. Decisions made now in our post-industrial age to redevelop the railway system will certainly leave their mark on future society, and there are strong motives to reinvest in railways today. The most progressive governments will favor construction of new tracks at the expense of new motorways because of the mounting difficulties linked to automobile congestion and pollution; channeling road traffic is being considered as a forced option. Proposed channeling, the directing of traffic away from already congested or polluted urban areas or destination resorts, would deprive road traffic of the very thing which has always made it so attractive: the unbridled freedom to travel cheaply at any time to any destination, without delays, from door to door, in one's own vehicle. In place of this could come regulation with many characteristics which have always worked to the disadvantage of public transport: lack of freedom, delays, and transfers.

Channeled road traffic could, by way of detours, force the traveler to participate in a complicated and fragmented form of public transport. The private vehicle would have to be left somewhere and the journey continued by public transport. The use of the private vehicle would become less attractive in comparison with public transport. As a consequence, investments in modern railway systems could very well increase. This tendency could be strengthened by the following trends:

- Mobility is increasing, especially in the leisure sector. If the railways want to capture a greater share of this, investment will be needed in modern equipment and new tracks.
- Trains and tracks seem to be less environmentally unfriendly than automobiles and highways. A train produces less pollution per kilometer/passenger than equivalent road transport. Besides, space consumption for new tracks is more modest than for roads and motorways with a comparable capacity. Governments may therefore stimulate the use of rail transport.
- In some urban areas in Europe, there is in fact no free choice. Because of continued damage to scenery and nature from further highway construction, the only viable alternative to meet transport needs is a rail track. In Holland, for example, the railway company uses double-deck trains in connections between large towns. In France the railway company has been successful with the TGV high-speed trains.
- In more and more tourist destinations, one feels that the tourist's automobile not only is a polluter but also damages the scenery. In many Mediterranean resorts, plans are ready or under construction to exclude automobiles from boulevards near the beaches and from the cities, because of the noise, smell, and parking and traffic prob-

lems, and otherwise to encourage train travel by tourists. Spain, for example, is planning to adapt the width of its international railroads to the smaller European size in order to attract more tourists with the French TGV high-speed trains.

- In the past, railway companies have run trains perfectly from a technical point of view, but they have lacked a marketing orientation. However, from other transport companies, such as air carriers and ferry operators, they are learning modern management techniques and marketing approaches. This is bringing a different mentality into railway operation, as companies are becoming much more client-oriented. If this approach is successful, it may make new investment in the railways much more attractive. So far, however, this change in mentality is noticeable in only the more progressive countries like France, Switzerland, the Netherlands, and the Federal Republic of Germany.

V. New Products

There are some places where new product introduction has enhanced the appeal of railroads. In the Netherlands the national railway carrier is investing for the future on a very large scale by the placement of new tracks in the surroundings of Amsterdam and some other areas, adaptation of some tracks for high speed trains, and safeguarding the tracks in blocks so that trains will stop automatically when another train is on the same track-block. This project is nearly finished on all the important tracks. Every year the company opens new railway stations in suburbs and renovates old ones in need of restoration. There are new trains, like the double-deck trains for modal split, but also new excellent spring carriages on the intercity lines. The catering facilities on board have improved, as have services at railway stations. Staff people who work with passengers follow special courses in tactical behavior in "difficult circumstances." Many special tariffs have been introduced for different groups of travelers, such as for leisure day trippers.

The results have been encouraging, with a steady increase of passengers and revenues, though the whole process is still under way. Nevertheless, the Dutch company still does not break even and, therefore, the government plans to divide the operation and maintenance of the tracks from operation of the trains. The railway industry will then be able to compete more successfully with transport companies and entities using the road system because the implicit subsidy from government supplied roads and motorways will be corrected; highways are typically financed separately as government-provided infrastructure, and transport companies and individual travelers do not directly confront the full cost of the roadways when making individual transport decisions.

In France, the high speed TGV train is profitable and, therefore, new projects are under construction. In the Federal Republic of Germany, the same tendencies are seen with their fast trains. Other countries and their companies will follow; but for international travel and transport using railways on a European scale, the saying holds that the whole chain is as only strong as the weakest partner.

VI. Railways on a European Scale

High speed rail travel, considered to start at 200 kilometers per hour on the up-graded lines and even 250 kilometers per hour on the new lines, provides new dimensions for travel in Europe. The current lack of infrastructure has meant, however, that European transport has not yet felt the benefits of these technological advances. Considerable economic advantages could be derived as, in many cases, high speed trains will be able to go twice as fast as automobiles and will be twice as cheap as planes. The European high speed trains meet the greater mobility requirements of the Single United Market, particularly in the light of the worsening congestion affecting the future of other means of travel.

For over twenty years, air and road transport have been the preferred means of travel in Europe. Between 1970 and 1985, air and road traffic rose respectively by 6 percent and 3.2 percent a year on average, while rail travel only grew by 1.6 percent per annum. These growth patterns may change as time and energy resources are considerably wasted as a result of road traffic jams and air space and airport congestion.

Aware of the challenge for the railways, the Community of European Railways (the railway companies of the twelve European Community member countries plus Austria and Switzerland) presented, in 1989, a project for a European high speed network. This project covers infrastructure, rolling stock, and timing for the future connections, thereby redrawing the European railway map.

This revival of the European railways is seen as a necessity. The question is no longer simply whether investments should be made, but particularly why and how. Western Europe is very busy with goal-oriented investments in the quality of life for the future. That is not a promise that the train will recover its historic market share, however, but numerous European governments are trying to favor the position of the train at the expense of the automobile and perhaps even the plane. This policy will have great implications for tourism as well.

VII. The Challenges for the Railway Companies

In reducing distances within Western Europe through greater speed and new connections with major tourist destinations, there is an exciting challenge for railway companies. They have a chance now to profit from the political climate to reorient transportation for several reasons, as already indicated in this analysis. They have the chance now to fight back to increase their market share, especially in leisure travel. It should be possible to regain their market with a good and competitive product. However, improvements are just beginning and the whole process will take some decades, so that the final result will not be determined until the long run; even then customers may not come spontaneously in great numbers. Therefore marketing specialists must develop new strategies as well, and a very sophisticated marketing policy will be necessary.

In formulating such a policy, the following points should be considered:

- There are subjective constraints to reaching people. There are so many advertising messages in the world that more and more consumers do not pick up the essence; they often do not have the feeling that the message is meant for them. This is a psychological problem. The potential client has indeed seen the advertisement and can even talk about it, but does not take the message to him- or herself. The message is for other people. This kind of problem demands a new and fresh approach to marketing, especially for such a challenging product as train travel.
- As society becomes more and more fragmented and segmented customers can be divided into groups with special characteristics. Judging by different groups' behavior during leisure time and consumption, lifestyles are a clear reflection of the conditions of their lives and choices that can be made with respect to the manner of living in industrial societies in the Western world. Lifestyles are an increasingly important dimension of the social structure. For railway companies, it will be necessary to identify lifestyle characteristics in order to communicate with potential markets for train travelers in the right language and with the right arguments.

Harmut Lüdtke (1989) tried to describe characteristics of interesting lifestyles which may be strong potential markets for train travelers. These would include:

- active persons with varied interests;
- trend and fashion conscious, leisure-oriented people;
- intrinsically motivated young people;
- alternatively oriented intellectuals;
- successful work-oriented citizens;
- conventional family persons;
- open-minded athletic skilled workers;
- authoritarian workers;
- conscientious senior citizens;
- resigned discontented people.

More research will be necessary to define which lifestyles are interested in traveling by railway and how to reach people of a given lifestyle or psychographic profile.

When railway companies can identify their new target groups and know their market potentials, they need to translate the demand in product differentiation. The core problem would then be, how one train with a limited number of carriages going from Point A to destination B can be arranged in such a way as to respond to the different demands of the leisure travel market. It is a problem already solved by automobile manufacturers. With computerized production techniques, they are able to make small changes in the standardization of production in order to meet the very special wishes of various clients.

It needs to be kept in mind that transportation is not a self-fulfilling preference but rather part of a total product. In tourism the final product is an attraction, and transportation is needed to reach that attraction and perhaps also accommodations. Therefore rail transportation should be packaged to deal more with other producers in tourism. This approach demands flexible management and sales approaches; however, partnership may offer attractive product combinations.

Transportation is also an enterprise with risks. A railway company should therefore take risks with investments to anticipate the demands of trend-setting groups, particularly in leisure and tourism. Up to now, European railway companies have been seen as public utilities, without regard to market needs. This process is changing. Railway companies in some countries do utilize a stronger market approach at this time. It is clear, however, that the new approach is not a question of just turning on the electricity switch. In Europe several hundred thousand people work for the railway companies, and it will take years to adapt a new mentality suitable to taking new risks.

The abolishing of inner boundaries in Western Europe is a first step towards a united Europe. But there will still be twelve independent countries with twelve independent state-owned railway companies. Cooperation is a nice word, but as yet every country and every company still has its own specifications for loads and carriages, electricity, tariffs, timetables, social obligations, and so on. However, the beginning of cooperation is a reality that market opportunities and economic and political forces are strongly encouraging.

With the help of modern techniques, railway companies have much more to communicate to their clients. On board a plane the pilot can give all the relevant information through a microphone; this is an information communication system that works. On trains, such communication is still an exception. The same applies to railway stations, although the situation is improving. Good communication is an integral part of the quality of the product.

VII. Conclusion

In Europe the train still holds an important position in passenger transportation. It is true that the train lost its dominant position in tourism and that today train travel is a secondary means of tourist travel relative to automobiles and air carriers; however, the current political climate is very good for a resurgence in train-based tourism. The train will be able to acquire a new and important role in society if managers of railway companies and politicians give way to new ideas and marketing approaches. The increasing mobility of European people demands new investments. This means that new injections of investment and development will also appear in tourism and that trains in the next century could very well fulfill a critical role in tourism for industrialized countries, such as those in Europe.

Chapter 10
Tourism Alternatives in an Era of Global Climatic Change

Geoffrey Wall

I. Introduction

The tourism industry and tourism destinations are often not in control
of their own destinies. Critical decisions which impinge upon the volume and quality of tourism are frequently made outside of destination
areas. These include decisions concerning airline routes and sched-
ules, investments in infrastructure, tour packaging and marketing, and
the influences of travel agents on the potential clientele. Tourists, by
definition, are located elsewhere and are typically confronted with a
bewildering variety of destinations and vacation packages from which
to choose. Furthermore, there are many factors which are external to
the tourist economy but have major influences upon it. Examples of
such factors include exchange rates and consumer prices, energy availability and costs, natural hazards, terrorism, and other political events,
such as strikes, coups, and wars. Such factors influence the very existence of tourism industries in specific places, as well as the types of
tourism which may be viable.

This lack of self-determination has triggered many of the criticisms
that have stimulated the discussions of alternative tourism. Yet, even if
a destination were able to accomplish perfect control over those things
which are controllable, there are still powerful external factors that
would influence the direction of tourism industry development and
performance. Researchers, government officials, industry representatives, and affected citizens are used to thinking about such forces as
economic, political, or environmental in nature, and most of the analytical tools that are typically brought to bear on such situations look at
short term or intermediate term strategies for mitigation. Beginning
in the 1980s, however, there has been a growing body of evidence that

global climate changes, such as "global warming," may be in the process of leading to significant and permanent transformations of climate patterns in many parts of the world. This certainly adds a new dimension to issues confronting the future of tourism.

This article is concerned with the influence of climate and weather upon tourism. In particular, it is concerned with the possible implications of global climate change. It will be suggested that changes in global climate, which are beyond the control of the tourism industry, may have far-reaching consequences for many current tourist destinations and for places contemplating involvement in tourism. Global climate change may place constraints upon and provide new opportunities for the tourism industry and may encourage the search for alternative types of tourism which are compatible with the new climatic regimes.

II. Climate, Weather, and Recreation

Atmospheric processes are among the most variable aspects of our natural environment. "Climate" is a generalization of the atmospheric conditions which have occurred over a long period of time, usually at least thirty years, while the term "weather" refers to atmospheric conditions over a specified period of time such as a day, week, season, or year. However, in recognition of this variability, climate may include information on the likelihood of the occurrence of extreme events as calculated from past records. In simplistic terms climate is what is expected and weather is what one actually gets.

It has already been implied that atmospheric processes vary on a wide range of time scales. Normal day-to-day variability is often of sufficient magnitude to mask longer term trends, making it difficult to estimate the speed and direction of change over longer time scales. However, there is ample historical evidence, such as the manifestations of glaciation, to indicate that there have been major fluctuations in climate in the past and to suggest that there may be comparable changes in climate in the future.

It is important to note that while human adaptations can be made to climate, they may be less flexible with respect to weather, as it is a short term phenomenon. Adaptive strategies may be severely tested if climate change is marked and its onset is rapid.

In much the same way as there are temporal changes in climate, so there are also spatial variations in atmospheric processes. These can be studied at a variety of scales from macro to meso to micro, and any conclusions which one may make may be scale-specific. One often thinks of spatial changes in climate in association with latitude but such broad generalizations may break down in specific locations, particularly when climate is modified by the uneven distribution of large water bodies and mountain ranges.

It can be concluded that the variability of atmospheric processes is such that it is likely to have important repercussions for a wide variety of human activities, including tourism. At the same time, the temporal and spatial variations in climate and weather make it difficult to isolate their precise significance at present, let alone their possible ramifications for the future.

III. The Climate-Tourism Interface

Following the suggestions of Riebsame (1985), there are at least four perspectives from which the relationships between climate and tourism can be viewed. The first is climate as setting. From this perspective, climate constitutes part of the environmental context in which tourism takes place. There are numerous studies which briefly describe the climatic characteristics of destination areas before discussing the activities which take place in them. In the majority of these studies, however, climatic variables do not constitute an element in subsequent analyses, and such studies are of limited use in leading to an understanding of impacts of climate change.

A second perspective views changes in atmospheric processes as generators of change in participation in tourism. Studies of this type include some of the more thorough studies of atmospheric processes in relation to tourism and recreation, and their findings have been reviewed elsewhere (Wall 1985). However, most such studies stress relationships between weather and recreation rather than implications of longer term climate change.

A third perspective sees climate as hazard. Hazard implies loss or harm in the context of chance, risk, or accident. The actual climatic phenomena thus termed can range in scale, character, and effect from slight, common variations, to rare, isolated effects, from global occurrences to local incidents. Resultant situations can vary from relatively minor inconvenience to unmitigated disaster. Although there is a large literature on hazards, there is little specifically on tourism, but there are passing references to the destruction of accommodation for visitors in coastal locations (Burton, Kates, and Snead 1969; Kreutzwiser 1982; Platt, Pelczarski, and Burbank 1987) and calculations of the loss of tourist business resulting from a volcanic eruption (Kreck 1981). As an aside, it is interesting to note that impacted sites may become tourist attractions as visitors come to gaze on the misfortune of others or stop at the site of a major disaster.

Lynch, McBoyle, and Wall (1981) have combined the hazard approach with the fourth perspective, which sees climate as a resource as well as a resistance. Since human activity imposes limits on the favorable and unfavorable valuation of meteorological conditions and human beings determine the socioeconomic activity for a specific time and place, they, in effect, define the hazardousness and utility of the phenomena which interact with their activities. That is, if the conditions vary beyond acceptable limits, the weather becomes a liability rather than a resource. This liability is a function of human built-in vulnerability or, in other words, the sensitivity of the activities and environments which one exposes to the elements.

Lynch, McBoyle, and Wall (1982) suggest that two important implications arise from these statements. First, the range of interactions resulting from the limitless variation in weather and social systems indicates an exceedingly complex system to examine and generalize. Second, the observation that human beings are the resource and resistance determinants suggests that they have some control in reducing the sensitivity of human activities to weather and climate. Lynch, McBoyle, and Wall argue that in order to make rational, objective decisions concerning responses to the vagaries of climate, it is essential that the decision maker (in this case the tourist or the proprietor of a tourist enterprise) has an explicit understanding of weather-activity relationships. The identification and measurement of the economic impact of weather variation is a key exercise in the establishment of this interaction. The economic assessment of weather hazards, or "weather costing," is not only possible and practical, but it enables comparisons to be made between sites and greater efficiencies to be achieved (Taylor 1970).

Masterton (1982) has suggested that changes in the weather give rise to both physiological and psychological responses that influence levels of comfort that, in turn, can be modified by the addition or subtraction of clothing. She proposes that climatic classifications can be devised based on comfort, leading to studies of tourist destinations on either a regional or a local scale, and of individual recreational activities. While such studies are unlikely to be mutually exclusive, both of them constitute potential directions for future research. Mieczkowski (1985) has employed the notion of comfort in his assessment and mapping of the tourism climates of the world.

The influence of weather conditions on tourism varies from region to region and activity to activity. Rain occurring in a region with a climate of twenty rain-days annually will likely have a greater influence upon human behavior than rain of the same intensity and duration occurring in a climate of one hundred rain-days annually (Crapo 1970). Similarly, weather variables become more influential in affecting activities as the amount of atmospheric contact increases. However, weather influences both indoor and outdoor activities. Unsuitable weather for outdoor activities will drive people indoors, and covered stadiums are built to protect participants in outdoor activities from the vagaries of the weather.

One of the major attributes of most tourist destinations is seasonality. Not only is there a regular round of activities associated with the seasons, there is also variation in activity in areas lacking a marked seasonal climate. This is because seasonality in areas of demand results in seasonal variations in visitation to areas of supply. Thus, for example, the desire for many Canadians to escape the Canadian winter to warmer climates creates a seasonal demand in temperate and tropical areas which do not have the same degree of annual variation in temperature.

The length of the season is also of crucial importance, particularly for private sector operators of tourist facilities. Capital is invested all year round but, for many activities and destinations, the operating period is limited and profits must be made in a short period of time. Furthermore, use is further peaked in a limited number of holidays and weekends, and a few inclement weekends may tip the balance between profit and loss. Anything which influences the length of operating seasons, be they climatic factors or otherwise (such as the length and timing of school holidays), is likely to have an impact upon the viability of tourist businesses.

It should also be remembered that the climatic and weather parameters which influence tourism, both singularly and in combination, vary from activity to activity. It may be very important, for example, to know whether precipitation falls as rain, snow, sleet, freezing rain, or ice pellets. Also, some activities are more sensitive to meteorological conditions than others. Although there is some information on the minimum climatic conditions necessary for particular activities to take place (Crowe, McKay, and Baker 1978) and suggestions have been made concerning the responses of participants in different activities to changes in the weather (Paul 1972), more work in these areas is needed.

In addition to the relatively direct impacts of climate upon tourism which have been considered, climate also impinges on tourism in a less direct fashion. Thus, for example, an abundance of snow may make the skiing conditions in a particular region very good but the journey to the slopes impossible. On a longer time scale, climatic change will influence the distribution of vegetation types, wildlife, and fish species on which some forms of tourism depend.

Much tourism takes place on or near the shoreline, and the presence of water enhances many forms of tourism even if water contact is not required. Fluctuations in climate at meso and macro scales have implications for water levels and discharge, and influence amenity and property values. Hare (1985) has pointed out that, at the low-water point of the mid-1960s in the Great Lakes, the water retreated hundreds of meters from some of the beaches and shores of Lake Huron. Furthermore, the volume of water has implications for water quality and, in some locations, such as parts of the Mediterranean and the Great Lakes where beaches are closed periodically because of pollution, this is already marginal for body-contact recreations.

The above discussion has indicated the far-reaching consequences of weather and climate for tourism. Most studies to date, however, have been based upon short term fluctuations in weather and climate; little has been written in the context of tourism on the implications of long term climatic change. Future climates will influence the viability of tourism, whether it is mass tourism or any of the alternative types suggested in this volume, and will provide challenges and threats to some destination areas while enhancing opportunities for others.

IV. The Greenhouse Effect and Climate Change

Most of the gases in the atmosphere have little effect upon the earth's radiation balance; both solar and terrestrial radiation pass through them with little hindrance. On the other hand, there are a number of gases which constitute only a small proportion of the atmosphere but which have a profound effect. These so-called "greenhouse gases" act somewhat like a greenhouse, permitting incoming radiation to pass through but absorbing heat that radiates from the earth's surface and emitting some of this heat downwards, warming the climate. Without this greenhouse effect, the earth would be about 30° C (60° F) colder than it is today. Human activities are now increasing the atmospheric concentration of greenhouse gases on a global basis, thus intensifying the greenhouse effect.

The major greenhouse gases are carbon dioxide, which is particularly associated with fossil fuel combustion and deforestation; methane, which is probably derived from agriculture, especially rice cultivation and animal husbandry; nitrous oxide, which results from the use of nitrogenous fertilizer, land clearing, biomass burning, and fossil fuel combustion; and halocarbons, particularly chlorofluorocarbons, which were introduced into the atmosphere for the first time this century. Concentrations of each of these gases continue to rise with far-reaching consequences for global climate.

The 1985 Villach meeting of the International Council of Scientific Unions, the United Nations Environment Program, and the World Meteorological Organization arrived at the following conclusions (as reported by Hare 1989). All greenhouse gases are known to be increasing as the result of human activities, and their combined future effect may be the equivalent of a doubling of carbon dioxide by the 2030s, in less than half a century. Such a doubling may induce global surface temperature increases of between 1.5 and 4.5 degrees Celsius. The impact of this warming will be greatest in high latitudes, particularly in autumn and winter. Equatorial regions will experience a lesser but still substantial warming. Much less confidence can be placed in assessments of the implications for rainfall and the hydrological cycle. However, there may be reduced moisture availability, particularly in middle latitudes, because of increased evapotranspiration coupled with an increased demand for water. Sea level may rise between 20 and 140 centimeters chiefly because of the thermal expansion of ocean waters (and only secondarily because of glacial melting). These predictions are based on direct measurement of temperature and atmospheric concentrations of greenhouse gases, estimates of future energy use and technological change, and on elaborate modeling of both the economic and ocean-atmosphere systems.

The eminent climatologist Kenneth Hare (1989) suggests that this would be a revolutionary change in world climate on a scale which is unprecedented in the history of civilization. He points out that not since the end of glacial climates a little over 10,000 years ago have temperatures changed so much or so rapidly. Possible changes in world climates resulting from the greenhouse effect are summarized in Figure 1 and Table 1. Such changes must have profound consequences for tourism, although it is not easy to suggest what these might be.

V. Implications for Global Patterns of Tourism

Since scientists and social scientists lack a crystal ball, it is not possible to indicate precisely what the implications of the greenhouse effect will be for tourism or for any other activity. It is possible, however, to make some pertinent observations.

Other things being equal, countries whose economies are currently highly dependent upon tourism would appear to be at the greatest risk. Table 2 indicates that patterns of international tourism, whether indicated by arrivals or receipts, are dominated by activity emanating from Europe and, secondarily, from North America. The leading destination countries for international tourists are indicated in Table 2. These

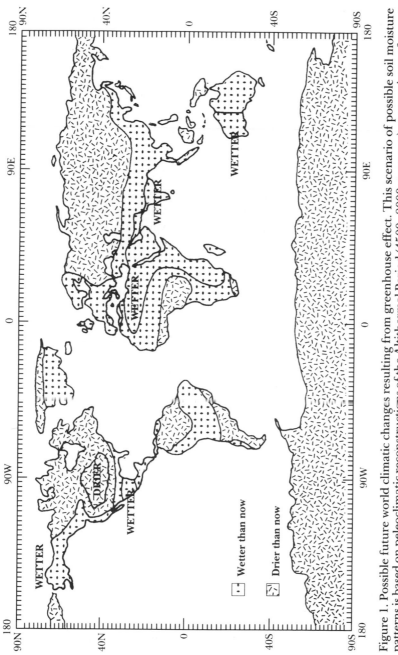

Figure 1. Possible future world climatic changes resulting from greenhouse effect. This scenario of possible soil moisture patterns is based on peleoclimatic reconstructions of the Altithermal Period (4500–8000 years ago), comparisons of recent warm and cold years in the northern hemisphere, and a climate model experiment. Where two or more sources agree on the direction of the change, the area of agreement is indicated with a dashed line and a label. Source: W. W. Kellogg and R. Schware, *Climatic Change and Society: Consequences of Increasing Atmospheric Carbon Dioxide* (Boulder, CO: Westview Press, 1981). Used by permission.

TABLE 1 Global Climate Warming Scenario

Region	Relative temperature increases	Relative change in moisture
Canada		
North	Large	Wetter(?)
South	Large	Drier
Rest of North and Central America		
United States	Moderate	Drier
Mexico	Small	Wetter
South America		
North	Small	Drier in most regions, central region may
South	Moderate	become wetter
Europe		
North	Large	Wetter
South	Moderate	Drier(?)
Africa	Small	Wetter in most regions, central region may become drier
USSR		
North	Large	Wetter(?)
South	Large	Drier
Asia		
China	Moderate	Drier
India	Small	Wetter
Oceania	Small	Wetter

countries, along with many smaller countries whose economies are dominated by tourism, have the greatest at stake.

As discussed by de Kadt and Smith in this volume (Chapters 4 and 7), many Third World countries have turned to tourism in recent years, and the rates of growth in such areas have been greater proportionately than in Europe or North America (Table 3). Absolute numbers of international tourist arrivals grew from 214.4 million in 1975 to more than 350 million (Table 4) so that even relatively small proportionate increases constitute large increases in absolute numbers. It may be unfortunate that many Third World destinations, with restricted alternative economic opportunities and limited economic buffers, have turned to tourism at a time when the natural resource base for tourism may be changing.

International tourism is only the peak of the tourist iceberg, for perhaps four out of five tourist trips do not cross international borders. The distribution of domestic travel is highly correlated on a global scale with discretionary income, and this is highly concentrated in the devel-

TABLE 2 Leading Destinations of International Tourism, 1985

	Arrivals[a]		Receipts[b]	
	Million	Rank	US $ million	Rank
Europe				
Austria	15.248	5	5 085	7
France	36.748	1	7 929	4
Germany FR	12.686	8	5 889	6
Italy	25.047	4	8 757	2
Spain	27.477	2	8 084	3
Switzerland	11.900	9	3 164	8
UK	14.449	6	6 995	5
North America				
Canada	13.171	7	3 101	9
USA	25.417	3	11 675	1
	30 other countries with 1 million +		20 other countries with US $ billion +	

[a]Arrivals at frontiers, except in Austria and Germany which refer to arrivals in registered tourist accommodation.
[b]Receipts of amounts spent in the country, except for Austria which include international fare payments.

oped nations of the western world. Domestic travel patterns are likely to be more stable than international travel in the face of global climate change because the former often take place in relatively short periods of free time, and time limitations place constraints on the destination choices of travelers (Lundgren 1989). On the other hand, outside of Europe where there are many relatively small countries in close juxtaposition, a larger proportion of international travel is long haul, and potential travelers have a multitude of destinations from which to choose. Should locations become less inviting, the international traveler may be able to switch destinations more readily than the domestic traveler. Many Third World destinations depend upon long-haul travelers and thus lack the security of a large domestic market. Hence, from this perspective also, many Third World destinations face greater uncertainty than their counterparts in the western world.

Tourists travel for a variety of motivations and not all are drawn solely by the attributes of the natural environment of the destination area. For example, many travel to visit friends and relatives, and the distribution of these travelers may remain largely unchanged unless modifications of global climate induce large, permanent migrations. Similarly, the distribution of major cities and historic sites is likely to remain much as it is today, at least in the short term.

On the other hand, destinations which rely primarily upon their

TABLE 3 Regional Distribution of International Tourism, 1975/1985
(percents)

	Arrivals		Receipts	
	1975	1985	1975	1985
Europe	72	68	65	57
North America	14	12	16	13.5
Latin America + Caribbean	6	6	9	11
East Asia + Pacific	4	8	5	10.5
Africa + M East + S Asia	4	6	5	8
World	100	100	100	100

natural resource base to attract tourists may be more at risk. Mountains and coasts are examples of such environments. Mountain ranges are extremely complex environments with major differences in climate and weather occurring over short distances. The level of resolution of the currently available general circulation models used for projecting global climates does not permit us to make statements about future climates of mountainous areas with confidence. The sea-sun-sand attractions of coastal areas as well as some historic resources, such as Venice, Italy, and the shoreline temples of Bali and Tamil Nadu, India, appear to be threatened by rising sea levels and associated increases in flooding and erosion.

Although such destinations are to be found in both temperate and tropical areas, there are many developing countries, including those of the Caribbean and elsewhere in the "south," whose tourist industries depend upon warm climates and attractive beaches. Such countries may lack the resources to combat rising sea levels and may be short of alternative attractions of sufficient quality to capture international markets. Furthermore, many such destinations have been developed with the assistance of multinational corporations which may respond to changing circumstances by seeking new opportunities elsewhere.

Temperatures are expected to increase more markedly in high rather than low latitudes. This may extend the lengths of summer seasons in middle latitudes and, coupled with milder winters, may reduce the allure of tropical climates. High latitude destinations may become more attractive and high altitude hill stations may prosper. In addition, if the tropics become even warmer, demands on energy for air conditioning and water consumption may increase in areas where such commodities are in short supply, for tourists are voracious consumers of such commodities, as is pointed out by Smith and Farrell in this volume.

The remainder of this analysis describes four case studies, all from

TABLE 4 International Tourism Arrivals and Receipts, 1975–1985, 1986, 1987

	Arrivals		Receipts	
	Million	*± percent*	*US $ bil*	*± percent*
1975	214.4		40.7	
1976	220.7	+3.0	44.4	+ 9.2
1977	239.1	+8.3	55.6	+25.2
1978	257.4	+7.6	68.8	+23.7
1979	274.0	+6.5	83.3	+21.1
1980	284.8	+4.0	102.4	+22.8
1981	285.1	+0.1	101.7	− 0.7
1982	286.8	+0.6	98.6	− 3.0
1983	292.8	+2.1	98.8	+ 0.2
1984	319.3	+9.0	103.6	+ 4.9
1985	333.8	+4.6	108.6	+ 4.8
1986 P	341.4	+2.3	129.2	+19.0
1987 P	355.0	+4.0	150.0	+16.1

P = provisional

Canada, which evaluate the implications of climate change for specific settings. These illustrate the kinds of research that can be undertaken given the current availability of information.

VI. Case Studies

As in much research assessing the socioeconomic implications of climate change, two scenarios for climate change associated with a doubling in atmospheric concentrations of carbon dioxide have been employed here and their implications assessed. Scenario A is based on a model developed by the Geophysical Fluid Dynamics Laboratory at Princeton University, whereas Scenario B uses output from a similar analysis undertaken by the Goddard Institute for Space Studies.

While these and similar models constitute the most sophisticated attempts to project carbon-induced climatic change, their limitations should be considered. First and foremost, it should be recognized that the projections are uncertain and cannot be verified. Second, the models employ coarse and different grids so that they are not completely comparable, and extrapolations have to be used to obtain information for specific locations. Given these and other related problems, the scenarios are best regarded as possible futures rather than predictions of the future. Nevertheless, in spite of their limitations, these scenarios constitute the best estimates of future climate, and thus they are the sources of data on future climate employed in the case studies.

Even if the scenarios evolve as projected, it is improbable that they will be experienced in a world which has not changed in other ways. It is an impossible task to predict what the world will be like in fifty years. Thus, in order to proceed, the assumption was made that, except for the changes in climate, all other things will remain as they are. No allowances were made for technological changes or policy initiatives which might modify the climate changes. Furthermore, it was assumed that future tourists will respond to the new climates in a similar fashion to which they respond to weather and climate at present. It was further assumed that variability about future climatic norms will be similar to that which is experienced at present. Tourism was examined in isolation: little attempt was made to investigate the implications of changes in tourism for other activities or economic sectors or, conversely, to assess the impacts of changes in those activities or society as a whole for tourism. Certainly it may be misleading to consider climate and tourism out of context, but it is necessary to do this when that context cannot be established.

Four case studies were undertaken. Two considered changes in the resource base: a national park (Prince Albert National Park, Saskatchewan) and selected wetlands (Point Pelee and Presqu'île in Ontario) were chosen for examination. Detailed investigations were also undertaken of the implications of climate change for skiing (a winter activity) and camping (a summer activity) in Ontario.

Space does not permit the detailed discussion of either methods or results. The interested reader can gain further information from the sources for each study which are identified below. The following sections present brief highlights of these studies.

Prince Albert National Park

The Canadian National Park System, which is an important tourism resource, is based to a considerable extent on biophysical factors and ecological principles. Biophysical factors play a role in the definition of national parks, park selection processes, ongoing management, and interpretation. In addition, management tools such as zoning, the content of interpretive programs, and the determination of appropriate recreational activities are based upon the biophysical attributes of each park. Management of natural phenomena, such as flora and fauna, is directly associated with ecology and habitat and, therefore, climate. Should climate changes occur, the implications for the national park system and for individual parks are likely to be far reaching.

Selecting vegetation as the central variable of concern since it is the basis of habitat and a good indicator of environmental change, the objectives of the research were to describe future climatic conditions and corresponding vegetation changes for Prince Albert National Park and to explore the array of potential implications of climate change for the study area and for the management of national parks (Vetsch 1986; Wall in press). Climate scenarios suggest that Prince Albert National Park is likely to experience a warmer, drier climate in the future. Detailed examinations of theories of vegetation responses to environmental stimuli, climatic impacts upon vegetation, historical evidence of vegetation distributions, species ecology, disturbance factors such as fire and grazing, and factors affecting species distribution constitute the basis for speculating on the vegetation changes to be expected in Prince Albert National Park under the climate change scenarios.

Based on these analyses, likely vegetation changes in Prince Albert National Park include an increase in the proportion of grassland in the park at the expense of boreal forest. Special resources within the park will be impacted by climate change with associated implications for park zoning, interpretive themes, and recreation. Five such changes are outlined below.

1. The Transition from Grasslands to Boreal Forest

The transition zone, or ecotone, between Boreal Forest and Grassland biomes is an important resource management and interpretive theme represented in the park. The edges of the biomes may be among the first areas to respond to an environmental change, with implications for the position and prominence of the transition zone. If climatic change is prolonged, it is conceivable that the bulk of the transition zone may move north of the park. These vegetation changes may create the need to reevaluate the unique and representative features of the park. In the immediate to short term future, opportunities may exist to increase the emphasis placed on dynamic environmental processes in interpretation.

2. Fescue Grasslands

The small areas of Fescue Grasslands are regarded as a special feature of the park because they are an outlier of the larger areas of Fescue Grasslands occurring approximately 60 kilometers to the south and because, for the past several decades, aspen has been encroaching onto the grasslands, decreasing suitable habitat for elk and bison. Climatic change will promote the perpetuation of grassland communities in the park and could decrease the need for their special preservation as presently exists. However, continual alterations in the natural state of similar grasslands outside the park suggest that the Fescue Grassland communities contained within the park will still remain an anomaly for the region.

3. American White Pelicans

The only protected breeding colony of American white pelicans in Canada is situated on Heron Island in Lavalee Lake near the north-western border of the park. Changes in climate, as depicted in the scenarios, may have deleterious effects by changing lake water levels, exposing nesting islands to the shore and allowing the invasion of predators. However, the zero degree (centigrade) April isotherm approximates the southern boundary of American white pelican range, as it reflects the availability of fish at the time of the birds' arrival in their nesting areas. Climatic change will extend the ice-free period, potentially opening up suitable habitat north of present park boundaries.

4. Woodland Caribou

Woodland caribou in Prince Albert National Park are at the southern margin of their range and are concentrated in the northern portion of the park. They are considered a special feature of the park since they are generally found in more northern regions and because they are considered to be a rare species in Canada. The herd of approximately 38 animals migrates in and out of the park but does not move great distances. Preferred habitat is mature coniferous forest, such as black spruce muskeg, but this should decrease under warmer, drier climatic conditions. This might force caribou to find suitable habitat farther north, leaving no woodland caribou in the park.

5. Free Roaming Bison

The park supports a herd of free roaming bison whose primary habitat is the ecotone between grassland and forest. Encroachment on grassland by aspen and other woody growth has decreased bison habitat, causing them to move out of the park more frequently to neighboring agricultural lands. Bison in this situation are not protected and have caused some conflicts with landowners. A future warming trend should increase the area of bison habitat in the park, reduce their need to roam, and help to reduce land use conflicts.

Thus, under scenario conditions, changes could occur in the resources currently deemed special or rare. For instance, the Fescue

Grasslands may no longer require special management for preservation but portions of the Boreal Forest may increase in significance. The summer recreation season will elongate and the winter season shorten, possibly resulting in greater recreation pressures. Increased land use pressures brought on by more frequent drought (as depicted in the scenarios) might result in a desire to convert currently marginal lands to agricultural uses. Such pressures may be manifest in increased conflicts between parks and uses of land for other purposes.

Climatic change also has implications for the amount of land devoted to parks, the size of each individual park, park selection and designation, and boundary delineation. The parks have a mandate to protect endangered species and to act as ecological reserves. Prospects of climatic change, and increased vulnerability of resources to such change, suggest a greater relevance of climatic criteria to the processes for designating parks and other reserves. For example, where possible, boundary designation should allow for the migration of ecosystems. The scenarios suggest a greater magnitude of climatic change in more northerly latitudes; hence, in such situations, greater emphasis should be given to placing parks in locations which are climatically optimal for the species being protected. There is a greater need for large parks with ecologically responsive boundaries. In northern regions, the concept of ecological islands is not viable because of the extensive migratory paths of many animals. How does one successfully design ecologically optimal locations when the impending climatic change is wide ranging and the animals that are being protected are highly mobile? It is clear that climatic change has far-reaching consequences for individual parks and for park systems which are beyond the scope of this report but which merit further investigation.

Wetlands

The consensus of climatologists is that the future climate of Canada may be warmer and drier than at present. One of the consequences of this is likely to be a lowering of lake levels with implications for the character and tourism potential of shoreline ecosystems. Some of the greatest impacts of lake level changes will occur along the margins of the Great Lakes where wetlands constitute important waterfowl habitat and a source of recreation for many people.

Point Pelee National Park and Presqu'île Provincial Park in southern Ontario were selected as study sites (Wall et al. 1986a). Both contain large areas of marsh which are of considerable importance for wildlife and recreation; however, they also constitute two different kinds of wetland systems with the potential to respond differently to changes in water level. Point Pelee is a closed, protected marsh which is separated from the lake by natural barrier beaches. In contrast, the marsh of Presqu'île is an open wetland system. In both cases, the marshes are not influenced to any great degree by runoff from the mainland, and water levels in Lake Ontario are a primary determinant of vegetational composition and functioning of the marshes.

In naturally confined marshes such as Pelee, lowered lake levels will cause the marsh to revert to marsh meadow and, eventually, to dry land. Because of the protective sand spits, the marsh will be prevented from moving lakeward and vegetation will shift from hydric to mesic conditions. Some plant species may change growth form to accommodate to drier conditions, but vegetation will change dramatically as species intolerant of drying die and are replaced by species emerging from buried seeds. The trees which mark the landward edge of the marsh may advance due to a lowering of the flood line.

Wetland species diversity will decline and the suitability of the marshes as a habitat for recreationally and commercially valued species, such as migrating waterfowl and muskrats, will be reduced. Sport fishing may also be affected by the reduced quality of shoreline marshes where fish feed and spawn. Other non-consumptive activities, such as canoeing and ice skating, will decline due to the lack of open water. The frequency of fires is likely to increase. In time, the marsh may lose its wetland character and, under extreme conditions, the waterfowl migration route may change, resulting in the collapse of hunting and, more importantly, bird watching.

In open shoreline marshes such as Presqu'île, the effects of lowered lake levels are unlikely to be as severe. Instead of a draining of the marsh and a trend toward dry land, there will probably be a shift in the vegetation in a lakeward direction. The extent of this shift depends on the magnitude of the lake level change, the slope of the bottom profile, and the suitability of the substrate. It is evident that the impacts of climatic change on shoreline ecosystems will vary considerably with the physiography of the littoral.

Presumably, should water levels in the Great Lakes fall, then, other things being equal and given sufficient time, a new equilibrium will develop that will include the establishment of new wetlands in locations where the physiography of the littoral is suitable. However, unfortunately, other things are unlikely to be equal. Many of the major wetlands are currently under protection in national, state, or provincial parks or some other heritage designation. There is no guarantee that locations with wetland potential will be under public jurisdiction, and existing users may discourage the development of new areas adjacent to their property. The requirements of other users, such as navigation and power generation, which may encourage dredging and filling or stabilization of water levels, will also militate against the formation of new wetlands. What are managers of existing wetlands to do if their holdings become less interesting ecologically and the reasons for their designation removed?

The points which have been made with respect to wetlands and Prince Albert National Park are applicable in a more general form to other ecosystems. A warming trend should lead to a poleward movement of biomes. In many parts of the world, however, natural areas are islands embedded in vast areas of modified landscapes, and in the absence of obvious routes for the spread of species or assemblages, it is unclear how the relocation of ecosystems will occur. Many parks, including the Canadian national and Ontario provincial parks, have been established partly on ecological criteria. In some cases they have been designated as being representative of existing natural regions and, in others, as an attempt to preserve particular species. What is natural in an era of pervasive, human-induced change? Climate change thus poses fundamental questions concerning both the designation and management of natural areas and the natural resource base for tourism and recreation.

Downhill Skiing

As has been discussed, much tourism is seasonal and there are strict climatic requirements for tourist activities to be possible or enjoyed. It follows that anything which alters the length of seasons is likely to have repercussions for the activities of tourists and for businesses which cater to them. Downhill skiing is one such activity.

Two areas of Ontario were selected for detailed study (McBoyle and Wall 1986). The South Georgian Bay area was selected as a southern ski area and the Lakehead, near Thunder Bay, was chosen from northern Ontario. Together, these two areas constitute the major downhill ski areas in the province. The following procedures were undertaken:

1. Snow cover periods suitable for skiing were determined for present-day conditions as well as for conditions suggested by the scenarios using criteria suggested by Crowe, Baker, and McKay (1978).
2. Data on current skier visits and expenditures were used in conjunction with estimated season lengths to calculate changes in the number of skier visits and the economic consequences of the climate scenarios.
3. Sensitivity analyses were conducted to determine the likely im-

pacts of various small changes in temperature and precipitation combinations.

The ski season was divided into two major categories: the "reliable season" in which there is a 75 percent or greater probability of there being suitable snow cover for skiing, and the "marginally reliable" in which there is a probability of between 50 and 75 percent of there being suitable snow cover. For the Lakehead under scenario A, the present marginally reliable or better season will be reduced from 131 days to 91 days, a reduction of 30.5 percent (Figure 2). Further reductions in both the reliable and marginally reliable seasons occur under scenario B. Although the reductions in the ski seasons are large, the key Christmas break, when 20 percent of the year's business is done, and the university/college mid-February break still fall within the reliable ski season. The elimination of skiing in March, when 20 percent of skier visits currently occur, is the major loss and, under scenario A, will result in a reduction of annual skier expenditures at the resorts of $1.9 million in 1985 Canadian dollars. However, it may not be necessary to endure all of this reduced business because of the possibility of an enhanced ability to draw upon the southern Ontario market.

The South Georgian Bay region, which is climatically marginal for skiing at present, does not fare as well as the Lakehead. The present-day marginally reliable ski season of 70 days will be reduced to 40 days under scenario A and will disappear altogether under scenario B. There will be no reliable ski season under scenario A or B.

The calculations associated with both scenarios suggest the virtual elimination of the ski industry in the South Georgian Bay area with a loss to the resorts in 1985 Canadian dollars of $36.5 million per annum in skier spending and a reduction of $412.8 million per annum in the retail trade of Collingwood, the major service center. This is in addition to the millions of dollars invested in infrastructure by the ski industry.

These conclusions, particularly with respect to the South Georgian Bay area, may appear to be extreme. However, an analysis of climatic variability indicates that this is not the case, and average conditions as indicated by the scenarios are experienced occasionally under the present climatic regime. Furthermore, it is not necessary for climatic change to be as great as that suggested in the scenarios for there to be a marked decrease in the length of the ski season in the South Georgian Bay area.

Tourists are extremely mobile and may be able to divert their patronage from one destination to another with relative ease. It follows that the evaluation of specific sites, in the absence of a consideration of broader opportunities, may lead to misleading results. Detailed results

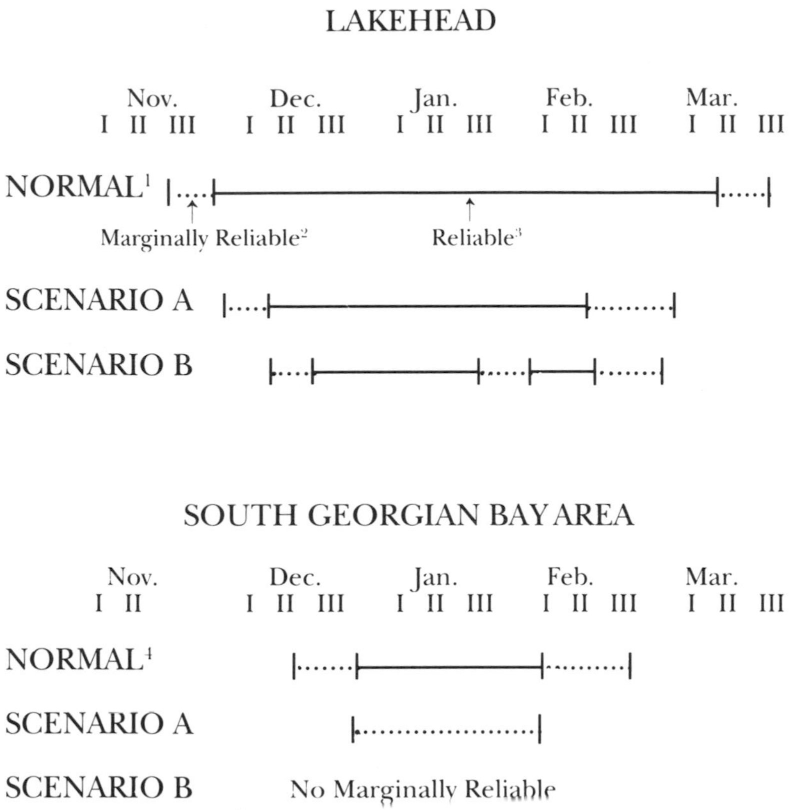

LAKEHEAD

	Nov.	Dec.	Jan.	Feb.	Mar.
	I II III	I II III	I II III	I II III	I II III

NORMAL[1] |...|├────────────────────────┤|.....|

↑ Marginally Reliable[2]   ↑ Reliable[3]

SCENARIO A |....|├──────────────┤|.........|

SCENARIO B |...|├──────────┤|....|├──┤|......|

SOUTH GEORGIAN BAY AREA

	Nov.	Dec.	Jan.	Feb.	Mar.
	I II	I II III	I II III	I II III	I II III

NORMAL[4] |......|├────────────┤|.........|

SCENARIO A |├....................┤|

SCENARIO B   No Marginally Reliable

I: - 1st to 10th day of month.
II: - 11th to 20th day of month.
III:- 21st to end of month.

1 Present day snow cover suitability percentiles for skiing calculated using data from Thunder Bay Airport.
2 Marginally Reliable: 50-74% probability of suitable snow cover for skiing.
3 Reliable: 75% or greater probability of suitable snow cover for skiing.
4 Present day snow cover suitability percentiles for skiing calculated using average values from Essa, Meaford and Thombury.

Figure 2. Periods with suitable snow cover for skiing in the Lakehead and South Georgian Bay areas under normal, scenario A, and scenario B conditions. Source: G. McBoyle and G. Wall, "Recreation and climatic change: a Canadian case study," *Ontario Geography* 28 (1986): 51–68. Used by permission.

have been presented above for two areas in Ontario, but results of analyses of other areas are beginning to emerge. For example, research on the Laurentians in Quebec indicates that skiing may also be curtailed in that location (McBoyle and Wall 1987; Lamothe and Periard 1988). Unpublished results for Michigan suggest similar results as for Ontario, that is, that the downhill ski resorts in the south of the state will struggle, but resorts in the north may continue to operate successfully but with slightly diminished operating seasons.

Diversification of activities, such as the addition of golf courses or water slides, is suggested as a management response, for the summer season may be lengthened and, in such ways, it may be possible to defray winter losses through summer gains.

Camping

Camping is both an activity undertaken by tourists and a form of tourist accommodation, and it was selected as being a good indicator of summer activities. Much as was done in the preceding section of skiing, present and future lengths of the camping season were calculated for eight provincial parks in Ontario (Wall et al. 1986b). It was assumed that any elongated season would result in the same amount of activity in the additional weeks as is present at the margins of the current, normal season.

There are considerable regional differences in season length, with parks in the south experiencing a longer season climatically (although not necessarily administratively) than those farther north. Because of lake effects, however, a simple north-south pattern does not exist. In all cases, the reliable camping season is extended under both scenarios, sometimes by as much as 40 days. Marginally reliable seasons are displaced earlier in the spring and later in the fall.

Information on numbers of campers, their lengths of stay, and their expenditures were then used to calculate the economic implications of the extended seasons. Should campers take advantage of the extended potential camping seasons, there would be positive economic implications which vary in magnitude in different parts of the province. However, these economic benefits may occur at the expense of increased environmental deterioration, as the parks host more visitors for longer periods of time.

It is important to acknowledge that impacts are not always negative, that change need not necessarily be bad, and that climate change may create opportunities as well as problems. The outlook is rosy for Ontario enterprises catering to the summer tourist provided that they are not likely to be adversely affected by declining water levels or the reduced availability of water.

VII. Summary and Conclusions

This analysis has been concerned with the implications of atmospheric processes for tourism. Although a literature has evolved elsewhere which examines aspects of the links between climate and tourism, virtually nothing has been written concerning the implications of climate change for tourism. This is a serious oversight at a time when mankind may be facing one of the most rapid, global climate changes in human history. The greenhouse effect and the likely climate changes to which it will give rise will likely impinge upon tourism at a global scale and may lead to diverse and profound consequences of global climate change for tourism.

The tourism development alternatives available to destination areas will be modified by global climate change. Global climate change will present both problems and opportunities for destination areas. The climate changes which have been discussed are projected to occur within the lifetimes of many current investment projects and within the lifetimes of many of the earth's present residents. Although the implications for tourism are likely to be profound, very few tourism researchers have begun to formulate relevant questions, let alone develop methodologies which will further understanding of the nature and magnitude of the challenges which lie ahead.

Epilogue: A Research Agenda on the Variability of Tourism

Dennison Nash

I. Introduction

The articles in this volume represent an interesting attempt to come to grips with some of the implications of tourism's variability. At the Academy seminar in which many of the original papers were presented, in Zakopane, Poland, in the summer of 1989, the increasingly popular concept of Alternative Tourism was subjected to intense scrutiny. Some participants eventually came to accept a point of view, suggested by Lanfant and de Kadt, that the term often represents an ideology that has emerged in reaction to the undesirable consequences of mainstream Western tourism; others noted the term was fraught with ambiguity, as is discussed in Butler's contribution to this volume. After a series of contentious sessions, the participants at the seminar came to feel that the term had little value as a scientific concept and that, considering the variety of touristic forms—each with the potential for generating desirable and undesirable consequences—it would probably be better to replace the term with the phrase "Alternative Forms of Tourism."

Thus, the seminar seemed to have rejected the politically or morally informed viewpoint that has characterized a good deal of consideration of the subject, a position that Jafari (1990) has referred to as the Adaptancy Platform (if one thinks that tourism is something benign) or the Cautionary Platform (if one thinks that it is necessary to be on guard against tourism or even reject it outright). A well-known illustration of the latter platform is to be found in Davydd Greenwood's angry denunciation of the tourism-induced degeneration of the Basque *alarde* ritual in Fuentarrabia, a position that he has subsequently regarded as unfortunate (1977/1989). Confronted with a concept which seemed to crystallize all of the implications of such a position, the members of the seminar took the significant step of arguing for the adoption of a line of inquiry in which, ideally, scientific concepts are generated only by scientific questions and theoretical necessity, a position that Jafari (1990) has termed the Knowledge Based Platform. (See also the Preface to this volume for a summary of Jafari's discussion.)

The phrase Alternative Forms of Tourism recognizes the obvious fact that tourism, however viewed, is variable within and across cultures. The theoretical implications of this fact are only lightly touched on in the papers in this volume, but the way does appear to be open for research that will work through these implications. What I want to do here is sketch out the nature of the theoretical foundation that will permit us to carry out such a research program.

II. A Conceptual Overview

However tourists and tourism are ultimately defined, the fact of travel must be taken into account. This means that tourism, whether domestic or international, involves transactions between different peoples, which is implied by the title of one of the preeminent works in the field, *Hosts and Guests,* edited by Valene Smith (1977/1989). Nash (1981:562) points out that such transactions take place in a *touristic process* "originating with the generation of tourists in some society or subsociety, continuing as these tourists travel to other places where they encounter hosts with a different culture, and ending as the give and take of the encounter affects the tourists, those who serve them, and the various societies or subsocieties involved."

In addition, Nash points out that this process may take the form of a *touristic system* "which can be embedded in some broader context." Barbados may thus be seen to be part of a farflung touristic network that includes potential clients in a number of countries, travel agencies, cruise lines, airlines, investors, food and other providers, and the like. Lanfant (1980:22) alludes to this in her pieces on international tourism in which she suggests that "tourism indirectly causes the different national societies to become gradually interlinked in economic, social, and cultural networks that are organized internationally on the basis of a central decision-making body and at the same time cut across national reference systems." She may be overdoing the power of tourism to effect such a development, as well as the concentration of decision making, but the fact that such systems do exist in the modern world would seem to be indisputable.

Where does the emergence of the concept of Alternative Tourism fit into all of this? It would seem to stand for a reaction by Third World interests and their sympathizers to the present world touristic system, which, in its mainstream form, they see as exploitative of Third World hosts. Important exponents of this point of view are the Ecumenical Coalition on Third World Tourism and the Third World Tourism European Ecumenical Network (ECTWT 1986; Millman 1988; Srisang 1990) which have condemned such tourism as an imperialistic arrangement in which powerful metropoles impose their leisure ways to the detriment of peoples in the Third World (the Cautionary Platform). Alternative Tourism is seen as a way in which these peoples can increase their control and promote a more sustainable and humane form of tourism development (the Adaptancy Platform).

The depredations of mass tourism in the Third World are real enough for people to be moved ethically or politically, but researchers committed to the Knowledge Based Platform could profit by seeing the issue as framed in terms of the concepts of *touristic process* and *touristic system*, as mentioned above. Seen in this way, tourism may or may not be the root of the troubles experienced by hosts in the Third World. The issue is, rather, dependency, which can be promoted not only by tourism but through other transactions. For example, Smith (1989:75–77) has argued that tourism is not a major agent of change among Alaskan Eskimos. Instead, one should consider the development of extractive industries, the contest between the United States and Russia, and U.S. governmental policies on welfare. The student of tourism would see the Alternative Tourism movement as an attempt by Third World interests to shape touristic and possibly other transactions in which they are involved to their better advantage.

The notions of *touristic process* and *touristic system* permit us to go still further in considering the forces that are responsible for the Alternative Tourism movement. An important protest against Western, mainstream tourism may also be generated in the metropoles that produce the tourists who find their way to the Third World. There, a host of movements to save the environment and the world's peoples from various industrial and other excesses (e.g., Krippendorf 1986) may contribute to the reaction against mass tourism. All such protests could be instrumental in getting the purveyors of modern tourism to recognize, however dimly, that practices which are not sustainable may not be viable. Then, as de Kadt suggests in Chapter 3 in this volume, the decision makers in some international tourism system, wherever they are, will feel the pressure to reorient themselves and consider the sustainability of their tourisms in making their calculations. How, otherwise, can we account for the fact that cruise operators are becoming more careful with the processing and disposal of the garbage they generate?

All this suggests that there are a number of actors in a specific touristic process and that each of these actors has more or less power to shape the nature of touristic transactions and, therefore, their consequences. The concepts of *touristic process* and *touristic system* invite us to consider the relevant actors in any specific case and how they operate. As John Pigram suggests in Chapter 4, any one of these actors (including, presumably, applied researchers) can propose a course of action. How the proposal will be greeted and ultimately disposed of is up to the other actors. Who are they who have the power to propose and dispose, and what are the consequences of their actions? We need much theoretically informed, methodologically adequate research to tell us about that.

III. The Variety of Tourism

The existence of a multiplicity of tourism forms in the contemporary world was recognized early on by Cohen (1972), who spoke of four kinds of tourists, and Smith (1977), who speaks of seven. Nash (1979a) points out that different forms of tourism in a society also can be discerned in premodern societies such as ancient Greece. Nevertheless, it does seem possible to agree with the contention that there has been an increase in touristic diversity in the modernizing process. Modernization generally is thought to involve increasing social differentiation; a multiplication of touristic forms appears to go hand in hand with that. As Nash (1979a:22) points out: "The intrasocietal distinctions in touristic activity that are barely apparent among horticulturalists are more obvious in agricultural societies with cities and states." Do the differences continue to increase in all industrial societies? The case of socialist societies with their purported leveling mechanisms gives one pause in making an affirmative generalization, but in any case, the fact of touristic variability in modern societies is well established and has suggested to de Kadt that in them "new alternative forms of tourism will continue to evolve spontaneously." Boyer (1972:19, 66) points out that the French take a number of different kinds of vacations, and approximately half of them do not take any vacation at all. And in the Soviet Union, routine statistics have been compiled on different forms of Russian tourism (see, e.g., Pirojnik 1989).

At any point along the touristic process, it is possible to discern a variety of touristic forms. Consider the host end where tourism development takes place. The Alternative Tourism movement may see only two general kinds of development here: good or bad. Douglas Pearce's contribution in this volume (Chapter 1) expresses the inadequacy of such a view where science is concerned. He points out that there are many forms of tourism development more or less depending on the point of view used to make the classification. Each of these is seen to have its own nature and to be capable of producing desirable or undesirable consequences.

The fact that different forms of tourism exist in a given context raises an interesting question of integration that is only lightly touched on in these articles. At any point along the touristic process, the issue of integration is the same, that is, how do different parts of any touristic system fit together? It would seem that mountain climbing and skiing are mutually compatible. What about power boating and sailing? That a considerable range of touristic activities can go together simultaneously and sequentially is obvious in any modern resort where an attitude of "the more-the-merrier" seems to be the rule. The range of activities offered at St. Moritz or a Club Med vacation village is dizzying to contemplate. In economic terms, the management of a modern resort seems to be constantly seeking to increase the diversity of the product offered at any given time and sequentially throughout the course of the year. Thus, what was formerly a specialized ski resort becomes a mecca for hikers and a center for golf, tennis, swimming, "culture," and business conferences. And with the addition of facilities that control the environment, as, for example, indoor tennis and swimming, it becomes possible to extend the range of activities still further. But there must be natural and sociocultural constraints that set limits on what activities will hang together and dictate the nature of their integration. What is the central principle that informs the various elements of a given tourist complex? Some notion of such a principle must have guided a consulting agency to recommend three centers of tourism development for one Third World location, in a situation known to the author. One center would be concerned with the active renewal of the individual, another for rest and relaxation, and another for promoting family vacation life. Each of these centers would offer a range of presumably compatible activities. An interesting line of research would attempt to uncover the underlying principles involved.

Our awareness of the variety of touristic forms has been increased still further by cross-cultural investigation. Initial research on tourism tended to concentrate on more developed metropoles such as in Europe and the United States and their domestic or foreign host satellites. This research has been expanded to include contemporary metropoles at all levels of development ranging from hunting and gathering to industrial (Nash 1979a). There have been studies that involve tourist generating situations in Sri Lanka (Pfaffenberger 1983), India (Ichaporia 1983), Japan (Moeran 1983; Ikkai 1988), and Mexico (Passariello 1983). And at last we are becoming acquainted with the tourism of centrally planned economies (Mosher 1988; RDNTA 1989; Allcock and Przeclawski 1990).

Further information about tourism's variability has come from historically oriented scholars. As far as Western history is concerned, we now know more about tourism in Salzburg from the Middle Ages to the present (Stadler 1975); aristocratic tourism in Nice from the eighteenth to the twentieth century (Nash 1979b); the famous Grand Tour of Europe (Brodsky-Porges 1981; Towner 1985, 1988); and tourism in the Middle Ages (Jusserand 1929/1980), ancient Rome (Balsdon 1969), and ancient Greece (Becker 1895).

There is, then, a growing body of information about the variety of tourism in contemporary and past societies. We now know a good deal more than we did before, but how sound is the information at our disposal? Dann, Nash, and Pearce (1988) do not give the field of tourism studies very high marks for methodological rigor. Until we are reasonably certain of the empirical grounding of our data, it will not be possible to make the kind of comparisons on which the analytical approach called for by Crick (1989; 338) depends. At this stage of tourism study, inadequacy of data should make us cautious about explanations. Still, the way seems open to pursue them.

IV. Explanations

How do we explain the variability of tourism within and between societies? Though the explanation of tourism in general may be beyond us at the moment, the question of why different forms of tourism emerge and continue to exist can be addressed. Why did the English at one time ignore the mountains, but later take to them with so much enthusiasm? Why is summer now the high season on Mediterranean shores while a century ago it was winter? Why do some people visit their relatives when on vacation while others do not? Why do some people tramp about on their own while others prefer organized tour groups in motor coaches? Why do some tourists travel farther than others? These and a host of other questions involving various forms of tourism call out for explanations.

Some steps along this research road have been taken by Nelson Graburn and his associates in a special issue of the *Annals of Tourism Research* devoted to the anthropology of tourism. Graburn (1983) suggests in his introduction to that volume a number of actors that may account for a society's or subsociety's touristic styles. These factors certainly are not exhaustive and need to be tested further in the cross-cultural domain, but they do give us a start toward explaining different forms of tourism. Such factors may be included in a general theoretical perspective that has been fairly broadly accepted in sociology and anthropology. In this view, any sociocultural system contains behavior, to which the term superstructure can be applied, and other behavior that can be referred to by the term infrastructure. There may be some terminological problems here because the word "infrastructure" has had a slightly different connotation where tourism development is concerned. Such things as roads, electricity, and water are often considered to be infrastructural elements. The intent is the same, however. It is that without these elements, tourism, or a specific form of tourism, could not develop.

Depending on one's specific theoretical perspective, it has been argued that such infrastructural factors as social relations, productive relations, personality structure, and wealth tend to initiate things, while superstructural phenomena such as art, philosophy, and religion tend to respond. Though superstructural elements have not been conceived as wholly reactive nor infrastructural factors wholly determined, the view has been that certain aspects of any sociocultural system may be thought of primarily as independent variables and others as dependent. From the tourist-generating end of the touristic process, it would seem that tourism can be seen mainly as a dependent variable and, therefore, an aspect of superstructure. The notion of tourism as a form of leisure, which Nash (1981; Nash and Smith 1991) has insisted on, suggests this.

From some specific theoretical viewpoint then, one can propose a series of hypotheses that account for the variability of tourism as superstructures in terms of infrastructural differences. Consider discretionary income, which has been proposed by Graburn (1983:19–20) as a factor that generates and maintains touristic patterns. Clearly, it helps to explain why some people take vacations and others don't; moreover, it sets up an array of explanations of touristic forms in terms of income. This line of explanation has been used by the Research Department of the National Tourism Administration, People's Republic of China (RDNTA 1989) by employing standard of living as an infrastructural element. This is only a simple beginning, of course, but it shows how a theoretically oriented research program could proceed.

At this moment, no one specific theoretical viewpoint seems to provide the best orientation for such a research program. This would seem to be due to the fact that research on tourism by social scientists has not so far been very sophisticated theoretically. Consider the article by Patricia Albers and William James (1983) on picture postcards of the Great Lakes Indians, which fits nicely into the infrastructural-superstructural perspective. These authors see picture postcards as reflecting and reinforcing the stereotyped image of the American Indian generated in American society. But what infrastructural aspect of that society best explains the production of this image, and thus, touristic preoccupations? A good deal of theoretical work needs to be done before questions like this can be answered.

At the host end of the touristic process, particularly in a place like the U.S. Virgin Islands where tourism has become the dominant institution (see Lewis 1972), tourism acts in the way infrastructures are supposed to act. That is, it plays a significant role in shaping the society as a whole and its environment. What are the consequences of different kinds of touristic input for different host societies and their environment? On this important question, the Alternative Tourism movement is not alone in rushing to judgment. As has been mentioned above, early tourism researchers often jumped to scientifically unjustified conclusions. As Dann, Nash, and Pearce (1988) make clear, the demonstration that a particular touristic input has a particular consequence is not always easy to accomplish. Studies that are more adequate methodologically and theoretically sophisticated need to be carried out. Hypotheses raised by earlier research, as, for example, in the well-known compendiums edited by de Kadt (1979) and Smith (1977/1989), can serve as a useful starting point. Such research can also be made to address the applied issue raised in this volume by Bryan Farrell and Richard Butler (Chapters 6 and 2) concerning sustainability. De Kadt, Pigram, and Wall as well treat this matter in ways that surely will involve readers in this pressing issue.

It now seems possible to envisage research in various host situations that will help us form a working understanding of the range of possibilities here. But such research will have to keep in mind the constituent elements of the touristic system that are operative in a given case. From a broad, Olympian perspective, one might be able to ask: what are the infrastructural elements that generate the tourism that extends out to host satellites to produce certain consequences for them?

It should be clear by now that research on any aspect of tourism requires an understanding of where it fits into some touristic system and its context as well as an identification of the relevant actors in it. The Alternative Tourism movement appears to have been heavily influenced by Dependency Theory, which tends to divide the capitalist world into two camps: the exploiters and the exploited. Satellite host societies in the Third World are seen to be relatively powerless to affect touristic events and are therefore exploited.

Viewed this way, the kind of tourism a society gets, the manner in which it operates, and the effects that follow are mostly dictated by outside centers. Such a view may be appropriate for exploring small, weak countries like the Gambia. But what about cases where more powerful countries such as those in Europe have become hosts in some touristic system? Or consider even some lesser developed countries such as Albania and North Korea (see Hall 1990), which still have the power to shape the tourism they get. Obviously, the distribution of power in different touristic systems varies. This means that theories other than Dependency will have to be considered to account for some tourism development. Thus, an increased awareness of the variety of touristic systems forces us to become more sophisticated theoretically. Needless to say, we have a long way to go in this regard.

V. Conclusion

The consideration of the concept of Alternative Tourism in this volume has been scientifically productive in a number of ways. First, it has identified the term for what it is, that is, an ideological concept that leaves something to be desired as a scientific or social scientific tool. By seeing it as a reflection of a contemporary social movement, the contributors to this volume have attempted to put it in its proper place. One wonders whether this could have been so easily accomplished if there had been more Third World participants in the seminar in Zakopane at which many of the papers were originally presented and the concepts rigorously discussed. It may not be easy to strive for scientific purity in the midst of the pressing problems that have played a part in the development of the concept. Furthermore, by proposing the phrase "Alternative Forms of Tourism" as a replacement, the participants in the seminar recognized the obvious variability of contemporary tourism which, though not new, seems to have increased during the course of modernization. This volume clearly shows that the recognition of such variability provides fertile ground for research on tourism.

The foundations for exploring the variety of tourism, its sources and consequences, already have been laid. By keeping in mind the concepts of *touristic process* and *touristic system,* in which various actors play a part in creating and maintaining different forms of tourism, the student of tourism will be able to comprehend fully what is going on in a specific case. Then the idea that tourism acts as a kind of superstructure can be used to account for what transpires in the process or system. The scientific agenda for analyzing tourism's variability, therefore, would seem to be set. All of the social sciences have something to contribute to our understanding of the subject. There has been an active give and take and some sharing between disciplines, but as Crick (1989:312) points out, it does not seem possible to "envisage a change in the fragmentary multidisciplinary nature of the field." It now seems clear that any synthesis that develops will neither involve some unified theory of tourism nor some specific methodology to study it. But it may be possible for researchers in the various disciplines to share an overview of touristic phenomena that lends coherence to their investigations into the variety of touristic forms that have been celebrated in this volume. Here, I have simply tried to point out that such an overview already exists.

References

Adler, J. 1985. On the road: reflections on the history of tramping. *Annals of Tourism Research* 12(3):335–54.

Aisner, P. and C. Pluss. 1983. *La ruée vers le soleil: le tourisme à destination du Tiers-Monde.* Paris: L'Harmattan.

Albers P. and W. James. 1983. Tourism and the changing image of the Great Lakes Indian. *Annals of Tourism Research* 10:123–48.

Allcock, J. and K. Przeclawski. 1990. Introduction to Special Issue: Tourism in centrally planned economies. *Annals of Tourism Research* 17(1):1–6.

Altman, J. 1989. Tourism dilemmas for Aboriginal Australians. *Annals of Tourism Research* 16(4):456–76.

Androniku, C. 1988. Personal communication. Nicosia, Cyprus.

Apthorpe, R., and D. Conyers. 1982. Decentralisation, recentralisation and popular participation in developing countries: towards a framework for analysis. *Development and Peace* 3 (Autumn):47–59.

Aristotle. *Ethique à Nicomaque.* Paris: Vrin, 1984.

———. *Organon. II: De l'Interprétation.* Paris: Vrin, 1984.

Bachmann, P. 1988. *Tourism in Kenya: Basic need for whom?* Doctoral thesis, Université de Lausanne, Faculté des Lettres, Berne, Frankfurt, New York, and Paris: Peter Lang.

Bacon, P. R. 1987. Use of wetlands for tourism in the insular Caribbean. *Annals of Tourism Research* 14(1):104–17.

Balsdon, J. 1969. *Life and leisure in ancient Rome.* New York: McGraw-Hill.

Bandyopadhyay, J. and V. Shiva. 1989. Political economy of ecology movements. *IFDA Dossier* 71 (May/June):37–60.

Baptistide, J. C. 1979. Tourisme et développement de la Guadeloupe. Thèse de Troisième Cycle (unpublished), Institut de Géographie, Faculté des Lettres et des Sciences Humaines de Rouen, Rouen.

Barbaza, Y. 1970. Trois types d'intervention du tourisme dans l'organisation de l'espace littoral. *Annales de Géographie* 434:446–69.

Barètje, R. 1987. La contribution nette du tourisme international à la balance de paiements. *Problems of Tourism* 10(4):51–88.

Barker, M. L. 1982. Traditional landscape and mass tourism in the Alps. *Geographic Review* 72(4):395–415.

Bazin, C. M. 1987. Capital industriel, patrimoine culturel: vers un capital touristique? *Problems of Tourism* 10(2):63–75.

————. 1988. Dans le processus de touristification: obsolescence obsolète des patrimoines. *Problems of Tourism* 11(4):92–97.

Becker, E. 1895. *Charicles*. Third edition. London: Longman's Green.

Best, M., R. Murray, and M. Pezzini. 1989. Industrial consortia and the third Italy. In R. Murray, ed., *Report on fourth stage of the Cyprus Industrial Strategy*. Institute of Development Studies, University of Sussex, Brighton.

Bilsen, F. 1987. Integrated Tourism in Senegal: an alternative. *Tourism Recreation Research* 13(1):19–23.

Blaikie, P. and H. Brookfield. 1987. *Land degradation and society*. London: Methuen.

Blanche, R. 1957. *Introduction à la logique moderne*. Paris: Armand Colin.

Blanchet, G. 1981. Les petites et moyennes enterprises Polynesiennes. Travaux et Documents de l'ORSTOM 136. Paris: ORSTOM.

Boerma, T. 1984. Work camps and other forms of alternative tourism from the Netherlands. In P. Holden, ed., *Alternative tourism*.

Boudon, R. and F. Bourricaud. 1982. Mouvements sociaux. In *Dictionnaire critique de la sociologie*, pp. 374–82. Paris: Presses Universitaires de France.

Boyer, J. C. 1980. Residences sécondaires et "reurbanisation" en région parisienne. *Tijdschrift voor Economische en Sociale Geografie* 71(2):78–87.

Boyer, M. 1972. *Le tourisme*. Paris: Éditions du Seuil.

Brett, E. A. 1987. States, markets and private power in the developing world: problems and possibilities. *The retreat of the state? IDS Bulletin* 18(3)(July):31–37.

British Tourist Authority, 1988. *The Channel Tunnel: an opportunity and a challenge for British tourism*. London: British Tourist Authority.

Britton, R. A. 1977. Making tourism more supportive of small state development: the case of St-Vincent. *Annals of Tourism Research* 6(5):269–78.

Britton, S. G. 1982. The political economy of tourism in the Third World. *Annals of Tourism Research* 9(3):331–58.

————. 1987. Tourism in small developing countries: development issues and research needs. In Britton and Clarke, eds., *Ambiguous alternative*, pp. 167–87.

————. 1989. Tourism. Dependency and development: a mode of analysis. In Singh et al., eds., *Towards appropriate tourism*, pp. 93–116.

Britton S. G. and W. C. Clarke, eds. 1987. *Ambiguous alternative: tourism in small developing countries*. Suva: University of the South Pacific.

Brodsky-Porges, E. 1981. The grand tour: travel as an educational device, 1600–1800. *Annals of Tourism Research* 8:171–86.

Broggi, M. F., ed. 1985. Sanfter Tourismus: Schlagwort oder Chance für den Alpenraum? Vaduz: Commission Internationale pour las Protectioń des Regions Alpines (CIPRA).

Bromberger, C. and G. Ravis-Giordani. 1977. La deuxième phylloxera? Facteurs, modalités et conséquences de migrations de loisir dans la région Provence-Côte d'Azur. Étude comparée de quelques cas. Aix-en-Provence: Service Régional de l'Équipement/CETE.

Brookfield, Harold. 1988. Sustainable development and the environment. *Journal of Development Studies* 25(1):126–35.

Brougham, J. E. and R. W. Butler. 1981. A segmentation analysis of resident attitudes to the social impact of tourism. *Annals of Tourism Research* 8(4):569–90.

Brugger, E. A., G. Furrer, B. Messerli, and P. Messerli. 1984. *The transformation of the Swiss mountains*. Berne: Paul Haupt.

Bruner, E. M., ed. 1984. *Text, play, and story: The construction and reconstruction of self and society.* Washington, DC: American Ethnological Society.

———. 1989. Of cannibals, tourists, and ethnographers. *Cultural Anthropology* 4(4):439–46.

Bruner, E. M. and B. Kirshenblatt-Gimblett. 1987. Mayers' Ranch and the Kedong Maasai Manyatta. *Problems of Tourism* 10(3):25–29.

Brundtland Report. See WCED.

Bruntland, Gro Harlem. Global change and our common future. Sixth Benjamin Franklin Lecture, May 2, 1989, reprinted in *Environment* 31(5) (June 1989):16–20, 40–43.

Budowski, G. 1976. Tourism and conservation: conflict, coexistence, or symbiosis. *Environmental Conservation* 3:27–31.

Burns M., D. Damania, and L. Heathcote. 1988. The environmental impacts of travel and tourism. Consultancy Paper prepared for the Industries Assistance Commission, Flinders University, Adelaide.

Burton, I., R. W. Kates, and R. E. Snead. 1969. The human ecology of coastal flood hazard in Megalopolis. Department of Geography Research Paper No. 115, University of Chicago.

Butler, R. W. 1980. The concept of a tourist area cycle of evolution and implications for management. *Canadian Geographer* 14:5–12.

———. 1990. Tourism, heritage and sustainable development. In J. G. Nelson and S. Woodley, eds., *Heritage conservation and sustainable development*, pp. 49–66. Heritage Resources Center, Waterloo: University of Waterloo.

Caribbean Ecumenical Consultation for Development. n.d. *The role of tourism in Caribbean development.* Barbados: Caribbean Conference of Churches.

Carpenter, Edmund. 1973. *Oh! what a blow that phantom gave me!* New York: Holt, Rinehart and Winston.

Carpenter, Richard A. and John A. Dixon. 1985. Ecology meets economics: a guide to sustainable development. *Environment* (June):6–11, 27–32.

Casson, Lionel. 1974. *Travel in the ancient world.* London: Allen & Unwin, Ltd.

Cazes, G. H. 1983. *Le tourisme international dans le Tiers-Monde: la problématique géographique.* Thèse pour le Doctorat d'État des Lettres, Université de Bordeaux III.

———. 1986/1987. Le tourisme alternatif: reflexion sur un concept ambigu. *Problems of Tourism/Problemy Turystiky* 10(3):18–24.

———. 1989a. *Le tourisme international. Mirage ou stratégie d'avenir?* Paris: Hatier.

———. 1989b. Alternative Tourism: reflection on an ambiguous concept. In Singh et al., eds., *Towards Appropriate Tourism,* pp. 117–26.

CBS (Government Census Bureau) 1986. Statistiek van het Personenvervoer 1986. Gravenhage, Netherlands: CBS.

———. 1987. Statistiek van het Personenvervoer 1987. Gravenhage, Netherlands: CBS.

———. 1988. Struktuuronderzoek dag- en verblijfrecreatie, 1988. Gravenhage, Netherlands: CBS.

Chambers, R. 1988. Sustainable livelihoods, environment and development: putting poor rural people first. Discussion Paper No. 240, Institute of Development Studies, University of Sussex, Brighton.

Chesneaux, J. 1989. *Modernité-monde.* Paris: La Découverte.

Chico Enterprise Record. 1987. Gringo express, March 8, p. 4C. Chico, California.

Christaller, W. 1963. Some considerations of tourism location in Europe: the peripheral regions—underdeveloped countries—recreation areas. *Papers of the Regional Science Association* 12:95–105.

Ciaccio, C. 1982. Consummation. Aménagement et protection des espaces littoraux en Sicile: le cas des Eoliennes. Colloque Franco-Espagnol sur les Espaces Littoraux. Madrid: Publications Agrarias, 75–80.

Clark, L. 1988. Planning for tourism in Far North Queensland. Unpublished paper presented at Conference on Frontiers in Australian Tourism, Canberra, June.

Clark, W. C. and R. E. Munn, eds. 1986. *Sustainable development of the biosphere.* Cambridge: Cambridge University Press.

CNUCED (United Nations Commission on Commerce and Development). 1963. *Actes de la Conférence des Nations Unies sur le commerce et le développement.* New York: United Nations.

————. 1973. *Les éléments de la politique du tourisme dans les pays en voie de développement.* New York: United Nations.

Cohen, E., 1972. Towards a sociology of international tourism. *Social Research* 39(1):164–82.

————. 1973. Nomads from affluence: notes on the phenomenon of drifter-tourism. *International Journal of Comparative Sociology* 14(1–2):89–103.

————. 1982. Marginal paradises: bungalow tourism on the islands of southern Thailand. *Annals of Tourism Research* 9:189–228.

————. 1983. Insiders and outsiders: the dynamics of development of bungalow tourism on the islands of southern Thailand. *Human Organization* 42:158–62.

————. 1984. The sociology of tourism: approaches, issues, and findings. *Annual Review of Sociology* 10:373–92.

————. 1987/1989a. Alternative tourism—a critique. *Tourism Recreation Research* 12(2):13–18. Reprinted in Singh et al., eds., *Towards Appropriate Tourism*, pp. 127–42.

————. 1988a. Authenticity and commoditization in tourism. *Annals of Tourism Research* 15(3):371–86.

————. 1988b. Tourism and AIDS in Thailand. *Annals of Tourism Research* 15:467–86.

————. 1989. Primitive and remote: hill tribe trekking in Thailand. *Annals of Tourism Research* 16:30–61.

Council for National Parks. 1989. Tourism update. *Tarn and Tor* 15:11.

Countryside Commission. 1989. Charter for green tourism. *Countryside* 35:2.

Cox, J. 1985. The resort concept: the good, the bad and the ugly. Keynote paper presented to National Conference on Tourism and Resort Development, Kuring-gai College of Advanced Education, Sydney, November, pp. 4–11.

Crapo, D. M. 1970. The effects of weather on recreational activity choice. Unpublished Ph.D. dissertation, Michigan State University.

Crick, M. 1989. Representations of international tourism in the social sciences: sun, sex, sights, savings, and servility. *Annual Review of Anthropology* 18:307–44.

Crowe, R. B., G. A. McKay, and W. M. Baker. 1978. *The tourist and recreation climate of Ontario.* Downsview: Atmospheric Environment Service.

Dalen, E. 1989. Research on values and consumer trends in Norway. Paper presented to conference co-sponsored by Tourism Management and the University of Surrey, London, March 13–14.

Daltabuit, M. and O. Pi-Sunyer. 1990. Tourism development in Quintana Roo, Mexico. *Cultural Survival Quarterly* 14(1):9–13.

Dann, G., D. Nash, and P. Pearce. 1988. Methodology in tourism research. *Annals of Tourism Research* 15:1–28.

Dann, G. and R. Potter. 1989. Yellow man in the Yellow Pages: sex and race typing in the Barbados Telephone Directory. Paper presented to the Caribbean Studies Association, Barbados, May.

David Davis, H., and J. A. Simmons. 1982. World Bank experience with tourism projects. *Tourism Management* 3(4):212–17.

Dearlove, J. 1987. Economists on the state. The retreat of the State? *IDS Bulletin* 18(3)(July):5–11.

Dernoi, L. A. 1981. Alternative Tourism: towards a new style in North-South relations. *International Journal of Tourism Management* 2(4):253–64.

———. 1988. Alternative or community-based tourism. In L. D'Amore and J. Jafari, eds., *Tourism—a vital force for peace*. Montréal: L. D'Amore and Associates.

Dogan, H. Z. 1989. Forms of adjustment: sociocultural impacts of tourism. *Annals of Tourism Research* 16(2):216–36.

Dombrink, J. and W. N. Thompson. 1990. *The last resort: campaigns to legalize casinos in America.* Reno: University of Nevada Press.

Dorfmann, M. 1983. Régions de montagne: de la dépendance à l'autodéveloppement. *Revue de Géographie Alpine* 71(1):5–34.

Dowling, R. 1989. Integrating tourism and conservation. Paper presented to Conference of Institute of Australian Geographers, Adelaide, February.

Drabek, Anne Gordon, ed. 1987. *Development alternatives: the challenge for NGOs.* Supplement to *World Development* 15 (Autumn).

Dubarle, R. P. 1957. *Initiation à la logique.* Paris: Gauthier-Villars.

Dunning, J. H. and M. McQueen. 1983. The eclectic theory of the multinational enterprise and the international hotel industry. In A. M. Rugman, ed., *New theories of the multinational enterprise*, pp. 79–106. London: Helm.

Durkheim. E. 1912/1979. *Les formes élémentaires de la vie religieuse. Le système totémique en Australie.* Reprinted Paris: Presses Universitaires de France.

———. 1915/1969. Note sur la notion de civilisation. Reprinted in *Journal sociologique*, pp. 681–85. Reprinted Paris: Presses Universitaires de France.

Durst P. and C. Ingram. 1988. Nature-oriented tourism promotion by developing countries. *Tourism Management* 26:39–43.

Eadington, W. R. 1990. Issues and trends in world gaming. In C. Campbell and J. Lowman, eds., *Gambling: golden goose or Trojan horse?* Vancouver: Simon Fraser University.

Eadington, W. R. and M. Redman. 1991. Economics and tourism. *Annals of Tourism Research* 18(1):41–56.

Eco, U. 1985. *La guerre du faux.* Paris: Grasset.

The Economist. 1989. Third world tourism: visitors are good for you. March 11:19–22.

ECTWT (Ecumenical Coalition on Third World Tourism). 1986. *Third World peoples and tourism: approaches to a dialogue.* P.O. Box 9-25, Bangkok, Thailand.

Edwards, F., ed. 1988. *Environmentally sound tourism development in the Caribbean.* Calgary: University of Calgary Press.

Ekins, P., ed. 1986. *The living economy.* London: Routledge.

————. 1988. Green ideas on economics and security and their political implications. In Friberg, ed., *New social movements in Western Europe*, pp. 98–112.

Elliott, C. 1987. Some aspects of relations between north and south in the NGO sector. In Drabek, ed., *Development alternatives*, pp. 57–68.

Elliott, J. 1983. Politics, power and tourism in Thailand. *Annals of Tourism Research* 10(3):377–93.

English, E. P. 1986. *The great escape: an examination of north-south tourism.* Ottawa: The North-South Institute.

Erisman, H. M. 1983. Tourism and cultural dependency in the West Indies. *Annals of Tourism Research* 10(3):337–61.

FAO/ECE (UN Food and Agriculture Organization). 1982. Report on the Symposium on Agriculture and Tourism. Mariehamn, June. Helsinki: Government Printing Centre.

Farrell, B. 1986. Cooperative tourism and the Coast Zone. *Coastal Zone Management Journal* 14(1–2):113–30.

————. 1990. Sustainable development: whatever happened to Hana? *Cultural Survival Quarterly* 2:25–29.

FEDOMASEC (Federation of Ecological Societies of the Dominican Republic). 1989. Dominican Republic: tourism vs. natural resources. A call for international support. *IFDA Dossier* 72 (July/August):65.

Fichtner, U. and R. Michna. 1987. *Freizeitparks: allgemeine Zuge eines modernen freizeitangebotes, vertiert am Beispiel des EUROPA-PARK in Rust/Baden.* Freiburg: Institute für Kulturgeographie der Albert-Ludwig-Universitat.

Frey, J. and W. R. Eadington, eds. 1984. Gambling: views from the social sciences. *Annals of the American Academy of Political and Social Sciences* 474 (July).

Friberg, M. 1988. Three waves of political mobilization in Western Europe and the coming of a fourth. In Friberg, ed., *New social movements in Western Europe*, pp. 1–55.

————, ed., 1988. *New social movements in Western Europe.* UNU European Perspectives Project 1986–87. Göteborg: PADRIGU.

Frommer, A. 1988. *The new world of travel.* Englewood Cliffs, NJ: Prentice–Hall.

Galbraith, J. K. 1967. *The new industrial state.* London: H. Hamilton.

Ganapin, D. 1985. Ecological assessment and guidelines for tourism site development: Boracay case. Manila: Unpublished manuscript.

Garrett, W. E. 1989. La Ruta Maya. *National Geographic* 176(4):424–79.

Geertz, C. 1986. *Savoir local, savoir global.* Paris: PUF.

Goldfarb, Gabriela. 1989. International ecotourism: a strategy for conservation and development. Unpublished Policy Analysis Exercise, John F. Kennedy School of Government, Harvard University (typescript).

Gonsalves, P. S. 1984. Tourism in India: an overview and from leisure to learning: a strategy for India. In Holden, ed., *Alternative Tourism.*

————. 1987. Alternative tourism—the evolution of a concept and establishment of a network. *Tourism Recreation Research* 12(2):9–12.

————, ed. n.d. *Equations (Equitable Tourism Options).* Bangalore: Alternative Network Letter.

Graburn, N. H. H. 1983. The anthropology of tourism. *Annals of Tourism Research* 10:9–34.

————. 1983. *To pray, pay, and play.* Aix-en-Provence: CHET.

Gray, H. P. 1970. *International travel—international trade.* Lexington: D. C. Heath.

Graycar, A. 1979. *Welfare politics in Australia.* Melbourne: Macmillan.

Greenwood, D. J. 1977/1989. Culture by the pound: an anthropological perspective on tourism as cultural commoditization. In Smith, ed., *Hosts and guests,* pp. 171–86 (1989 ed.).

Grosjean, G. 1984. Visual and aesthetic changes in landscape. In E. A. Brugger, G. Furrer, B. Messerli, and P. Messerli, eds., *The transformation of Swiss mountain regions,* pp. 71–79.

Gunn, C. 1979. *Tourism planning.* New York: Crane, Russak.

———. 1988. Small town and rural tourism planning. In F. Dykeman, ed., *Integrated rural planning and development,* Department of Geography, Mount Allison University, Sackville, pp. 237–51.

Gunn, C. and A. Worms. 1973. *Evaluating and developing tourism.* College Station: Texas A & M. University.

Gurin, J.-P. 1984. *L'aménagement de la montagne en France: politiques, discours et production d'espace dans les Alpes du Nord.* Ophyrs.

Haider, W. 1985. Small accommodation development in the Caribbean: an appraisal. In L. Pulsipher, ed., *Proceedings of the Conference of Latin Americanist Geographers.* Muncie, IN: Ball State University.

Hall, D. 1984. Foreign tourism under stress: the Albanian "Stalinist" model. *Annals of Tourism Research* 11:539–56.

———. 1990. Stalinism and tourism: a study of Albania and North Korea. *Annals of Tourism Research* 17:36–54.

Ham, C. and M. Hill. 1986. *The policy process in the modern capitalist state.* Bristol: Harvester Press.

Hammitt, W. and D. Cole. 1987. *Wildland recreation.* New York: Wiley.

Hanna, N. 1989. *Tropical beach handbook* (BMW). London: Fourth Estate.

Hardin, G. 1969. The Tragedy of the Commons. *Science* 162:1243–48.

Hare, F. K. 1985. Climatic change in the Great Lakes Basin: an appraisal. Paper presented at the Workshop on Climate Impact Assessment in the Great Lakes Basin: Research Strategies, King City, Ontario.

———. 1989. The global greenhouse effect. In *Conference Proceedings: The Changing Atmosphere,* pp. 59–69. Geneva: World Meteorological Organization.

Harrigan, N. 1974. The legacy of Caribbean history and tourism. *Annals of Tourism Research* 2:13–25.

Harvey, C. 1988. Non-marginal price changes: conditions for the success of floating exchange rate systems in Sub-Saharan Africa. *Stabilisation —for growth or decay? IDS Bulletin* 19(1) (January):67–74.

Hasslacher, P. 1984. *Virgental: Sanfter Tourismus.* Innsbruck: Oesterreichischer Alpenverein.

Hayward, S. J., V. H. Gomez, and W. Sterner. 1981. *Bermuda's delicate balance.* Nassau: Bermuda National Trust.

Helber et al. 1984. Resort development concept plan for Boracay Island, Philippines. Honolulu: Unpublished manuscript.

Hettne, Bjorn. 1985. World development, world peace and European options. *EADI Bulletin:*2.

Hills, T. L. and J. Lundgren. 1977. The impact of tourism in the Caribbean: a methodological study. *Annals of Tourism Research* 8 (3) pp. 462–74.

Hilts, S. and T. Moull. 1988. Toward a theory of rural planning. In F. Dykeman, ed., *Integrated rural planning and development,* Department of Geography, Mount Allison University, Sackville, pp. 105–12.

Holden, Peter, ed. 1984. *Alternative Tourism: Report on the workshop on Alternative Tourism with a focus on Asia.* Bangkok: Ecumenical Coalition on Third World Tourism.

Holder, J. S. 1988. The pattern and impact of tourism on the environment in the Caribbean. In Edwards, ed., *Environmentally sound tourism development in the Caribbean.*

Hong, E. 1985. The third world while it lasts: the social and environmental impact of tourism with special reference to Malaysia. Penang: Consumers' Association of Penang.

Howe, A. 1983. The implementation gap in social policy. In J. Dixon and D. Jayasuriya, eds., *Social policy in the 1980s.* Canberra: College of Advanced Education.

Hupkes, S. 1987. Gasgeven of afremmen, Toekomstscenario's voor ons vervoersysteem. Deventer, Netherlands.

IDS. 1987. The Retreat of the State? *IDS Bulletin* 18(3)(July).

———. 1988. Stabilisation—for growth or decay? *IDS Bulletin* 19(1) (January).

Ibn Talal, H. 1989. Quelle culture, quel développement? *IFDA Dossier* 71 (May/June):19–24.

Ichaporia, N. 1983. Tourism at Khajuraho: an Indian enigma? *Annals of Tourism Research* 10:75–92.

Ikkai, M. 1988. Traditional reciprocity among Japanese tourists. *Kroeber Anthropological Society Papers* 67–68:62–66.

International Academy for the Study of Tourism. 1989. *Theoretical Perspectives on Alternative Forms of Tourism.* Zakopane, Poland, August 19–25.

International Sociology. 1988. Universalism and indigenisation. Symposium on Universalism versus Indigenisation in Sociological Theory, Xth World Congress of Sociology, Mexico City, 19-8-82. *International Sociology* 3(2):155–99.

Jackson, E. L. 1984. Energy development, tourism and nature conservation in Iceland. In R. Oldson et al., eds., *Northern Ecology and Resource Management,* pp. 387–403. Edmonton: University of Alberta Press.

Jackson, I. 1986. Carrying capacity for tourism in small tropical Caribbean Islands. *UNEP Industry and Environment* 9(1):7–10.

Jafari, J. 1977. Jamaica: why don't you stop and say hello? *Annals of Tourism Research* 4(3):295–98.

———. 1984. Unbounded ethnicity: the tourist network and its satellites. *Revue de Tourisme* 3:4–21.

———. 1987. The tourist system: sociocultural models for theoretical and practical application. *Problems of Tourism* 10(3):3–17.

———. 1989a. An English language literature review. In J. Bystrzanowski, ed., *Tourism as a factor of change: a sociocultural study,* pp. 17–60. Vienna: Centre for Research and Documentation in Social Sciences.

———. 1989b. Soft tourism. *Tourism Management* 9(1):32–84.

———. 1990. Research and scholarship: the basis of tourism education. *Journal of Tourism Studies* 1:33–41.

Jansen-Verbeke, M. C. 1989. Ean toekomstverkenning van de positie van de train in het vrijetijdsverkeer. Breda/Tilburg, Netherlands.

Jayal, N. D. 1986. Speech by Mr. N. D. Jayal, Advisor, Planning Commission, Government of India. In Jayal and Motwani, eds., *Conservation, tourism and mountaineering in the Himalayas,* pp. 65–70.

Jayal, N. D. and M. Motwani, eds. 1986. *Conservation, tourism and mountaineering in the Himalayas.* Dehra Dun: Natraj Publishers.

Jenkins, C. L. 1982. The effects of scale in tourism projects in developing countries. *Annals of Tourism Research* 9(2):229–49.

Jenkins, J. 1988. The development of fossicking for recreation and tourism in the New England region. Unpublished B. A. Honour Thesis, Department of Geography and Planning, University of New England, Armidale, Australia.

de Jetley, A. 1988. Town report: heavenly Hana going to hell? *The Mauian* (April/May):52–57.

Jeudy, H. P. 1986. *Mémoires du social.* Paris: Presses Universitaires de France.

Jokiel, L. 1988. Holding on to Hana. *Hawaii Business* (May):42–53.

Jones, A. 1987. Green Tourism. *Tourism Management* 26:354–56.

Jusserand, J. 1929/1980. *English wayfaring life in the Middle Ages.* 4th ed., 1950, reprinted New York: Putnam.

de Kadt, E., ed. 1979. *Tourism—passport to development? Perspectives on the social and cultural effects of tourism in developing countries.* New York: Oxford University Press for the World Bank and UNESCO.

———. 1985. Dilemmas of development: reflections on the universal and unique, the utilitarian and utopian. First Anniversary Lecture, Central Bank of the Seychelles, Mahé.

———. 1989. Making health policy management intersectoral: issues of information analysis and use in less developed countries. *Social Science and Medicine* 29(4):503–14.

Kalinowski, G. 1972. *La logique des normes.* Paris: PUF.

Kanahele, G. 1982. Hawaiian Renaissance. Hawaiian Values, Series 1 (pamphlet). Honolulu.

Kariel, H. 1989. Tourism and development: perplexity or panacea? *Journal of Travel Research* 28(1):2–6.

Kellogg, W. W. and R. Schware. 1981. *Climatic change and society. consequences of increasing atmospheric carbon dioxide.* Boulder, CO: Westview Press.

Kingma, S. en M. 1989. Jansen-Verbeke, Sporen naar de vrije tijd van de toekomst. Tilburg/Breda, Netherlands.

Korten, D. C. 1987. Third generation NGO strategies: a key to people centered development. In Drabek, ed., *Development Alternatives,* pp. 145–59.

Kosters, M. J. 1985. *Focus op Toerisme.* second edition, Gravenhage, Netherlands: CBS.

———. 1990. Vakantietoerisme van Nederlanders slaat alle records. *Nederlands Vervoer* (August).

Kozlowski, J. 1985. Threshold approach in environmental planning. *Ekistics* 311 (March/April):146–53.

Krapf, K. 1961. Les pays en voie de développement face au tourisme: introduction méthodologique. *Revue de Tourisme* 16(3):82–89.

———. 1963. *Tourism as a factor of economic development: role and importance of international tourism.* Rome: United Nations Conference on International Trade and Tourism.

———. 1964. *La consommation touristique: une contribution à une théorie de la consommation.* Aix-en-Provence: Centre d'Études du Tourisme.

Kreck, L. A. 1981. When Mt. St. Helens blew its top. *Journal of Travel Research* 19:16–22.

Kreutzwiser, R. D. 1982. An evaluation of government response to the Lake

Erie shoreline flood and erosion hazard. *Canadian Geographical Journal* 26(3):263–73.

Krippendorf, J. 1982. Towards new tourism policies. *Tourism Management* 3:135–48.

———. 1986. Tourism in the system of industrial society. *Annals of Tourism Research* 13(4):517–32.

———. 1987a. *The holiday makers*. London: Heinemann.

———. 1987b. *Les vacances et après? Pour une nouvelle comprehension des loisirs et des vacances*. Paris: L'Harmattan.

Krutilla, J. and A. Fisher. 1975. *The economics of natural environments*. Baltimore: Johns Hopkins University Press.

Lalande, A. 1960. *Vocabulaire technique et critique de la philosophie*. Paris: Presses Universitaires de France.

Lamothe and Periard. 1988. Implications of climate change for downhill skiing in Quebec. *Climate Change Digest* 88-03.

Lane, B. 1988. Rural Tourism. Countryside Recreation Conference, Countryside Commission, Cheltenham.

Lanfant, M.-F. 1980. Introduction: tourism in the process of internationalization. *International Social Science Journal* 32:7–43.

———. 1987. "L'impact social et culturel du tourisme international" en question: réponse sociologique. *Problems of Tourism* 10(2):1–36.

———. 1989a. International tourism resists the crisis. In A. Olszewska and K. Roberts, eds., *Leisure and lifestyle: a comparative analysis of free time*, pp. 178–93. London: Sage/ISA.

———. 1989b. Le tourisme dans le processus d'internationalisation. *Revue Internationale des Sciences Sociales* 32(1):14–45 (English and Spanish translation).

Lanfant, M. F., M. H. Mottin, M. Picard, D. Rozenberg, and J. de Weerdt. 1978. *Sociologie du tourisme: positions et perspectives dans la recherche internationale*. Paris: CES/CNRS.

Lanfant, M. F., C. Bazin, M. Picard, and J. de Weerdt. 1988. *Les problématiques de l'impact social et culturel du tourisme international*. Paris: URESTI/CNRS.

Languar, R. 1984. Nouveaux patrimoines, nouveau tourisme. *Revue de Tourisme* 4:12–16.

———. 1986. L'analyse des impacts socio-culturels du tourisme par l'Organisation Mondiale du Tourisme (WTO): une doctrine et un bilan. Table Ronde Internationale, Marly-le-Roi, France, June.

Lefevre, V. and J. Renard. 1980. Tourisme, agriculture et habitat dans l'intérieur des Marais Monts. *Cahiers Nantais* 18:45–65.

Le Goff, J. 1988. *Histoire et mémoire*. Paris: Gallimard.

Le Monde. 1989. Penser local, agir global: la développement local en ordre dispersé. *Le Monde*, 15 Novembre.

Lévi-Strauss, C. 1962. *Le totémisme aujourd'hui*. Paris: Presses Universitaires de France.

———. 1973. Humanisme et humanité. In *Anthropologie structurale deux*, pp. 319–422. Paris: Plon.

———. 1983. *Le regard éloigne*. Paris: Plon.

Lewis, G. 1972. *The Virgin Islands: a Caribbean Lilliput*. Evanston, IL: Northwestern University Press.

Lüdtke, H. 1989. Veränderungstendenzen in Freizeitkonsum und Lebensstillen: Versuch einer Typologie. Amsterdam: Congres. NS.

Lundberg, D. E. 1974. *The tourist business.* Boston: Cahners Books.

Lundgren, J. 1974. On access to recreational lands in dynamic metropolitan hinderlands. *Tourist Review* 29(4):124–31.

———. 1989. Patterns. In G. Wall, ed., *Outdoor recreation in Canada,* pp. 133–61. Toronto: Wiley.

Lynch, P., G. R. McBoyle, and G. Wall. 1981. A ski season without snow. In D. W. Phillips and G. A. McKay, eds., *Canadian climate in review—1980.* Downsview: Atmospheric Environment Service.

———. 1982. Skiing, snow and solvency. Geographical Inter-University Resource Management Seminars, 12:31–70.

MacCannell, D. 1976. *The tourist: a new theory of the leisure class.* London: Macmillan.

———. 1986. Tourisme et identité culturelle. *Communications* 43:169–86.

Mader, V. 1988. Tourism and environment. *Annals of Tourism Research* 15(2): 274–76.

Malempre, G. 1982. Le tourisme comme industrie culturelle. *Revue de Tourisme* 1:2–5.

Masterton, J. 1982. Skiing, snow and solvency: the climatological perspective. Geographical Inter-University Resource Management Seminars 12:72–79.

Mathieson, A. and G. Wall. 1982. *Tourism: economic, physical and social impacts.* New York: Longman.

Mauss, M. 1969. Les civilisations: éléments et formes. In *Essais de sociologie.* Paris: Minuit.

———. 1980. Essai sur le don: formes et raison de l'échange dans les sociétés archaiques. In *Sociologie et anthropologie,* pp. 145–279. Paris: Presses Universitaires de France.

McBoyle, G. and G. Wall. 1986. Recreation and climatic change: a Canadian case study. *Ontario Geography* 28:51–68.

———. 1987. The impact of CO_2-induced warming on downhill skiing in the Laurentians *Cahiers de Géographie de Quebec* 31(82):39–50.

McElroy, J. and K. de Albuquerque. 1989. Tourism styles and policy responses in the open economy-closed environment context. Paper presented to the Caribbean Conservation Association Conference on Economics and the Environment, Barbados, November 6–8.

McIntosh, R. and C. Goeldner. 1990. *Tourism: principles, practices, philosophies.* 6th edition. New York.

McKean, P. F. 1973. *Cultural involution: tourists, Balinese and the process of modernization in an anthropological perspective.* Ph.D. dissertation, Brown University.

———. 1977/1989. Towards a theoretical analysis of tourism: economic dualism and cultural involution in Bali. In Smith, ed., *Hosts and guests,* pp. 93–108 (1977ed.); pp. 119–38 (1989 ed.).

Meadows, D. H., D. L. Meadows, J. Randers, and W. W. Behrens III. 1972. *The limits to growth.* New York: Universe Books.

Medlik, S. 1988. International tourism: past, present and future. Public lecture, University of Guelph, Ontario.

Meganck, R. and B. S. Ramdial. 1984. Trinidad and Tobago cultural parks: an idea whose time has come. *Parks* 9(1):1–5.

Merleau-Ponty, M. 1960. De Mauss à Claude Lévi-Strauss. In *Signes,* pp. 143–57. Paris: Gallimard.

Messerli, P. and E. A. Brugger. 1984. Mountain areas between self reliance and dependence, between economy and ecology: a summary. In E. A. Brugger, et al. *The transformation of the Swiss mountains,* pp. 603–19.

Mieczkowski, Z. T. 1985. The tourism climate index: a method of evaluating world climates for tourism. *Canadian Geographer* 29:220–23.

Millman, R. 1988. Just pleasure: the churches look at tourism's impacts. *Annals of Tourism Research* 15:555–58.

Milne, S. 1987. The economic impact of tourism in the Cook Islands. Occasional Paper 21, Department of Geography, University of Auckland.

Minc, A. 1982. *L'après-crise est commencé.* Paris: Gallimard.

Ministerie van Verkeer en Waterstaat. 1989. Tweede Struktuurschema Verkeer en Vervoer. Gravenhage, Netherlands.

Mishra, H. R. 1984. A delicate balance: tigers, rhinoceros, tourists and park management vs. the needs of the local people in Royal Chitwan National Park, Nepal. In J. A. McNeely and K. R. Miller, eds., *National parks, conservation and development,* pp. 197–205. Washington, D C : Smithsonian Institution.

Moeran, B. 1983. The language of Japanese tourism. *Annals of Tourism Research* 10:93–108.

Molnar, E., M. Mihail, and A. Maier. 1976. Types de localités touristiques dans la République Socialiste de Roumanie. *Revue Roumaine de Géologie, Géophysique et Géographie,* Série de Géographie 20:189–85.

Morin, E. 1962. *L'esprit du temps: essai sur la culture de masse.* Paris: Grasset.

Morris, A. and G. Dickinson. 1987. Tourist development in Spain: growth versus conservation on the Costa Brava. *Geography* 72(1):16–25.

Mosher, M. 1988. A case study of tourism in Chinese peasant society. *Kroeber Anthropological Society Papers* 67–68.

Mouy, P. 1944. *Logique et philosophie des sciences.* Paris: Hachette.

Mukerji, C. 1978. Bullshitting: road lore among hitchhikers. *Social Problems* 25(3):241–52.

Murphy, P. 1985. *Tourism: a community approach.* London: Methuen.

Musgrave, W. 1984. The economics of sustainable development. Keynote paper to Conference on Conservation and the Economy, Sydney, September.

———. 1988. Some notes on the concept of sustainability. Unpublished paper, Department of Agricultural Economics, University of New England, Armidale, Australia.

Nash, D. 1977/1989. Tourism as a form of Imperialism. In Smith, ed., *Hosts and guests,* pp. 37–52 (1989 edition).

———. 1979a. *Tourism in pre-industrial societies.* Aix-en-Provence: Centre des Hautes Études Touristiques.

———. 1979b. The rise and fall of an aristocratic tourist culture—Nice, 1763–1936. *Annals of Tourism Research* 6:61–75.

———. 1981. Tourism as an anthropological subject. *Current Anthropology* 22:561–81.

Nash, D. and R. Butler. 1989. Report of the First Meeting of the International Academy for the Study of Tourism in Zakopane, Poland, August 21–23. *Newsletter of the International Academy for the Study of Tourism* 2(3):2–4.

Nash, D. and V. Smith, 1991. Anthropology and tourism. *Annals of Tourism Research* 18(1):12–25.

Nederlandse Spoorwagen. 1989, 1990. Congres "Vrije tijd en Mobiliteit," 1989. Utrecht, Netherlands.

Nielson, L. B. 1984. A critique of alternative tourism in Bali. In Holden, ed., *Alternative tourism.*

Nora, P., ed. 1984. *Les lieux de mémoire I. la république.* Paris: Gallimard.

———. 1986. *Les lieux de mémoire II. la nation.* 3 vol. Paris: Gallimard.

Norbu, N. 1984. Cultural preservation in Sogarmatha. *Parks* 9, 2:14–15.

NRIT, 1990, 1989, 1988, 1987. Trendrapport Toerisme. Breda, Netherlands.

Nyoni, S. 1987. Indigenous NGOs: liberation, self-reliance, and development. In Drabek, ed., *Development alternatives*, pp. 51–56.

O'Grady, R., ed. 1975. *Tourism: the Asian dilemma.* Singapore: Christian Conference of Asia.

———. 1980. *Third world tourism.* Singapore: Christian Conference of Asia.

Okotai, T. 1980. Research requirements of tourism in the Cook Islands. In Pearce, ed., *Tourism in the South Pacific*, pp. 169–76.

OMT (Organisation Mondiale du Tourisme; see also WTO). 1979. *Étude sur la contribution du tourisme a l'échange des valeurs spirituelles et à une meilleure compréhension entre les peuples.* Madrid: WTO.

———. 1985. *Rôle de l'état dans la sauvegarde et la promotion de la culture comme facteur de développement touristique et dans la mise en valeur du patrimoine national de sites et de monuments à des fins touristiques.* Madrid: WTO.

Oppedijk van Veen, W. M. and T. W. M. Verhallen. 1986. Vacation market segmentation: a domain-specific value approach. *Annals of Tourism Research* 13(1):37–58.

Organization of American States (OAS). 1984. Enhancing the positive impact of tourism on the built and natural environment. In *Reference Guidelines for Enhancing the Positive Socio-Cultural and Environmental Impacts of Tourism*, vol. 5. International Trade and Tourism Division, Department of Economic Affairs, Washington, DC.

Passariello, P. 1983. Never on Sunday: Mexican tourists at the beach. *Annals of Tourism Research* 10:106–22.

Paul, A. H. 1972. Weather and the daily use of outdoor recreation areas in Canada. In J. A. Taylor, ed., *Weather forecasting for agriculture and industry*, pp. 132–46, Newton Abbot: David and Charles.

Pearce, D. G. 1978. Tourist development: two processes. *Travel Research Journal:*43–51.

———, ed. 1980. *Tourism in the South Pacific: the contribution of research to development and planning.* UNESCO Man and the Biosphere Report no. 6. Christchurch, N.Z.: National Commission for UNESCO/Dept. of Geography, University of Canterbury.

———. 1984. Planning for tourism in Belize. *Geographical Review* 74(3):291–303.

———. 1987. *Tourism today: a geographical analysis.* Harlow: Longman; New York: Wiley.

———. 1989. *Tourist development.* Second edition. Harlow: Longman; New York: Wiley.

Pearson, C. S. 1985. *Down to business: multinational corporations, the environment and development.* World Resources Institute. January.

Peck, J. G. and A. S. Lepie 1977/1989. Tourism and development in three North Carolina coastal towns. In Smith ed., *Hosts and guests*, pp. 203–22 (1989 edition).

Pepper, D. 1987. "New Economics" and the deficiencies of green political thinking. *Political Quarterly* 58(3):333–38.

Perez, L. 1974. Aspects of underdevelopment: tourism in the West Indies. *Science and Society* 37:473–80.

Perpinan, M. 1984. Philippine women in the service and entertainment sector. Second International Interdisciplinary Congress on Women. Gröningen, the Netherlands 17–21 April.

Perroux, F. 1982. *Dialogue des monopoles et des nations: équilibre des unités actives.* Grenoble: Presses Universitaires de Grenoble.

Pfaffenberger, B. 1983. Serious pilgrims and frivolous tourists: the chimera of tourism in the pilgrimages of Sri Lanka. *Annals of Tourism Research* 10:57–74.

Pfafflin, G. F. 1987. Concern for tourism: European perspective and response. *Annals of Tourism Research* 14(4):576–79.

Picard, M. 1979. *Sociétés et tourisme: reflexions pour la recherche et l'action.* Paris: UNESCO.

———. 1990. "Cultural Tourism" in Bali: cultural performances as tourist attractions. *Indonesia* 49:37–74.

Pigram, J. 1985. *Outdoor recreation and resource management.* London: Croom Helm.

———. 1987. Tourism in Coffs Harbour. Armidale, Australia: University of New England.

Pirojnik, I. 1989. Évolution du tourisme en URSS. *Problems of Tourism/Problemy Turystyki* 12:71–79.

Platt, R. H., S. G. Pelczarski, and B. K. R. Burbank, eds. 1987. Cities on the beach: management issues of developed coastal barriers. Department of Geography Research Paper No. 224, University of Chicago.

Plog, S. C. 1973/1977. Why destination areas rise and fall in popularity. *Cornell Hotel and Restaurant Association Quarterly* (Nov.):13–16. Reprinted in E. M. Kelly, ed., *Domestic and international tourism.* Wellesley, MA: Institute of Certified Travel Agents.

Poon, A. 1987. Information technology and innovation in international tourism—implications for the Caribbean tourism industry. Unpublished Ph.D. dissertation, University of Sussex.

———. 1988a. The future of Caribbean tourism—a matter of innovation. *Tourism Management* 9(3):213–20.

———. 1988b. Tourism and Information Technologies. *Annals of Tourism Research* 15:431–549.

———. 1988c. Flexible specialization and small size—the case of Caribbean tourism. DRC Discussion Paper 57, Science Policy Research Unit, University of Sussex.

———. 1989. Global developments in all-inclusive hotels—with special reference to the Caribbean and St. Lucia. Barbados: Caribbean Tourism Organization.

———. 1990. Flexible specialization and small size: the case of Caribbean tourism. *World Development* 18(1):109–23.

Preau, P. 1968. Essai d'une typologie de stations de sports d'hiver dans les Alpes du Nord. *Revue de Géographie Alpine* 58(1):127–40.

Preau, P. 1970. Principle d'analyse des sites en montagne. *Urbanisme* 116:21–29.

Priestley, G. K. 1986. El turismo y la transformacion del territorio: un estudio de Tossa, Lloret de Mar y Blanes a traves de la fotografia aerea 1956–1981. In *Turisme i Mediambient Sant Feliu de Guixols—Costa Brava.* Barcelona: Jornades Tecniques Sobre.

Problems of Tourism. 1987. *L' "impact social et culturel du tourisme international"* *en question: réponses interdisciplinaires.* Table Ronde Internationale, Marly-le-Roi, France, 9–11 Juin 1986, vol. 10, nos. 2, 3.

Ranck, S. 1980. The socio-economic impact of recreational tourism on Papua New Guinea. In Pearce, ed., *Tourism in the South Pacific,* pp. 55–68.

Raynouard, Y. 1986. L'économie des stations de sports d'hiver. *Espaces* 80:14–15.

Research Department of the National Tourism Administration, People's Republic of China (RDNTA). 1989. Tourism and change in life style: the China case. *Problems of Tourism/Problemy Turystyki* 12:66.

Regier, H. A. and G. L. Baskerville. 1986. Sustainable redevelopment of regional ecosystems degraded by exploitive development. In Clark and Munn, eds., *Sustainable development of the biosphere,* pp. 75–100.

Richter, L. K. 1983. Tourism politics and political science: a case of not so benign neglect. *Annals of Tourism Research* 10(3):313–35.

———. 1984. The political and legal dimensions of tourism. In Holden, ed., *Alternative Tourism.*

———. 1987. The search for appropriate tourism. *Tourism Recreation Research* 12(2).

———. 1989. *The politics of tourism in Asia.* Honolulu: University of Hawaii Press.

Richter, L. K. and W. M. Richter, 1985. Policy choices in South Asian tourism development. *Annals of Tourism Research* 12(2):201–17.

Riebsame, W. 1985. Seven challenges of climate impact research. Paper presented at the Workshop on Climate Impact Assessment in the Great Lakes Basin: Research Strategies. King City, Ontario.

Riley, P. 1988. Road culture of international long-term budget travelers. *Annals of Tourism Research* 15:313–28.

Rist, G. 1987. La "dimension socio-culturelle" occidentale du développment. Mimeo. EADI Fifth General Conference, Amsterdam.

Ritchie, J. R. B. and C. R. Goeldner, eds. 1987. *Travel, tourism and hospitality research: a handbook for managers and researchers.* New York: Wiley.

Robert, P. 1964. Argument cornu. In *Dictionnaire alphabétique et analogique de la langue française* 6:232. Paris: Société du Nouveau Lettres.

Roberts, H. 1987. Editorial. *Politics in Command? IDS Bulletin* 18(4) (October):1–6.

Rostow, W. W. 1961a. *The stage of economic growth: a non-communist manifesto.* Cambridge: Cambridge University Press.

———. 1961b. *The process of economic growth.* New York: Norton.

Rodenburg, E. E. 1980. The effects of scale in economic development: tourism in Bali. *Annals of Tourism Research* 7(2):177–96.

Roekaerts, M. and K. Savat. 1989. Mass tourism in South and South East Asia: a challenge to Christians and churches. In Singh et al., eds., *Towards Appropriate Tourism,* 35–70.

Romeril, M. 1983. A balanced strategy for recreation, tourism and conservation. *Tourism Management* 2:126–28.

Rosewood Hotels, Inc. 1987. Hana community meeting: information package. June 19. Hana (typescript).

Sadler, B. 1987. Sustaining tomorrow and endless summer: on linking tourism and environment in the Caribbean. In Edwards, ed., *Environmentally sound tourism development in the Caribbean.*

Saglio, C. 1979. Tourism for discovery: a project in Lower Casemance, Senegal. In de Kadt, ed., *Tourism—passport to development?*

———. 1985. Sénégal: tourisme rural integré en Basse-Casamance. *Espaces* 76:29–32.

Seers, D. 1969. The meaning of development. *International Development Review* 11, 4.

Sfez, L., ed. 1977. *L'objet local.* Paris: 10/18.

Shook, V. E. 1985. Ho'oponopono. East-West Center and the University of Hawaii, Honolulu.

Sigaux, G. 1966. *History of tourism.* Translated by J. White. London: Leisure Arts.

Simonis, U. E. 1989. Ecology and economic policy. *IFDA Dossier* 70 (March/April):59–64.

Singh, N. D. 1986. Speech delivered by Cmdr Joginder Singh, Deputy Commercial Manager, Air India. In Jayal and Motwani, eds., *Conservation, tourism and mountaineering in the Himalayas.* pp. 75–78.

Singh, T. V., H. L. Theuns, and F. M. Go, eds. 1989. *Towards Appropriate Tourism: the case of developing countries.* Frankfurt am Main: Peter Lang.

Smit, B. 1989. Climate warming and Canada's comparative position in agriculture. *Climate Change Digest* 89-01. Downsview: Atmospheric Environment Service.

Smith, T., 1973. The policy implementation process. *Policy Sciences* 4:197–209.

Smith, V. L., ed. 1977/1989a. *Hosts and guests: the anthropology of tourism.* Philadelphia: University of Pennsylvania Press. First edition 1977, revised 1989.

Smith, V. L. 1977/1989b. Eskimo tourism: micro-models and marginal men. In Smith, ed., *Hosts and Guests,* pp. 55–82 (1989 edition).

———. 1981. Controlled vs. uncontrolled tourism: Bhutan and Nepal. *RAIN* (Royal Anthropological Institute Newsletter) 46:4–6.

Société des Nations (League of Nations). 1936. *Étude sur les mouvements touristiques considérés comme un facteur économique international.* Geneva.

de Soto, Hernando. 1986. *El otro sendero: la revolución informal.* Bogotá: Ed. Oveja Negra.

Srisang, K. 1990. An ecumenical coalition on Third World tourism. *Annals of Tourism Research* 16:119–21.

Stadler, G. 1975. *Von der Kavalierstour zum Sozialtourismus.* Salzburg: Universitätsverlag Anton Pustet Salzburg.

Stankey, G. 1989. Conservation, recreation and tourism. Paper prepared for Conference of Institute of Australian Geographers, Adelaide. February.

Stankey G., Cole D., Lucas R., Peterson M., and Frissell S. 1985. The limits of acceptable change (LAC) system for wilderness planning. General Technical Report INT-176, Intermountain Forest and Range Experiment Station, Ogden, Utah.

Stepien, Edward R. 1988. M'ihau: A Brief History. Working Paper Series, Center for Pacific Island Studies, University of Hawaii, Honolulu.

Swizewski, C. and D. I. Oancea. 1978. La carte des types de tourisme de Roumanie. *Revue Roumaine de Géologie, Géophysique et Géographie.* Série Geographie 23(2):291–94.

Taylor, J. A., ed. 1970. *Weather economics.* Memorandum No. 11. Aberystwyth: University College of Wales.

Teas, J. 1988. I'm studying monkeys: what do YOU do? Youth and travelers in

Nepal. *Kroeber Anthropological Society Papers* 67–68:42–54. Berkeley: University of California.

Theuns, H. L. 1989. Multidisciplinary focus on leisure and tourism. *Annals of Tourism Research* 16(2):189–204.

Touraine, A. 1982. *Solidarité.* Paris: Fayard.

——. 1984. *Le retour de l'acteur: essai de sociologie.* Paris: Fayard.

Tourism Industry Association of Canada. 1985. Comments on a Canadian Tourism Strategy, Tourism Industry Association of Canada, Ottawa.

Towner, J. 1985. The grand tour: a key phase in the history of tourism. *Annals of Tourism Research* 12:297–334.

——. 1988. Approaches to tourism history. *Annals of Tourism Research* 15(1):47–62.

Toye, J. 1987. *Dilemmas of development.* Oxford: Basil Blackwell.

Travis, A. S. 1982. Managing the environmental and cultural impacts of tourism and leisure development. *Tourism Management* 3/4:256–62.

——. 1985. The consequences of growing ecological consciousness, and changing socio-cultural needs, on tourism policy. In *Trends of tourism demand.* AIEST, Bregenz. September.

Tuchman, B. 1984. *The march of folly: from Troy to Vietnam.* New York: Ballantine.

Tumaob, L. 1988. Principal, Boracay Elementary School. Personal communication.

Turner, L. and J. Ashe. 1975. *The golden hordes—international tourism and the pleasure periphery.* London: Constable.

Turner, V. and E. M. Bruner, eds. 1986. *The anthropology of experience.* Urbana: University of Illinois Press.

Turner, R. K., ed. 1988. *Sustainable environmental management: principles and practice.* Boulder, CO: Westview Press.

Tüting, L. n.d. Introduction. In L. Tüting and K. Dixit, eds., *Part III: Tourism and ecology in Bikas-Binas development—Destruction, the change in life and environment of the Himalaya.* Geobuch.

Tüting, L. and J. Krippendorf. 1989. *Tourismus mit Einsicht.* Starnberg: Arbeitsgemeinschaft Tourismus mit Einsicht.

United Nations. 1963. *Recommendations on international travel and tourism.* Geneva.

United Nations Commission on Commerce and Development. See CNUCED.

United Nations Economic Commission for Latin America and the Caribbean. Forthcoming. *The socio-cultural impact of tourism in Barbados, Curacao, St. Lucia and Tobago.* Port-of-Spain: UNECLAC.

United Nations Environment Program. 1981. *The Cocoyoc declaration: in defense of the earth.* Nairobi.

UNESCO. 1982. *Déclaration de Mexico sur les politiques culturelles.* Paris.

United Nations Food and Agriculture Organization. See FAO.

Vaitsos, V. 1974. *Intercountry Income Distribution and Transnational Enterprises.* Oxford: Clarendon.

van Doorn, J. W. M. 1979. The Developing Countries: are they really affected by tourism? Some critical notes on socio-cultural impact studies. Paper presented at Seminar on Leisure Studies and Tourism, Warsaw, 7–8 December.

de Varine, H. 1976. *La culture des autres.* Paris: Seuil.

Vetsch, J. 1986. The implications of CO_2-induced climatic change for Prince

Albert National Park, Saskatchewan. Unpublished MA thesis, University of Waterloo.

Virieux-Reymond, A. 1975. *La logique formelle*. Paris: Presses Universitaires de France.

Wall, G. 1985. Climatic change and its impact on Ontario: tourism and recreation Phase 1. Report submitted to Environment Canada, Ontario Region.

———. Forthcoming. Implications of climatic change for Prince Albert National Park, Saskatchewan. *Climate Change Digest*.

———. 1989. Economic aspects of tourism and heritage. To appear in Conference Proceedings, *Tourism and Heritage Preservation*, Trent University, Peterborough.

Wall, G., R. Harrison, V. Kinnaird, G. McBoyle, and C. Quinlan. 1986a. Climatic change and recreation resources: the future of Ontario wetlands? *Papers and Proceedings of Applied Geography Conferences* 9:124–31.

———. 1986b. The implications of climatic change for camping in Ontario. *Recreation Research Review* 13(1):50–60.

Watzlawick, P., J. H. Beavin, and D. D. Jackson. 1972. *Une logique de la communication*. Paris: Seuil.

WCED (World Commission on Environment and Development). 1987. Tokyo Declaration, 27 February. *Our common future* (the Brundtland Report). Oxford: Oxford University Press.

de Weerdt, J. 1987. Espace rural et tourisme en France: Orientations de la recherche. *Problems of Tourism* 10(2):83–93.

———. 1988. Espace rural et tourisme en France: la dialectisation du milieu rural par la logique du significant urbain. *Problems of Tourism* 11(4):76–91.

WES. 1988. Ready for the tunnel. In *Facetten van West-Vlaanderen*, nr. 32, Brugge, Netherlands.

Western Australian State Planning Commission. 1988. Shark Bay Regional Plan, Perth.

Wilkinson, P. F. 1988. Integrating tourism planning into comprehensive national development in island microstates. Paper presented to the First Global Conference, "Tourism, A Vital Force for Peace," Vancouver, October 23–27.

———. 1989. Strategies for tourism in island microstates. *Annals for Tourism Research* 16(2):153–77.

Wong, P. P. 1986. Tourism development and resorts on the East coast of Peninsular Malaysia. *Singapore Journal of Tropical Geography* 7(2):152–62.

WHO (World Health Organization)/UNICEF. 1978. *Primary health care. [Report of the International Conference on Primary Health Care.]* Alma Ata, USSR, 6–12 September 1978, Geneva: WHO.

WTO (World Tourism Organization; see also OMT). 1981. Manila Declaration. Madrid: WTO.

———. 1989. Statement on responsible tourism. Symposium, 26–30 November, Tamanhasset, Algeria.

World Wildlife Fund–Conservation Foundation. 1988. Research Agenda, WWF–CF Osborn Center for Economic Development. Unpublished.

Young, R. C. 1977. The structural context of the Caribbean tourist industry: a comparative study. *Economic Development and Cultural Change* 25(4):657–72.

Yugoslavia. 1988. *Statisticki godisnjak Jugoslavije 1988* (Statistical Yearbook of Yugoslavia). Belgrade.

Yum, S. M. 1984. Case report on attempts at alternative tourism, Hong Kong. In Holden, ed., *Alternative Tourism.*

Zimmer, R. 1988. Hana, Maui, Hawaii: a holistic approach toward tourism. Paper presented to the First Global Conference, Tourism—A Vital Force for Peace, Vancouver, October 23–27.

Author Index

Adler, J., 5
Albers, P., 222
Allcock, J., 221
Altman, J., 104
Androniku, C., 35
Apthorpe, R., 73
Ashe, J., 31

Bachmann, P., 54, 55
Bacon, P. R., 118
Baker, W. M., 198, 211
Balsdon, J., 221
Bandyopadhyay, J., 53, 54, 56, 63, 64
Baptistide, J. C., 17
Barbaza, Y., 20, 26
Barker, M. L., 20, 26
Baskerville, G. L., 116
Best, M., 74
Bilsen, F., 16, 50
Blaikie, P., 117
Blanchet, G., 16, 28
Boudon, R., 90
Boyer, J. C., 20
Boyer, M., 219
Britton, R. A., 15–17, 19
Britton, S. G., 25, 27, 29, 156
Brodsky-Porges, E., 221
Broggi, M. F., 15, 18
Bromberger, C. P., 20, 25, 26
Brookfield, H., 49, 60, 62, 64, 71, 117
Brougham, J. E., 34
Brugger, E. A., 35
Brundtland, G. H., 49, 57, 58, 60, 62, 65, 69, 73, 116
Budowski, G., 118
Burbank, B. K. R., 196

Burns, M., 79
Burton, I., 196
Butler, R. W., xi, 31, 32, 34, 43, 70, 159, 160, 164, 216, 223

Carpenter, E., 99
Casson, L., 4
Cazes, G. H., 15, 44, 50, 89, 135
Chambers, R., 64
Christaller, W., 32, 42
Ciaccio, C., 155
Clark, L., 86, 115
Clarke, W. C., 15
Cohen, E., 6, 10, 15, 31, 44, 47, 50, 51, 55, 152, 155, 164, 219
Cole, D., 84
Conyers, D., 73
Cox, J., 79
Crapo, D. M., 197
Crick, M., ix, 221, 224
Crowe, R. B., 198, 211

Dalen, E., 160
Daltabuit, M., 135
Dann, G., 158, 159, 221, 223
de Albuquerque, K., 159, 162, 163
de Jetley, A., 127
de Kadt, E., 47, 56, 58, 64, 70, 73, 162, 164, 216, 218, 219, 223
Dearlove, J., 66
Dernoi, L. A., 15, 17–19, 27
Dickinson, G., 26
Dogan, H. Z., 60, 61, 152
Dombrink, J., 7
Dorfmann, M., 27
Dowling, R., 81

Drabek, A. G., 72
Dunning, J. H., 97
Durkheim, E., 93, 104
Durst, P., 79

Eadington, W. R., vii, xi, xiii, 7, 9
Edwards, F., 44
Ekins, P., 49, 53, 58, 62
Elliott, C., 72, 73
Elliott, J., 67
English, E. P., 160
Erisman, H. M., 55, 68

Farrell, B., xi, 8, 10, 34, 115, 125, 204,
  223
Fichtner, U., 5
Fisher, A., 79
Friberg, M., 53, 59, 65, 72
Frommer, A., 135

Galbraith, J. K., 97
Ganapin, D., 148
Garrett, W. E., 135
Goldfarb, G., 118
Gomez, V. H., 40
Gonsalves, P. S., 18, 50
Graburn, N. H. H., xi, 89, 221, 222
Gray, H. P., 21
Graycar, A., 82
Greenwood, D. J., 102, 216
Grosjean, G., 43
Gunn, C., 83, 87
Gurin, J.-P., 27

Haider, W., 20
Hall, D., 5, 224
Ham, C., 82
Hammitt, W., 84
Hanna, N., 155
Hardin, G., 35
Hare, F. K., 199, 200
Harrigan, N., 160, 161
Harvey, C., 66
Hasslacher, P., 18, 19, 22
Hayward, S. J., 40
Helber, 136, 142, 143, 145, 146, 148, 154
Hettne, B., 49, 53
Hill, M., 4, 82, 204
Hills, T. L., 4, 19, 27
Hilts, S., 87
Holden, P., 15, 18, 50, 51, 73

Holder, J. S., 40, 44
Hong, E., 53, 141
Howe, A., 87

Ibn Talal, H., 55
Ichaporia, N., 220
Ikkai, M., 220
Ingram, C., 79

Jafari, J., viii, 10, 11, 103, 216, 217
James, E., 67, 180, 222
Jayal, N. D., 41
Jenkins, J., 27, 86
Jeudy, H. P., 100
Jokiel, L., 126, 129
Jones, A., 79

Kanahele, G., 131
Kariel, H., 159
Kates, R. W., 196
Korten, D. C., 66, 74
Kosters, M. J., xii, 5, 180
Kozlowski, J., 50
Krapf, K., 101, 102
Kreck, L. A., 196
Kreutzwiser, R. D., 196
Krippendorf, J., 15, 18, 54, 55, 79
Krutilla, J., 79

Lamothe, 214
Lanfant, M.-F., xii, 89, 94, 111, 216, 217
Languar, R., 94
Lefevre, V., 20
Lepie, A. S., 20
Lewis, G., 223
Lundberg, D. E., 19
Lundgren, J., 19, 20, 27, 203
Lynch, P., 197

Mader, V., 79, 87
Maier, A., 21
Masterton, J., 197
Mathieson, A., 34
McBoyle, G. R., 197, 211, 214
McCannell, D., 100
McElroy, J., 159, 162, 163
McKay, G. A., 198, 211
McKean, P. F., 105
McQueen, M., 97
Meadows, D., 53
Meganck, R., 44

Messerli, B., 35
Mieczkowski, Z. T., 197
Millman, R., 218
Milne, S., 29, 30
Moeran, B., 220
Molnar, E., 21
Morin, E., 101
Morris, A., 20, 26
Mosher, M., 221
Motwani, M., 41
Moull, T., 87
Mukerji, C., 6
Munn, R. E., 115
Murphy, P., 34, 72, 86
Murray, R., 74, 75
Musgrave, W., 80, 83, 85

Nash, D., xii, 5, 151, 216, 217, 219–23
Norbu, N., 44
Nyoni, S., 55

Oancea, D. I., 21
Okotai, T., 80
Oppedijk van Veen, W. M., 21

Passariello, P., 220
Paul, A. H., 126, 198
Pearce, D. G., xii, 6, 15–17, 19–22, 26,
  27, 50, 50, 61, 74, 78, 156, 164, 221,
  223
Pearson, C. B., 53, 57, 63, 68
Peck, J. G., 20
Pelczarski, S. G., 196
Pepper, D., 49, 50, 53, 65
Perez, L., 160
Pcriard, 214
Perpinan, M., 152
Pezzini, M., 74
Pfaffenberger, B., 220
Pfafflin, G. F., 47
Pigram, J., xii, 57, 77, 81, 156, 219, 223
Pirojnik, I., 219
Platt, R. H., 196
Plog, S. C., 21, 42
Poon, A., 68, 69, 74, 163, 164
Potter, R., 159
Priestley, G. K., 20, 26
Przeclawski, K., 221

Ramdial, B. S., 44
Ranck, S., 16, 28

Ravis-Giordani, G., 20, 25, 26
Raynouard, Y., 20
Redman, M., 9
Regier, H. A., 116
Renard, J., 20
Richter, L. K., 58, 67, 68, 70, 71, 73, 89
Riebsame, W., 196
Riley, P., 6, 51, 67, 136
Rist, G., 52
Robert, P., 62, 128, 129, 131, 134
Roberts, H., 70
Rodenburg, E. E., 20
Roekaerts, M., 39, 40
Romeril, M., 81
Rostow, W. W., 101

Saglio, C., 15, 16, 28, 50
Savat, K., 39, 40
Seers, D., 52
Shiva, V., 53, 54, 56, 63, 64
Shook, V. E., 131
Sigaux, G., 4
Simonis, U. E., 61, 63
Singh, T. V., 41
Smith, T., 82, 83
Smith, V., vii, xii, xiii, 6, 12, 21, 32, 75,
  102, 135, 156, 202, 204, 217, 218, 219,
  223
Snead, R. E., 196
Srisang, K., 218
Stadler, G., 221
Stankey, G., 84
Stepien, E. R., 132
Sterner, W., 40
Swizewski, C., 21

Taylor, J. A., 197
Theuns, H. L., 52, 67, 70
Thompson, W. N., 7
Toye, J., 48, 75
Travis, A. S., 50, 106
Tuchman, B., 156
Tumaob, L., 139
Turner, L., 31, 115
Tüting, L., 50

Vaitsos, C. V., 67
van Doorn, J. W. M., 26
Verhallen, T. M. W., 21
Vetsch, J. 207

Wall, G., xii, 34, 35, 42, 122, 194, 196, 197, 207, 209, 214, 223

Wilkinson, P. F., 57, 58, 62, 68, 72, 75, 155, 156, 159, 161, 162

Wong, P. P., 20

Worms, A., 87

Young, R. C., 6, 20, 135, 141, 146, 151, 152, 168, 176, 179, 186, 192

Yum, S. M., 51

Zimmer, R., 128, 129, 131, 134

Subject Index

Adaptancy Platform, 10, 11, 216, 218
Africa, 64, 66
Albania, 224
Alberta, 127
Algeria, viii
Alps, 20, 26, 27
alternative forms of tourism, viii, ix, xiii, 17, 32, 37, 39, 87, 158, 164, 166, 170, 172, 177, 179, 216, 217, 219, 224
alternative tourism, vii, viii, 3, 4, 10, 15–20, 22, 26–32, 34, 36, 37, 39, 40–45, 47, 48, 50, 51, 53, 56, 57, 62, 64, 66, 67, 69, 72, 74, 75, 78–88, 115, 126, 135, 136, 164, 165, 180, 182, 194, 216–19, 223, 224
Australia, xii, 7, 8, 77, 86
Austria, 18, 20, 190

Bahamas, 161, 168
Bali, xii, 20, 27, 204
Barbados, 158, 161, 162, 164, 171, 173, 174, 176, 217
Bavaria, 18, 20
Belize, 26, 135, 156, 164
Bermuda, 40
Bora Bora, 16
Boracay, 12, 135, 136, 139–43, 145, 146, 148, 150–52, 154–57. *See also* Philippines.
Brazil, 57
Brundtland Commission, 49, 57, 58, 60, 62, 65, 69, 73, 116. *See also* World Commission on Environment and Development.

California, xi, xii, 118, 135, 146

Canada, xi, xii, 7, 34, 77, 81, 167–70, 172, 173, 205, 208, 209
Cancun, 159
Caribbean Sea, 16, 19, 20, 27, 42, 69, 74, 80, 158–65, 167, 168, 173, 204
Cautionary Platform, 10, 216, 218
Channel Islands, 155
Chicago, 9
China, 59, 167, 222
Chur Declaration, 18
Club Med, 34, 163, 220
Club of Rome, 53
Cocoyoc Declaration, 115
Colombia, 167
Commission Internationale pour la Protection des Régions Alpines (CIPRA), 18
Cook Islands, 29
Costa Brava, 8, 20, 26, 36, 44
Costa Rica, 118, 135, 167
Côte d'Azur, 20
Cuba, 59, 160
Cyprus, 35, 75

Dallas, 126, 128, 129, 132
Disney World, 7
Disneyland, 7
Dominican Republic, 54

Eco-tourism, 8, 118
Ecuador, 167
Ecumenical Coalition of Third World Tourism (ECTWT), 18, 218
Egypt, 64
England, xi, xii, 81, 180
Epcot Center, 7

Europe, 2, 5, 18, 19, 27–29, 44, 47, 48, 59, 64, 65, 72, 74, 173, 180, 181, 182–88, 190–93, 200, 202, 203, 220, 221, 224
Externalities, 8, 9, 61, 66, 71, 117, 182, 184

farm tourism, 29
Fiji, 17
Florida, 7, 8
France, xii, 5, 7, 20, 27, 181, 183, 185, 188–90
Frankfurt, 154
French Polynesia, 16, 28

Gambia, 224
Germany, 29, 181–83, 185, 186, 189, 190
gites ruraux, 28
Greece, 182, 183, 219, 221
green tourism, 9, 10, 35, 79, 81
greenhouse effect, 66, 199, 200, 215
Greenpeace, 45, 53, 115
Grüne Band, 29
Guadeloupe, 16, 28, 164, 167
Guyana, 160, 169

Hana, 125–134
hard tourism, 19
Hawaii, xi, 8, 47, 119–21, 124, 126, 129, 132, 133. *See also* Maui.
Hungary, 59

India, 53, 204, 220
Indonesia, xii
Ireland, 28, 29, 169
Italy, 20, 74, 155, 204

Jamaica, 118, 163
Japan, 74, 121, 122, 128, 220

Ka'anapali, 120
Kahala, 120
Kapalua, 120
Kenya, 118
Kihei, 120
Knowledge-Based Platform, 11
Korea, 224

Labrador, 118
Lahaina, 120
Las Vegas, 7

London, xi
Los Angeles, 128

Madrid, 155
Malaysia, 20
Manila, 136, 139, 142, 146, 148, 152, 154, 156
mass tourism, 3, 8, 10, 11, 17–19, 22, 28, 30–32, 34–41, 43, 44, 50, 68, 79, 80, 81, 85, 87, 136, 159, 161, 165, 180, 182, 199, 218
Maui, 8, 119–25, 127–29, 131–33. *See also* Hawaii.
Mediterranean Sea, 20, 21, 26, 183, 188, 199, 221
Mexico, 8, 27, 135, 159, 167, 220
Miami, 6
Michigan, 214
Monaco, 5
Moorea, 16
Morocco, 55
Mozambique, 59

Naples, 4
nature-oriented tourism, 79
Netherlands, 178–91
New Zealand, xii, 81
Norway, 185

Oahu, 120
Ontario, xi, xii, 40, 206, 209–212, 214
Orlando, 7

Panama, 167
Papua New Guinea, 16
Paris, xii, 20
Philippines, 12, 121, 135, 136, 139–42, 150–52, 154, 156, 157. *See also* Boracay.
Point Pelee National Park, 206, 209
Poland, 59, 216
Portugal, 182
Presqu'ile National Park, 206, 209
Prince Albert National Park, 206–209
Provence, 20, 25
Puerto Rico, 16, 164

Quebec, 214
Queensland, 35

Romania, 21
Russia, 218

St. Moritz, 220
St. Vincent, 17, 164
Salzburg, 221
sanfter Tourismus, 18, 29
Santander, vii
Saskatchewan, 206
Savignac, 9
Senegal, 16
Seoul, 141
sex tourism, 152
Sierra Club, 115
Singapore, 141
skiing, 211–14
soft tourism, 10, 18, 29, 79
Statement on Responsible Tourism
   (Tamanrasset, 1989), 104
Stockholm, 53, 154
Sweden, 168, 182, 185
Switzerland, 18, 20, 169, 182, 185, 186,
   189, 190

Tahiti, 16
Thailand, 6, 67, 146, 148, 152, 155, 167
TGV. *See Train à Grande Vitesse.*
Third World, 6, 12, 17–20, 27, 28, 30,
   32, 34, 39, 47, 50, 54, 56, 59, 60, 64,
   73, 87, 155, 158, 166, 180, 202, 203,
   217, 218, 220, 223, 224
Tivoli, 4
Tobago, 20, 163, 164
Tokyo, 7, 116, 141

Toronto, 167
Train à Grande Vitesse, 181, 188–90
Trinidad, 163, 167, 170
Turkey, 183

United Kingdom, 68, 74, 166, 173
UNESCO, 17
United Nations Conference on the Human Environment, 115
United States, 6, 7, 68, 73, 118, 121, 122,
   139, 155, 156, 161, 166, 167, 171–73,
   180, 218, 220

Venice, 204
Virgin Islands, 161, 223

Waikiki, 6, 8, 120
Wailea, 120
World Commission on Environment and
   Development (WCED), 49, 115, 116.
   See also Brundtland Commission
World Conservation Strategy, 77, 115
World Tourism Organization (WTO), vii,
   viii, 1, 2, 9, 95, 107, 116, 148

youth tourism, 6
Yugoslavia, 59

Zaire, 118
Zakopane, viii, ix, 88, 216, 224